OIL LEADERS

CENTER ON GLOBAL ENERGY POLICY SERIES

CENTER ON GLOBAL ENERGY POLICY SERIES

Jason Bordoff, series editor

Making smart energy policy choices requires approaching energy as a complex and multifaceted system in which decision makers must balance economic, security, and environmental priorities. Too often, the public debate is dominated by platitudes and polarization. Columbia University's Center on Global Energy Policy at SIPA seeks to enrich the quality of energy dialogue and policy by providing an independent and nonpartisan platform for timely analysis and recommendations to address today's most pressing energy challenges. The Center on Global Energy Policy Series extends that mission by offering readers accessible, policy-relevant books that have as their foundation the academic rigor of one of the world's great research universities.

Robert McNally, *Crude Volatility: The History and the Future of Boom-Bust Oil Prices*

Daniel Raimi, *The Fracking Debate: The Risks, Benefits, and Uncertainties of the Shale Revolution*

Richard Nephew, *The Art of Sanctions: A View from the Field*

Jim Krane, *Energy Kingdoms: Oil and Political Survival in the Persian Gulf*

Amy Myers Jaffe, *Energy's Digital Future: Harnessing Innovation for American Resilience and National Security*

Oil Leaders

AN INSIDER'S ACCOUNT OF FOUR DECADES OF SAUDI
ARABIA AND OPEC'S GLOBAL ENERGY POLICY

Ibrahim AlMuhanna

Columbia University Press

New York

Columbia University Press
Publishers Since 1893
New York   Chichester, West Sussex
cup.columbia.edu

Library of Congress Cataloging-in-Publication Data
Names: AlMuhanna, Ibrahim, author.
Title: Oil leaders : an insider's account of four decades of Saudi Arabia
and OPEC's global energy policy / Ibrahim AlMuhanna.
Description: New York : Columbia University Press, [2021] |
Series: Center on global energy policy | Includes bibliographical references and index.
Identifiers: LCCN 2021038653 (print) | LCCN 2021038654 (ebook) |
ISBN 9780231189743 (hardback) | ISBN 9780231548496 (ebook)
Subjects: LCSH: Petroleum industry and trade—Saudi Arabia. |
Oil industries—Saudi Arabia. | Leadership—Saudi Arabia. | Energy policy.
Classification: LCC HD9576.S33 M84 2021 (print) | LCC HD9576.S33 (ebook) |
DDC 338.2/72809538—dc23/eng/20211006
LC record available at https://lccn.loc.gov/2021038653
LC ebook record available at https://lccn.loc.gov/2021038654

Cover design: Noah Arlow
Cover image: Getty Images

I did my utmost to obtain accuracy and I only wrote what I believed was the whole truth.

—IBN BISHER, ARABIAN WRITER AND HISTORIAN
FROM THE EARLY NINETEENTH CENTURY

CONTENTS

FOREWORD

ROBERT McNALLY

For most of the last five and a half millennia, the only way a man or woman could travel overland faster than running was to harness a horse. That changed in the late nineteenth century when two inventions—modern oil drilling and the internal combustion engine—revolutionized transportation, lifting swaths of humanity out of poverty and enabling the economic and social dynamism that make possible the high living standards enjoyed by much of the world. Oil has many uses, from medicine to plastics, but its widespread use in transportation makes it the lifeblood of modern civilization: Today's agriculture, industry, public and commercial services, defense, and other vital systems are unthinkable without mechanized transport fueled by oil.

Oil has downsides. A toxic and dangerous liquid, oil can foul soil, air, and water, endangering human health and global ecosystems. Its combustion is a significant contributor to anthropogenic greenhouse gas emissions. These externalities require attentiveness and regulation from both industry and government.

But oil's biggest drawback for use as a reliable energy source is its proneness to extreme price instability. Taming wildly gyrating oil prices requires supply managers, the subject of this superb book by Ibrahim AlMuhanna, *Oil Leaders*.

Oil prices are prone to wild boom and bust swings because demand and supply are notoriously insensitive to prices. Gasoline and diesel are must-have commodities that are essential for modern life and for which there are few scalable substitutes. And on the supply side, oil has high upfront capital costs, long lead times, and relatively low operating expenses. Equilibrating supply and demand for inelastic commodities like oil requires very large price swings. And when wars, pandemics, natural disasters, and economic turbulence trigger big supply-demand imbalances, the resulting oil price swings are larger and more jarring.

Oil price volatility hurts everyone. It shortens planning horizons, deters investment, increases unemployment, hammers consumers' pocketbooks, and hamstrings efforts by central bankers and fiscal authorities to promote stable, noninflationary growth. Soaring gasoline and diesel prices have triggered social unrest in Iran, France, Brazil, Nigeria, the United Kingdom, and Chile (to name a few recent examples) and contributed to the failed reelection bids of presidents Jimmy Carter and George H. W. Bush. Collapsing crude prices in the mid-1980s induced Saddam Hussein to attack Kuwait.

As early oil historian Norman Nordhauser wrote, the history of oil can be viewed as a "quest for stability."[1] The only practical solution, as noted above, is supply management. That entails a group of oil producers continually pouring over supply, demand, inventory, and price data, attentive to any signs of excessive and destabilizing imbalances. When supply-demand imbalances threaten to emerge, they must proactively—and usually collectively—adjust supply up or down to nip big price swings in the bud.

Oil companies have tried to tame prices by collectively managing supply since the inception of the modern oil era in 1859. Most attempts quickly failed due to internal mistrust and external competition. In over 150 years, only three supply managers achieved durable success: (1) John D. Rockefeller's Standard Oil; (2) the Texas Railroad Commission, in conjunction with other oil states, the federal government, and major international oil companies; and (3) OPEC, led by Saudi Arabia.

As history has shown, and AlMuhanna's book ably explains, the burden on supply managers is heavy. They must grapple with flawed and incomplete data and reconcile varying views about inherently uncertain future oil supply and demand. They must establish and enforce rules and norms to prevent free-riding and minimize distrust. Because oil is very political, the views of national leaders often influence supply decisions. Supply managers must push back, urging leaders to sacrifice autonomy and market share by reducing oil output for the sake of price stability. And they must invest in expensive but unused spare production capacity in case it is needed to address unexpected tightness. When they succeed at stabilizing oil prices, supply managers are largely taken for granted and ignored. But when booming or busting oil prices roil economies and markets, they become the villains of a startled and annoyed public.

The return of wild boom-bust oil price cycles since 2000 demands an improved understanding of how oil markets and supply managers work. Fortunately, Ibrahim AlMuhanna's timely and authoritative book contributes significantly to the existing literature. In his role as a senior Saudi official and OPEC delegate over the last thirty years, AlMuhanna has been part of a small team that shaped modern Saudi oil policy and steered OPEC policy making through several major crises. By illuminating the interplay of oil fundamentals and geopolitical trends and events with the personalities that helped define them, AlMuhanna provides a unique glimpse into major oil upheavals, including the First Gulf War, the Jakarta debacle of 1997, and the epic 2020 oil price collapse.

Although pressure on the energy industry to decarbonize will intensify, economic and technological realities dictate that oil will continue to dominate transportation. The world will still crave oil price stability. Thus AlMuhanna's seasoned and extensive insights about oil supply managers past and present will remain essential well into the future.

PREFACE

I was born in 1953, and until the age of sixteen I lived in a small village, Ad Dakhilah, Sudair, in central Saudi Arabia, with a population of about a hundred people. We had no electricity. We did not have enough food on the table. Actually, we did not even have a table; we ate on the floor. Our meals consisted of dates, wheat, and very rarely, meat. In the early years, we used wood and camel waste for cooking. Kerosene came along later, and it was a major revolution in the use of energy in our region. The first time I saw electricity was when I arrived in the city of Riyadh late one night at the age of ten. It was a cause for amazement, and I vividly remember it to this today. Five years later, our village was connected to the electricity grid, but it only worked during the night. We had a lot of health problems. Four of my siblings did not survive.

Like many Saudis my age, I was witnessing with my own eyes the rapid changes resulting from the kingdom's newly generated oil wealth, a successful political and economic system, and prudent oil management.

At the age of thirty-six, I found myself in the middle of major international events, seeing and participating in many energy-related decisions, meeting three Saudi kings as well as many heads of state and distinguished people, working with four Saudi energy ministers, and officially visiting more than fifty countries. I witnessed major political and economic crises that affected the oil market. These included the Iraq invasion of Kuwait, the Asian financial crisis, the political and energy upheavals in Venezuela, the U.S. invasion of Iraq, the global financial crisis of 2008, and the Iran nuclear standoff. Recently, the coronavirus pandemic has had a sweeping impact on the global economy and on energy usage, as well as on the way the oil market is managed.

Over the past three decades, I attended almost all Organization of of the Petroleum Exporting Countries (OPEC) and the combination of OPEC and other producers, known as OPEC+, ministerial conferences and related meetings. I witnessed firsthand the commencement and progress of the energy consumer-producer dialogue. My responsibilities at the Ministry of Energy involved me in many UN climate change conferences, from their beginning in Rio de Janeiro in 1992 through the Paris Agreement in 2015.

Before I joined the Saudi Ministry of Energy in 1989, I had no interest in oil. I thought it was dull and static. After I got involved, my thinking gradually changed, and I discovered two things. First, the oil market is very dynamic. It keeps changing and changing, not only by the year and by the month but even by the day. It is also subject to political, economic, and even weather-related surprises. Second, the oil market is a multidimensional subject in which market fundamentals, the environment, other sources of energy, politics, the media, rumors, companies, oil experts and analysts, official statements, and the psychology and beliefs of decision makers are all important. But what is critical is the way that these factors interact with each other, with no clear-cut beginning or end. It is an ongoing circular process.

Within this context, information, personality, and psychology are all important. This includes elements such as perception, misperception, and negative or positive sentiments at any given moment in time. Decision makers, with the intricacies of personality, information, and background, are significant players in these situations, and they are the subject of this book.

Oil leaders base their decisions on pure national interests, real or perceived. But they are influenced in return by the information they receive and their interpretation of that information. This includes predictions of how others—allies or adversaries—will think and behave. They might miscalculate the issue or the potential behavior of others.

My experience in "oil diplomacy" has shown me that oil leaders, whether heads of state or ministers, base their decisions on what they perceive to be in the national interest of their own country, but they are also influenced by the way they interact within the complex world. I was drawn to considering how the national interest is exercised in a collective framework—be it in

OPEC, OPEC+, or on the global scene—and how these interactions influence the national and global status of these leaders.

Throughout the history of oil, from the day it became a commercial commodity, different types of decision makers have made significant differences in the energy market and in the industry at large. They include political leaders, technocrats, ministers, heads of major energy companies, energy investors, geologists, engineers, and many more. Their power, influence, and international importance vary from country to country and from time to time.

Oil has a critical role to play as a source of energy in the future of global economy. Two directions seem possible in the next twenty or thirty years. In one direction, oil remains an important part of our economic base; demand for oil continues to rise, driven by economic growth, population growth, and the need for a better life, especially in developing and emerging economies. The second possibility is an energy transition based on political desires in which oil, gas, and coal use are gradually reduced and exchanged for an increased use of renewables such as solar, wind, and even nuclear. This transition is not going to be easy, and it is likely to lead to significant changes in industries, businesses, and investment directions, and to changes in the global economy, politics, and the national interests of all countries. Some unprepared countries, especially poorer ones and small oil exporters, are likely to suffer more than others.

We should be prepared for a lot of energy uncertainty in the coming decades, and the role of decision makers, regardless of the direction the world might go, will be more important than ever.

In addition to my personal observations and information, I conducted about fifty interviews over a period of four years with energy officials, economists, financial leaders, experts, journalists, and others in Saudi Arabia and around the world. Also, a good number of people read earlier drafts of the book and made comments, but responsibility for the information and the opinions expressed in the book are solely mine.

Equally important, I worked in the Saudi Ministry of Energy for about thirty years, and I still have close connections within the ministry. My job was to speak for and reflect the energy policies of Saudi Arabia, and I did so with consistent communication and approval from the ministers or their assistants. However, this book is not in any way a reflection of the ministry's policies and opinions regarding the events described here. The content reflects only my personal knowledge, experiences, understanding, and analysis, without revealing any information that might be considered secret or confidential.

Data is a major issue in the international energy market, and there are differences, small and large, between sources. I relied on OPEC's data for the most part, but I also considered data from other important sources, especially from the International Energy Agency and the International Energy Forum, as well as the World Bank and other institutions.

ACKNOWLEDGMENTS

This book is an analytical memoir, where I combine my own experiences and knowledge with that of other people through personal interviews as well as published primary and secondary sources in Arabic and English. It took me about four years from writing the proposal to completion of the manuscript. It covers more than four decades of development in the oil world and the key personalities who shaped global energy policies. Extreme caution was needed when dealing with such subjects. Accuracy and fairness came first. This was not an easy task. It required careful work and a lot of help in different formats from a variety of people, and I am indebted to all of them.

First and foremost, I must thank the Saudi energy ministers and the many people from within the ministry whom I had the privilege to associate with and learn from throughout my career. The ministers are H.E. Hisham Nazer (1989–1995), H.E. Ali al Naimi (1995–2016), H.E. Khalid al Falih (2016–2019), and H.R.H. Prince Abdulaziz bin Salman, who not only asked me to work at the ministry in the first place but also did his best to help me understand the oil market and OPEC and work with the international media in the most optimal way.

I also benefited from the abundance of knowledge and experience of H.R.H. Prince Faisal bin Turki, the special advisor to the Ministry of Energy from 1986 to 2018, about domestic energy and mineral issues, natural gas, and the relationship between energy and relevant industries.

I would also like to mention with special respect the late Mohammad Farouk al Husseini, who was an economic advisor when I joined the ministry. He was one of the most renowned and well-informed experts in energy economics and OPEC issues. He was always down to earth and truthful. Many people in the Saudi Energy Ministry were inspired by him, and I was one of them.

Other past and present ministry officials read the book, or parts of it, and offered discerning comments. I owe special thanks to H.E. Majid Al Moneef, the Secretary General of the Supreme Committee on Hydro-carbon Affairs, and former Saudi OPEC governor. I continuously talked with him about different issues relating to the book. He read two different drafts and gave valuable suggestions and information. I am grateful for his help and advice.

Two important figures who read drafts of the book were Jawad al Sakka, a respected Saudi energy legal expert, and the late Ahmed al Ghazzawi, another widely acknowledged expert on such issues as Saudi Arabia's borders with neighboring countries. They both provided valuable information, especially covering the era of Minister Yamani.

Many colleagues read all or part of the book and offered useful comments, for which I am very grateful. They include H.E. Abdelrahman Abdelkareem, former assistant minister of energy; Suleiman al Herbish, former president of the OPEC Fund for International Development; Ahmed Al Zahrani, the assistant to the Ministry of Energy for development and excellence; Turki al Thunayyan, the legal advisor at the Ministry; Adeeb al Aama, Saudi Arabia's OPEC governor; Nayef al Musehel, deputy minister of policies and strategic planning; Turki al Wosemer, general supervisor of the minister's office; Naser al Doseri; Mansour al Ayyaf; Awwad al Harthe; Yousif al Salem; Fahad al Toryf; Eissa al Zerma; and Samiha Khayyat.

Jamil al Dandany, a former advisor at the Ministry of Energy and former department director at Aramco, read two different drafts and made excellent remarks. James Connal, who was a speechwriter in the ministry, provided invaluable support relating to editing and advice on some of the contents of the book.

Outside the ministry, there are many distinguished Saudi officials who read the book and offered insightful information for which I am truly grateful. They include:

H.E. Mohammed Aba al Khail, the Saudi minister of finance (1975–1995). We had a lengthy discussion on a background basis.

H.E. Hamad al Sayari, former head of the Saudi Central Bank (1985–2009).

H.E. General Abdulrahman al Banyan, military advisor in the Royal Court.

H.E. Abdulrahman Al-Saeed, former advisor in the Royal Court.

H.E. Abdulrahman al Tuwaijri, former president of the Saudi Capital Market Authority (CMA).

H.E. Yousef al Sadoun, former undersecretary of the Ministry of Foreign Affairs for Economic and Cultural Affairs, who read the chapter about Prince Saud.

Abdulmalik al Ashaikh, former legal advisor to the Royal Court.

Abdallah Jum'ah, former president and CEO of Saudi Aramco.

Abdulaziz al Jarbou, former chairman of SABIC.

Abdulrahman al Rashed, chairman of the editorial board of al Arabiya News.

Turki Al-Dakheel, Saudi ambassador to the United Arab Emirates.

Abdulaziz bin Salamah, former deputy minister at the Saudi Ministry of Information, who read two drafts of the book.

Abdulaziz al Faiz, former Saudi ambassador to Kuwait.

Dr. Ahmed al Ghamdi, former member of the Shura Council and former advisor at the Ministry of Energy.

Abdulwahab al Faiz, a Saudi writer and media consultant.

There are multiple esteemed individuals within the energy and political scene from around the world who read a draft of the book or part of it and gave appreciated ideas and opinions. Notable people include Bassam Fattouh, the director of the Oxford Institute for Energy Studies (OIES); Walid Khadduri, the former editor-in-chief of the Middle East Economic Survey (MEES); and Bhushan Bahree, executive director at IHS Markit.

I had fruitful and continuous discussions regarding the events in the 1980s and 1990s with Abdul Samad al Awadi, the former head of marketing of Kuwait Petroleum Corporation in Europe and a member of the Kuwaiti delegation to OPEC, who offered invaluable information and suggestions. I highly appreciate his assistance.

Dan Yergin has read the book and offered impactful comments, which I highly appreciate.

I would like to give special thanks to Daniel Poneman, former U.S. deputy secretary of energy and Ambassador Douglas Silliman, the president of the Arab Gulf States Institute in Washington (AGSIW) and former U.S. ambassador in Kuwait, both of whom read the book, or parts of it, and offered important comments.

Besides the above-mentioned people, there are many distinguished decision-makers who gave me a great deal of their time to discuss various energy and political issues. They include Issam al Chalabi, former oil minister of Iraq (1987–1990); Abdallah el Badri, former secretary general of OPEC; and Luis Giusti, former CEO of the Venezuelan national oil company PDVSA, who read the two chapters related to him and to Venezuela and provided conversant remarks.

Two individuals were of great help in offering their insights, editorial assistance, as well as double-checking some data. They are Kate Dourian, contributing editor at MEES and former IEA official, and Diane Munro, energy analyst and former IEA official.

Others who offered their help and read the book include Rania el Gamal, chief energy correspondent in the Middle East at Reuters, and Amena Bakr, deputy bureau chief at Energy Intelligence.

Some organizations provided useful assistance. Saudi Aramco was so helpful in many aspects. I would also like to give special thanks to King Abdullah Petroleum Studies and Research Center (KAPSARC), where some were keen to help from the start. Aljawhara Al-Quayid at KAPSARC provided much needed information related to the first six chapters. Adam Sieminski, former KAPSARC president, read an early draft and provided good and constructive recommendations. Fahad al Turki, vice president at KAPSARC, offered his support.

The third institution was OPEC. I had lengthy and informative discussions with the secretary general, Mohammad Barkindo, which I highly appreciated. Ayed al Qahtani, the director of research, offered his help. Ms. Snjezana Cirkovic, the Information Center coordinator at OPEC double-checked data and information, and kindly gave her assistance. Shakir al Rifaiey from the office of the secretary general was very helpful in many aspects.

I received beneficial help in different ways from many people. They include Mohammad Wajjh Alyo, Ali Twairqi, Mohammed al Thomairi, Guy Caruso, Gro Anundskaas, Paul Mollet, Abdullah Al-Quwaiz, Khalid Al-Muhanna, Medlej al Medlej, Joel Couse, Ji Yeon Park, Abdullah al Bureathen, Abdullah al Furaih, and Yousef al Mohaimeed.

There are others I may have forgotten and to them I offer my apologies. I am also beholden to others who did not wish to be mentioned by name but whose help was greatly appreciated.

ACKNOWLEDGMENTS

Gary Ross, CEO of Black Gold Investors and the founder of PIRA, and Nathaniel Kern, President of Foreign Reports, all contributed information about certain issues in the book. Ross read the entire book and gave many suggestions which were very helpful.

I would also like to express my appreciation to two anonymous oil experts who read an early draft and gave constructive comments.

Two people deserve special appreciation for their invaluable assistance: first and foremost, Jason Bordoff, the founding director of the Center on Global Energy Policy at Columbia University. When I told him my idea of writing such a book, he was very enthusiastic and wanted it to be published by Columbia. He followed the process so attentively and gave it special attention; it was almost as if it was his project.

Second, I would like to give special gratitude to Caelyn Cobb, editor of global history and politics at Columbia University Press. Her timely editorial comments and suggestions were enormously helpful.

Monique Briones, the editorial assistant at Columbia University Press was very helpful and closely followed the later development of the book, offering constructive assistance. The copyeditor of the book, Kay Mikel, and the project manager, Ben Kolstad, have done an excellent job, which I highly appreciate.

I would like to give special thanks and gratitude to Bob McNally, the founder and president of Rapidan Energy Group, for writing the foreword of the book and his kind words about the contents and myself.

The book became a family project, especially during the 2020 Covid-19 lockdown in Saudi Arabia. My son Haitham and my daughter Haya took special care of the project and helped in so many ways, including typing, editing, and double-checking information and data, as well as doing extra research. Haya's contribution was extraordinary, including researching and collecting information, fact checking historical events, and relentlessly sending e-mails on my behalf when needed even though she was busy with university. Haitham proofread the book, double-checked data and information, and matched and double-checked the citations. My other son Alwaleed offered a lot of assistance, large and small, in many areas including data and information. The rest of my family were also very supportive. My wife Nesreen al Haqbani created a calm working atmosphere in the house despite the long hours I devoted to the book, and my youngest daughter Nora was charming and helpful when needed. I highly appreciate the kind support of my family from the start to the end. I would like to express my deep gratitude to my late sister Dulayyil and my eldest brother Abdullah. They both helped and inspired me in my early years, especially after the death of my father and the disability of my mother Haya al Aiban.

OIL LEADERS

DECISIONS, DECISION MAKERS, AND OIL

In 1985, Ahmed Zaki Yamani of Saudi Arabia and Ali al-Khalifa al-Sabah of Kuwait met privately and decided to change the oil pricing method and increase oil production in their countries. A couple of months later, oil prices collapsed, Yamani lost his job, and Saudi Arabia faced major financial and economic problems.

On May 28, 1990, Saddam Hussein addressed an Arab summit in Baghdad and referred to low oil prices and the increase in oil production by Kuwait (among other countries) as a "war against Iraq." Two months later, Iraqi troops invaded Kuwait.

In March 1994, Luis Giusti became chairman and CEO of the Venezuelan National Oil Company. His policy of increasing oil production without regard for the Organization of the Petroleum Exporting Countries (OPEC) contributed to the second collapse in oil prices in twenty years. This collapse led to the rise of a new Venezuelan government whose policies have had major consequences for the country in recent decades.

On March 7, 2020, after an unproductive OPEC+ meeting and after careful study and discussion, Saudi Crown Prince Mohammed bin Salman asked Prince Abdulaziz bin Salman, Saudi Arabia's minister of energy, to shift toward maximizing the Saudi oil market share. This later led to significant changes in the management of the international oil market.

These are just four of the many incidents that have played out on the world petroleum stage since 1985. Decisions made by individual heads of state, government ministers, CEOs, and others have had major impacts on the global petroleum market from the 1980s to the present day, and by extension these decisions have affected the world's economy and politics as well. Through my work for the Saudi energy ministry, I saw firsthand how decisions were made and what influenced those decisions. I believe that an in-depth analysis based on accurate information and personal observations of those who were part of, or close to, the decision-making process will help us better understand the influence of the oil markets on the world's economy: past, present, and future. That is the major goal of this book. My personal experience and interviews with many decision makers, as well as information from primary and secondary sources, contributes to our understanding of these topics. The decisions that shaped the oil market have had far-reaching consequences around the world, and they deserve special attention.

When I joined the Saudi Ministry of Petroleum (now the Ministry of Energy) in 1989, my main responsibilities involved media and information. I also worked hard to understand oil basics: the market, the industry, the economy, and the policies of the important energy-producing and energy-consuming countries. By the beginning of 1990, a major conflict was building in the region, and oil was the apparent reason.

Two individual decision makers contributed to an increase in tensions. The Kuwaiti minister of petroleum, Sheikh Ali al-Khalifa al-Sabah, did not want his country to lower its oil production and adhere to OPEC's quota. Meanwhile, Iraqi president Saddam Hussein saw the Kuwaiti policy as part of an international conspiracy to undermine his regime. Saddam Hussein was a belligerent leader who had many economic and financial problems at home—and he thought Kuwait should be under Baghdad's control. Therefore, Kuwaiti oil policy could be used as a pretext for something bigger (chapter 3).

As the conflict intensified, King Fahd of Saudi Arabia became involved. He believed that problems apparently rooted in oil policy and production should be solved at the energy ministerial level, and he asked the Saudi minister of petroleum, Hisham Nazer, to intervene and find a solution. King Fahd worked behind the scenes, and a small group of people in the ministry, including me, became involved alongside Nazer and Prince

Abdulaziz. King Fahd's goal was for all countries to stick to their quotas in order to attain higher and more stable price levels.

I went with Nazer to Abu Dhabi, where he delivered a letter from King Fahd and met with Sheikh Zayed of the United Arab Emirates. The meeting took place at Sheikh Zayed's farm. He was charming and friendly with everyone and had a simple life. Even before reading the letter, Sheikh Zayed told Nazer, "Tell His Majesty that I will do whatever he wants us to do." A couple of days later Nazer visited Baghdad and Kuwait to meet their leaders, and I regret not going with him when he asked. Although I missed meeting one of the most controversial Arab leaders in modern history, I later learned the details of the meeting from Nazer. He also discussed the meeting in the book about his life.

Events were evolving quickly. Day after day I worked directly for Nazer and Prince Abdulaziz (who was his leading adviser), taking directions from them on what needed to be done. We had a meeting in Jeddah on July 10, 1990, which was followed by a full OPEC meeting in Geneva on July 29. Shortly after that, on August 2, the Iraqi invasion of Kuwait began. Our focus at the Saudi ministry of energy was on OPEC and the oil market rather than on the geopolitical dimension. We got into a serious battle with Sadek Boussena, the Algerian oil minister and president of the OPEC conference, over the need to call an extraordinary OPEC ministerial conference. His position was that there was no need for such a meeting, and he was supported by Iran. The issue was whether Saudi Arabia and other capable nations could increase their production to replace missing Iraqi and Kuwaiti oil exports.

Walking into the OPEC conference with Nazer and Prince Abdulaziz on the afternoon of August 28, I remember Boussena calling me over to him. At the time, I was based in London and in charge of international media communications (chapter 3). Boussena quietly said, "Ibrahim, we are holding the conference now and would like to do what the Saudis want, so would you please stop the media attacks against us." During that meeting, we had another battle. Nazer said that Saudi Arabia would increase its production from 5.4 to 8.5 MBD within three months. But the markets, experts, and media were not convinced. It was my responsibility to persuade them, and I was successful with some.[1] Time after time, whenever we solved one problem—whether it was actual or perceived—we found ourselves dealing with a new one. The oil market, its players, and policies keep changing all the time.

In 1995, Ali Al-Naimi replaced Nazer as the Saudi minister of energy. I knew Al-Naimi very well, but I was unsure about my future in the organization. Before my work for the ministry, I had been teaching at King Saud University in Riyadh, but Al-Naimi asked me to stay on in my position. The next important oil policy change came with the Jakarta agreement in November 1997. Through our media program, we worked hard to convince the outside world of the merits of Al-Naimi's proposal to increase production (chapter 4). Before the end of the year, oil prices collapsed and a new and more difficult problem emerged. Saudi Arabia, Mexico, and Venezuela—with the help of OPEC—were struggling to bring the markets back to stability. Prince Saud al-Faisal, the Saudi minister of foreign affairs, became an important player (see chapter 5).

From 2000 to 2007, the market remained stable because Saudi Arabia and OPEC were able to smoothly deal with major oil-related events such as the U.S. invasion of Iraq, the Venezuelan oil strike, the loss of Nigerian production, and destructive hurricanes in the Gulf of Mexico. In 2008, however, the oil market suffered some serious shocks, and international leaders King Abdullah of Saudi Arabia, U.S. president George. W. Bush, British Prime Minister Gordon Brown, and others got involved (chapter 7). Rising oil prices in 2012 triggered another crisis that involved King Abdullah and U.S. president Barack Obama (chapter 8).

Oil prices began a steady decline in 2014, and the only serious international attempt to fix the market in April 2016 ended in a major failure. Twenty days later, on May 7, 2016, Al-Naimi was relieved of his position and Khalid al-Falih was installed as his replacement (chapter 9). Before the end of the year, Crown Prince Mohammed met with Russian president Vladimir Putin, and they decided to work together to take the leading role in managing the international oil market (chapter 10). However, oil prices went through a big swing in 2018–2019, and on September 8, 2019, Prince Abdulaziz replaced al-Falih as Saudi minister of energy.

But the biggest shock came in early 2020 with the global spread of COVID-19. The pandemic caused a major contraction in the global economy and led to the largest decline in oil consumption to date. This time it was U.S. president Donald Trump who took the leading role in international management of the oil market (chapters 7 and 8). During these years, I participated in almost all of the official international meetings that any of Saudi Arabia's energy ministers attended. My job was to reflect the kingdom's policy position to the outside world,[2] and I was widely quoted (not usually by name) by international media from many countries and in different languages. These quotes were attributed to "a Saudi Gulf official," "a Gulf source close to Saudi thinking," "an OPEC delegate," "a Saudi oil official," "a Saudi industrial source," and so on.[3]

In my thirty-plus years of work in the Saudi oil ministry, my experience and knowledge far exceeded the scope implied by these terms. I took part in the discussion of ideas behind the scenes and observed decision-making during many energy-related crises, including wars, hurricanes, and economic and oil crises. I have met with three Saudi kings and have worked closely with four Saudi energy ministers. I have also met with many world leaders, visited more than fifty countries on official trips, and engaged in discussions with hundreds of energy ministers and heads of major energy companies.

During these years, I observed and took notes about these events and trends. I was continually amazed at how individual decision makers can and do shape events and trends, a subject that has not been properly studied and has not received enough attention. I hope that sharing these insights will further our collective understanding of the power of these individuals and their influence on the world's economies.

OIL AND WORLD AFFAIRS

For thousands of years, energy has been an essential driver of human development. Thanks to steam engines and coal, the eighteenth century brought on the industrial revolution, which introduced mass production of manufactured goods and the beginnings of mass transportation via the rail network. It also ensured the dominance of Western countries, notably the United Kingdom, over the rest of the world and sparked increased development in the United States. The industrial revolution also led to faster printing presses, which gave rise to mass media, universal education, and a wider dissemination of information. With all of this occurring simultaneously, a new philosophy of political economy as well as revolutionary ideas took hold, transforming human history. These new ideas included socialism, capitalism, and the concept of the welfare state. The discovery of oil sparked another revolution and marked the beginning of the age of oil. Oil is the most versatile source of energy ever discovered. It is easy to transport, easy to store, and has a variety of uses. Reserves are huge and keep growing despite fears, now discounted, that production is peaking. In addition to its use in power generation and manufacturing, oil has paved the way for an unparalleled expansion in the last hundred years in modes of transportation, especially road and air travel. Its uses include fertilizers and petrochemicals, which are an essential part of modern life.

Economic growth and the rise of human prosperity have been possible thanks to oil. Billions of dollars have been invested in the entire oil value chain from exploration to final product manufacturing and marketing. Oil companies and related businesses, such as car manufacturers, airlines, and petrochemical producers, still drive the global economy even as technology and communication companies are beginning to make their mark.

The control of oil resources has been vital in times of both war and peace. In resource-rich countries and regions, particularly in the developing world, oil has led to internal strife and regional tensions. And in some countries, when rightly managed, oil has led to economic development and human prosperity. Daniel Yergin succinctly described humanity's relationship with oil when he wrote, "Today, we are so dependent on oil, and oil is so embedded in our daily doing, that we hardly stop to comprehend its pervasive significance. It is the oil that makes possible where we live, how we live, how we commute to work, how we travel."[4]

It is little wonder, then, that oil has received so much attention during the last hundred years. This attention has taken many forms, including creation of hundreds of national and international companies and governmental and nongovernmental organizations dedicated to energy issues, including oil. Similarly, hundreds of research centers—governmental, private, and commercial—focus on oil and energy more generally. New books and reports are published almost every week. Oil is one of the most important commodities of our time, and it is expected to remain so for many decades to come. Added to this, oil is becoming an important part of the global climate change discussion. Therefore, it is imperative that we study this commodity in all of its dimensions, including the oil market's leadership, processes of decision-making, and the power of its decision makers.

ADVENTURERS, ENTREPRENEURS, AND CEOS

The oil story begins with adventurers, including geologists who were focused on discovering and producing oil. Among the first were George

Bissell, founder of the first oil company, the Pennsylvania Rock Oil Company, and John Galey, the great wildcatter of the nineteenth century who, history recalls, could "smell oil." In Saudi Arabia one such adventurer was American field geologist Max Steineke of the Standard Oil Company of California (Socal). Steineke continued drilling to a deeper level without the knowledge and authority of his bosses in California and, in 1938, discovered well No. 7, which was the beginning of oil production in Saudi Arabia.

In the second category are the business entrepreneurs, those who looked for business opportunities that required access to oil. The first and most famous was John D. Rockefeller, who established Standard Oil Trust in the early twentieth century. Entrepreneurs in related businesses, such as Henry Ford of the automobile industry, are also included in this category.

CEOs of major oil companies make up a third category. Just as the age of great oil adventurers and oil entrepreneurs wound down, the era of strong corporate leaders ascended. Oil became a major economic force in the twentieth century, and following the breakup of Standard Oil Trust in 1911, a number of oil companies were formed in the United States and Europe, largely as joint-stock companies. There was intense competition among them, and the winner was typically the company with the most effective leader. In the early years, Henri Deterding, who engineered the merger of Royal Dutch with Shell in the early twentieth century, turned Shell into a major Dutch oil company that competes with the dominant U.S. oil companies to this day. There is also John Cadman, chairman of the Anglo-Iranian Company (later British Petroleum, now BP), who saved the company and made it a great enterprise in the early twentieth century. Walter C. Teagle, chairman of Standard Oil Company of New Jersey (now Exxon), saved the company after the 1911 breakup and made it the most important international oil company. Enrico Mattei founded the Italian oil company Eni, now a major multinational; and Armand Hammer built Occidental Petroleum, transforming it from a bankrupt firm into a major international company.

The number of state-owned oil companies increased dramatically during the 1970s when several oil-producing countries nationalized their oil industries and took over concessions previously held by the multinationals. National oil companies (NOCs) draw strength from the large reserves they manage in their respective countries, but their degree of success depends on their relationship with their respective governments. Even the CEOs and presidents of state-owned oil companies work under the constraints set by their shareholder—the government. In addition to the governance that applies to all companies, the state government oversees all NOC activities to one degree or another. Appointments to the NOC board are sometimes based on personal or political biases, and governments may limit spending and even sometimes force these companies to carry out unrelated activities. Few heads of national oil companies merit mentioning for making distinguished contributions. However, Ali al-Khalifa al-Sabah of Kuwait was responsible for transforming Kuwait's National Oil Company in the late 1970s and early 1980s from a purely crude oil–producing and operating company to a fully integrated company with global operations. He set an example that others would follow.

Individual adventurers, entrepreneurs, and all-powerful heads of oil companies dominated the oil industry for more than one hundred years, but their influence has declined in recent times. Today oil companies work in a more structured environment, and company boards, shareholders, accountants, engineers, finance directors, and lawyers all work together to make the company successful. So we turn to the next figures in the evolution of oil management: political leaders who, more than any other group, have dominated or influenced the oil market for the last fifty years.

POLITICAL LEADERS

Oil has become an important source of government revenues, political power, and influence, and political leaders have recognized its special importance. In major international upheavals during the first half of the twentieth century, such as the First and Second World Wars and major revolutions in Russia and China, oil played a part in and often determined the course of the conflicts. For example, during World War II, the United States, the United Kingdom, and Russia had enough oil resources under their direct or indirect control to out compete Germany, Japan, and Italy, which did not have any oil resources.

Before and during World War II, leaders of the great powers paid special attention to oil. Adolf Hitler's Central Plan, under which he instigated hostilities, was in part about the need to control oil. Japanese strategist Admiral Isoroku Yamamoto, who planned the attack on Pearl Harbor in 1941, was thinking about how to control the oil resources in Indonesia. In the

United States during the Roosevelt administration, Secretary of the Interior Harold L. Ickes became the central figure in U.S. oil policy for more than a decade and was the first political leader to craft the country's oil policy. He advocated for U.S. government control of Aramco, modeled on the British government's controlling interest in the Anglo-Iranian Oil Company. After the war ended, the policy focus in the United States and Europe shifted to reconstruction and economic development, and oil again became a central issue. One of the first major international postwar crises the United States faced was about oil. Iranian prime minister Mohammad Mosaddegh nationalized the assets of the Anglo-Iranian Oil Company in 1951, and the U.S. and UK governments backed a military coup that deposed Mosaddegh.

The next major oil crisis that pitted the Western allies against each other took place five years later when Egypt nationalized the Suez Canal. The United Kingdom and France formed an alliance with Israel in a military campaign to seize the waterway. All shipping, including oil, was stopped until the United States forced its allies to withdraw, allowing the canal to reopen and oil flows to resume. The Suez crisis and Mosaddegh's overthrow not only reinforced U.S. political domination over the oil business but also highlighted the lengths to which the United States was prepared to go to ensure the security of supply of this increasingly important commodity. For a large part of the twentieth century, a growing number of Western oil companies, mainly American, controlled the entire oil value chain outside the former Soviet Union and China, including exploration, production, transportation, refining, and, of course, pricing. However, the political leaders of oil-producing developing countries started to plan joint actions to defend their interests against the dominant Western international oil companies.

A revolution was brewing thanks to the efforts of two great individuals who belonged to prominent oil-producing countries, Abdullah al-Tariki of Saudi Arabia and Juan Pablo Alfonzo of Venezuela. Working together, they established OPEC in September 1960, but it took more than ten years for OPEC to gain control of oil pricing. It is interesting to note that OPEC was created in part as a reaction to the decision of one individual within the major oil-consuming countries: Standard Oil of New Jersey's chairman Monroe Rathbone, who unilaterally cut oil prices in 1959 and 1960.

In the early 1970s, OPEC took the lead in the oil market by deciding to set the price of oil. The consuming nations fought back. One of the most notable political leaders in this effort was Henry Kissinger, the former U.S.

secretary of state, who was instrumental in creating the International Energy Agency (IEA) in 1974, a body tasked with coordinating and representing the interests of the major oil-consuming (mainly Western) nations. This led to conflict between the IEA and OPEC that continued for sixteen years. When the IEA started analyzing the international oil market at the end of the 1970s, its reports were available only to member countries. The IEA's analysis was top secret and brief, totaling about seventeen pages. Today the IEA's *World Energy Outlook* could be more than six hundred pages long.

In an atmosphere of rising oil prices, changes in market leadership, the use of oil as a political tool, and many oil-related conflicts at all levels, individual decision makers became even more influential and their impact on the oil market, including oil prices, grew.

POLITICAL LEADERS AND DECISION-MAKING

Decision-making processes for individuals acting alone or with a small number of people are complex. Rational models and game theory, as well as psychological models (expectation, perception, misperception, and emotion), have been studied in an effort to explain and understand the behavior of decision makers at national and international levels in a political or economic context.[5] In addition to rational or psychological aspects of behavior, decision makers are influenced by six factors that stand out at different times and with different individuals and political leaders who have influenced the oil sector.

Timing and the Context of Decisions

Oil ministers normally take into account the state of the international oil market as well as their country's petroleum, political, economic, and financial interests. The importance of oil ministers in the international arena is largely a reflection of the importance of their respective countries within the oil market. For example, the Iraqi oil minister was marginalized within OPEC and in the international market during the economic embargo (1990–2003). However, Iraq and its oil minister became very important when their production started to rise in 2015. Oil ministers of small, oil-producing countries sometimes have an outsized role. In the 1970s and early 1980s, Algeria exerted greater weight in OPEC than was warranted by its size in the market because of its position in the nonaligned movement and the active participation of oil ministers such as Belaid Abdessalam.

During the 1980s, Ali al-Khalifa al-Sabah of Kuwait was very influential even though Kuwait's production was close to capacity, but the importance of Kuwait within OPEC declined in the 1990s due in part to its frequent changes of oil ministers (more than twenty since 1990). These oil ministers lacked good background knowledge of the workings of OPEC and the international oil market, and this applied even to those who were highly qualified.

Background, Knowledge, and Experience

English is the official language of OPEC and of the international oil market, so fluency in the English language is necessary for oil ministers. In addition, a thorough technical understanding of oil market dynamics is required for oil ministers who want to wield influence in the oil market. For example, Prince Abdulaziz, the Saudi minister of energy, is a logical thinker who speaks fluent English and has a rigorous understanding of oil issues, including technologies and market fundamentals. He also does his homework, carefully studying the issues and preparing for official meetings by getting the best information and counsel available. His close working relationship with Crown Prince Mohammed and his grasp of the issues and the weight of Saudi Arabia helped him achieve Saudi Arabia's goals in 2020 during a most difficult time for the oil market from March to December.

Age and Number of Years in Office

Age and experience are important factors for any decision maker anywhere and in any field. Younger decision makers tend to be more active and innovative, willing to make bold decisions and to take risks. This is less often the case for older decision makers. The longer ministers or decision makers are in office, the less active and innovative they are likely to be. For example, Ali Al-Naimi was sixty-three years old during the 1998–1999 energy crisis, and he had been a minister for just three years. He was willing to travel the world to find a solution to the crisis, making about fifteen trips in one year and visiting three countries (Russia, Norway, and Austria) in a single day in 1999. During the 2014–2015 oil crisis, Al-Naimi was more than eighty years old and had been the minister for more than twenty years. At that stage in his life, he was unwilling to take the initiative or to visit other countries in search of a solution (chapter 9).

Relationships with Higher Authorities and Colleagues

Oil ministers need to have a good working relationship with other stakeholders and above all with their bosses for decisions they make to hold—or even to keep their jobs. For example, Issam al-Chalabi, Iraqi minister of petroleum from 1987 to 1990, did not have direct communication with President Saddam Hussein during the Kuwait oil crisis of the 1990s. There is no doubt that this lack of communication contributed to inconclusive negotiations in the first eight months of 1990, and Iraq and Kuwait were unable to find a solution to the oil crisis between them. This failure contributed to the Iraqi invasion of Kuwait in the summer of 1990 (chapter 3).

Good personal relationships both at home and abroad are often cemented by dining together or by attending sporting events (hiking, fishing, and so on). These relationships help to build understanding, trust, and the ability to work together to find solutions to problems.

Personality Traits

Personality traits shape human behavior and affect decision makers. Traits such as love, fear, hatred, jealousy, communication skills, trustworthiness, ambition, loyalty, integrity, and willingness to take risks influence the attitude of decision makers. It is these personality traits that have made a clear difference in the oil policies of many ministers from all over the world, and especially those within OPEC. Saddam Hussein's belief in his greatness and his obsession with conspiracy theories led him to make a very damaging decision for Iraq, the region, and the oil market (chapter 3).

Information

Information and the way it is presented and interpreted is the foundation for decision-making in all fields, and oil and energy information and research is available from many sources today. Policies regarding the oil market, such as OPEC's decisions to increase or decrease oil production, are based on the best available information at that particular time. In 2014, some market watchers and some oil officials believed that low oil prices, ranging from $60 to $70 per barrel, would lead to the disappearance of at least half of the shale oil production in the United States. This mistaken belief was proved wrong in the following year (chapter 9).

Oil market information has burgeoned since the 1980s as an expanded number of producers, consumers, and interested companies—including banks and hedge funds—have become active participants in the oil and energy industries. Although the number of reports has grown, the quality of these reports has not improved in a noticeable way. Today a variety of specialized news agencies and other news outlets play important roles in providing information for the oil market, and these sources can be grouped in the following categories.

- **International governmental organizations:** OPEC, the IEA, the World Bank, and the International Monetary Fund, among many others, employ strong, respected, and widely quoted researchers.
- **Governmental information agencies:** Many oil-producing and oil-consuming countries have their own information bureaus. The most important one—not in terms of size but by range of activities and transparency—is the U.S. Energy Information Administration, which is administratively independent from the government. Other countries have information and research centers on a smaller scale. Some of this information and research is not made available to the public because of fears that it might be interpreted as reflecting official policy.
- **Academic and semiacademic research centers attached to universities:** Among these research centers are the Oxford Institute for Energy Studies, Columbia University's Center on Global Energy Policy, and the King Abdullah Petroleum Studies and Research Center in Riyadh, Saudi Arabia.
- **Oil companies:** Almost all oil companies have their own information and research departments. Some of them are very strong and collect and analyze data used in making internal decisions, but external distribution of this information is limited.
- **Banks and financial institutions:** With the increase in physical oil trading and financial derivatives, major banks have established their own research and information centers. Some of these banks, unlike oil companies, publicize their work and their predictions regarding market direction.

- **Energy and petroleum consultants:** These institutions have been growing in numbers and expanding their activities. Perhaps the most important ones are IHS Markit and S&P Global Platts in the United States, which merged in 2020. This merger created one of the largest market data providers worldwide. The transaction's valuation of $44.5 billion is a clear indication of the value of data and information. These kinds of research centers are influential on many levels, and decision makers are selective in their choice of research organizations. This information often plays a pivotal role in events, as you will see throughout this book.

- **Media:** Oil is an important media topic, especially during energy-related or political crises. In addition to the major news agencies and business journals, there are important specialized oil publications such as the *Middle East Economic Survey* (MEES), which began with the indirect support of Aramco in 1957. Equally influential is the *Petroleum Intelligence Weekly* (PIW), launched in 1960 by the American oil media star Wanda Jablonski with the full support of international oil companies. Specialized oil publications are the most important sources of information, not only for the international oil market but also, and more important, as channels of communication within the oil industry, including OPEC.

NOVEL CONTRIBUTION OF THIS BOOK

Oil is important today for the prosperity and well-being of humanity, and it will continue to be important for many years to come. In the chapters that follow, I examine the role of many individual decision makers in the oil market since the beginning of the 1980s. I explore the role of important political leaders in oil-rich countries, such as Saudi Arabia's King Fahd, King Abdullah, King Salman, Crown Prince Mohammed bin Salman, and Prince Saud al-Faisal, as well as presidents Hugo Chavez of Venezuela, Saddam Hussein of Iraq, Barack Obama and Donald Trump of the United States, and Vladimir Putin of Russia. I also discuss the work of important energy ministers such as Prince Abdulaziz bin Salman, Ahmed Zaki Yamani, Hisham Nazer, Ali Al-Naimi, Ali al-Khalifa al-Sabah, Issam al-Chalabi, Alexander Novak, and Ali Rodriguez; powerful and influential heads of oil companies including Adrian Lajous (Pemex), Luis Giusti (Venezuelan National Oil Company), and Igor Sechin (Rosneft Oil Company);

as well as the late Roberto Mabro of the Oxford Institute for Energy Studies, who played a notable role in the oil market in the 1980s and 1990s.

Through the lens of the personality of these leaders, I examine important events such as the fall of oil prices in the 1980s and 1990s, the Iraqi invasion of Kuwait, the political/financial instability in Venezuela, and the economic and oil crises caused by the coronavirus pandemic in 2020. To provide a comprehensive account, I rely on my personal observations and experience. For more than thirty years, I have been a senior adviser in the Saudi ministry of petroleum (now the Ministry of Energy) and worked closely with four important ministers (Nazer, Al-Naimi, al-Falih, and Prince Abdulaziz). I did not work with Yamani, but I talked extensively with many people who had worked with him. In addition to my firsthand knowledge, I have conducted more than one hundred interviews and discussions with current and former key decision makers both inside and outside Saudi Arabia and have consulted public documents and secondary sources.

This is the first book to be written in a few decades in English by a Saudi national about Saudi Arabia's oil policy, OPEC, and the international oil market. I have focused on Saudi Arabia for two reasons. First, Saudi Arabia has been the most important oil country in the world for the last fifty years in terms of its reserves, production, exports, and spare capacity and has played a moderate to leading role in international oil management and decision-making during this time. Second, for more than thirty years, I have held a variety of positions in the Saudi energy sector, gaining a wide range of experience inside Saudi Arabia and elsewhere. I offer new insights and provide a unique perspective on the oil industry during this time. I believe a better understanding of the oil and energy policies of Saudi Arabia, OPEC, OPEC+, the United States, the United Kingdom, Russia, and others can be gained by examining the decision makers and the decisions they have made that have shaped major energy and petroleum strategies since the early 1980s.

Chapter One

AHMED ZAKI YAMANI
Good Start, Difficult Ending

On October 29, 1986, Hassan Yassin, a Saudi businessman and government adviser who had worked at the Ministry of Petroleum in the 1960s, arrived in Riyadh from Europe. He had brought a reclining chair with him as a gift for the petroleum minister Ahmed Zaki Yamani and asked his driver to take him to Yamani's house. On the way there, Yassin heard the news on the radio that King Fahd had relieved Yamani of his duties and replaced him with Hisham Nazer, who was then minister of planning. Thinking quickly, Yassin immediately asked the driver to take him to Nazer's house instead of Yamani's, and Yassin offered the chair to the new minister. In a single day, one man lost the ministry and a chair, and another man won both.[1]

Yamani occupied the post of Saudi minister of petroleum and mineral resources for twenty-four years and six months (from March 1962 to October 1986) under three Saudi kings (King Faisal, King Khalid, and King Fahd). During his tenure, Yamani played an active role in a tumultuous period that saw the rise of OPEC, the oil crises of the 1970s, and a turbulent period for politics of the Middle East. Yamani came close to death in 1975 when militants held him and some OPEC ministers hostage.

Yamani was the external image of Saudi Arabia's oil policies during the 1970s and the first half of the 1980s, but his legacy is mixed. There was a period of upheaval in the international oil market three years before his departure in 1986, and some of Yamani's key decisions then have had negative repercussions that are still being felt today and are likely to remain with us for some time to come. When Yamani passed away in February 2021, hundreds of comments, both negative and positive, circulated inside Saudi Arabia about his personality and his policies.

Yamani was the longest-serving nonroyal minister in the Saudi cabinet. Yamani had his own way of dealing with his bosses and colleagues, fellow ministers within Saudi Arabia, and with OPEC. He had a unique personality and decision-making style and was an international star who drew a crowd wherever he went, appearing regularly on the cover of *Time* and *Newsweek*. Yamani's decisions had an impact not only on Saudi Arabia and OPEC but also on the international oil market and the global economy. He stood out for two reasons. First, he was an effective OPEC negotiator when dealing with major international oil companies during a period that saw a rapid rise, followed by a steady fall, in oil prices. Second, he expressed strong political views, especially regarding the Arab oil embargo and the Arab-Israeli conflict.

Initially, Yamani struggled to fill the shoes of his legendary predecessor, Abdullah al-Tariki, who had cofounded OPEC and enjoyed a short but distinguished career both nationally and internationally. As a young minister working under King Faisal, Yamani did what he was told and delivered exactly what the king asked of him. The 1960s were relatively quiet years in the oil industry, and Yamani followed legacy policies established by al-Tariki.

Yamani's relationships and his international status changed as the oil market evolved. At an early press conference after an OPEC meeting in June 1969, only one journalist was in the room, and the journalist asked Yamani about the weather. Ten years later hundreds of journalists from around the world would attend Yamani's press conferences. After his appointment and through the early 1970s, Yamani mainly focused on domestic issues and is credited for the following achievements:

1. Establishment of the General Petroleum and Mineral Organization (Petromin) in 1962 as a government-owned but independent body responsible for local refining and distribution as well as other related petroleum and mineral activities, including the right to develop new oil reserves. Petromin gave some oil concessions outside Aramco areas to international companies (for example, concessions in the Red Sea to the French company Auxirap and part of the

Empty Quarter to the Italian oil company Agip). When Petromin was established by royal decree, the objective was "the diversification of the sources of income to avoid political and economic risks which may result from dependence on one source, namely, petroleum." This goal has been stated repeatedly since then and remains a key Saudi government objective. It should also be noted that the idea of founding Petromin was floating around before Yamani became a minister.

2. Establishment of the Department of Aerial Survey. Its task was to prepare different scale maps covering all of Saudi Arabia, including the borders with neighboring countries. It has grown over the years and is active in mapping and conducting land surveys of Saudi territories.

3. Negotiation of a number of border agreements with neighboring countries. Yamani signed the partition of the Neutral Zone on behalf of the Saudi government with Kuwait (1969), Iran (1968), and Qatar (1965). He also negotiated the agreement with the United Arab Emirates (UAE), but it was signed by King Faisal and Sheikh Zayed of the UAE in 1974.[2]

4. A leading role in the establishment of the College of Petroleum and Minerals in Dhahran in 1963 to advance higher education in these two subjects in Saudi Arabia (now renamed the King Fahd University of Petroleum and Minerals). It is the leading university in the fields of science and engineering in Saudi Arabia and the Arab world. Many important figures in the history of Saudi Arabia graduated from this university. Some people, including Americans in Aramco, objected, arguing that there were not enough Saudis to justify setting up a college. However, Yamani went ahead with the plan because he believed in the need for the advancement of Saudis working in Aramco.

5. His contributions to the establishment of the Organization of Arab Petroleum Exporting Countries (OAPEC) in 1967 to disassociate international oil issues from intra-Arab political conflicts.

Internationally, Yamani came to prominence in the early 1970s when OPEC began negotiating oil prices with international oil companies. In the beginning, the Iranians and Libyans took the lead in these negotiations, but the Arab-Israeli war of 1973 and the subsequent oil embargo changed the equation. Saudi Arabia's King Faisal was galvanized into action, assuming leadership on the political and petroleum fronts. Yamani also assumed a more prominent role in OPEC, leading negotiations with international oil companies on behalf of some Arab Gulf countries regarding their oil concessions. He also became the kingdom's public face on both oil and politics, reflecting King Faisal's policy in the absence of a government spokesperson. When King Faisal was assassinated in March 1975, Yamani was standing near the king, an image that reinforced the perception of his special relationship with King Faisal.[3]

After King Faisal's death, the king's brother, Khalid, became king and his brother, Fahd, became crown prince and deputy prime minister, major roles with vast influence and power. Aided by the country's vast oil income, King Khalid and Crown Price Fahd ushered in an era of prosperity known as the days of Tafrah (or the days of plenty). King Khalid's administration featured a new generation of young highly educated ministers, and Yamani and Prince Sultan, who was the defense minister, were the only ministers who kept their posts. Under King Khalid's administration, new policies encouraged investing in the economic development of all sectors in Saudi Arabia including public housing, political and media restrictions were loosened, and government ministries were modernized and became functioning administrative units. As oil prices surged, the kingdom prospered, and multiple opportunities arose for people to make money and improve the quality of their lives.

The second half of the 1970s was good for Yamani, and he notched up some significant achievements, including the smooth acquisition of Aramco from the American oil companies. In 1973 the Saudi government bought a 25 percent stake of Aramco, followed by an additional 35 percent in 1974, and attained full ownership in 1976. Some OPEC members chose full-fledged nationalization of oil resources, but Yamani followed a different path, and in doing so, he managed to retain good relations not just with the U.S. government but also with the former U.S. Aramco partners.

Saudi Arabia's oil prices and production had been more moderate than those of the majority of OPEC members in the early 1970s, and following the Arab-Israeli war of 1973, the oil embargo, and the subsequent surge in oil prices, Yamani became an international celebrity. Suddenly Yamani was the protagonist not just of Saudi oil policy but also of foreign policy. Until 1975 when Prince Saud al-Faisal was appointed foreign minister, Saudi Arabia did not have a full-time minister of foreign affairs (it had a minister of state for foreign affairs), and King Faisal acted as the minister. So it is no wonder that Yamani assumed the role of spokesperson, especially with the Western media. Prince Saud al-Faisal had worked for Yamani at the

Ministry of Petroleum, and they were very close friends. Yamani still occasionally spoke on Saudi foreign policy in the late 1970s, but his tone became less strident.

Yamani did not appear to take seriously, or perhaps ignored, political decisions by the industrialized countries to reduce their dependence on OPEC and on oil in general. Maybe Yamani was driven by the theory, which was commonplace at that time, that the world was running out of oil.[4] However, this decision by the industrialized countries began to have a clear impact on OPEC in the late 1970s.

When King Fahd came to power in 1982, nothing changed for Yamani. The two men had developed a good rapport over twenty years, and the new king continued to allow Yamani to make key decisions, hoping perhaps that the days of plenty would continue. But Yamani failed to understand that the tide was moving against OPEC and that the old tools of market dominance would soon fail to work. More important, the system of fixed oil prices, which had existed for many decades, was transitioning to market-based prices. Yamani and OPEC were slow to understand this change, and it took about five years (from 1983 to 1987) for them to move from fixed prices to a market-based target price range.

YAMANI'S PERSONALITY, THINKING, AND RELATIONSHIPS

Yamani was born in 1930 in Mecca, an auspicious place for Muslims, and his father was well known and highly educated for the time. The young Yamani studied Law at Cairo University in Egypt and went on to obtain degrees from New York University and Harvard Law School. Upon his return to Saudi Arabia, Yamani had no difficulty securing an important job as a royal court legal adviser. He dressed very well in Arabic and Western clothes and had an elegant and charming manner that exuded confidence. His good looks, intelligence, confidence, and down-to-earth manner when dealing with the media endeared him to journalists. However, his peers sometimes found Yamani to be difficult and arrogant. He focused on the big picture, often ignoring the finer details, making him a somewhat one-dimensional man.[5]

Yamani spoke excellent Arabic and spoke English with an exotic accent. He chose his words carefully and expressed himself confidently and stylistically. He was logical and structured in both his thinking and his speech. "Yamani was one of the best quotable officials," noted Bhushan Bahree, a veteran journalist and oil analyst.[6] Yamani loved the media spotlight but did not want to appear to be an attention-seeker. He lobbied quietly to secure invitations to appear on U.S. TV networks and programs, such as Ted Koppel's *Nightline*.[7] "When he arrived in a hall, either for a lecture or a press conference, the whole room became electrified; he was like a king or the head of a great power," said publisher and oil analyst Pierre Terzian.[8]

On the international stage, Yamani's charismatic appeal did not fade when oil prices slumped, and his image remained untarnished for a couple of years after he left the ministry. But at home his star waned as soon as oil prices began to fall. Yamani's woes began in 1982 when a perfect storm hit the oil market. Shrinking global demand and rising non-OPEC supply led to a steady decline in the price of oil and a sharp fall in the "call on OPEC oil" (the difference between total demand and supply from non-OPEC sources). The global oil-pricing system based on official selling prices (OSPs) came under pressure, and Saudi Arabia and other OPEC oil producers faced economic and financial difficulties. Successive oil market collapses saw Saudi government oil revenues slump from $186 billion in 1982 to $42 billion in 1986. GDP gradually declined from $524 billion in 1982 to $322 billion in 1986, and the assets of the Saudi Central Bank shrank as the current account deficit surged. A deficit appeared in 1983 and continued to grow in the following years.[9]

By 1986, speculative pressure on the Saudi currency (the riyal) was so great that the government was forced to abandon its long-held peg to the U.S. dollar and to devalue the riyal from 3.31 to 3.75 to the dollar. That year, both the nascent stock market and the real estate market crashed, in some cases plunging by as much as 70 percent.

Many Saudis blamed Yamani for these problems, but Yamani pointed the finger at OPEC and non-OPEC oil producers. He even blamed a Western conspiracy against OPEC for the country's woes while arguing that the market would soon turn in OPEC's (and Saudi Arabia's) favor.[10] In the four years following the 1982 oil crisis, Yamani had to fight fires on multiple fronts, an effort that would test him to the limit. A new paradigm for decision-making was needed, but Yamani was hampered by incomplete information. To succeed, he would need foresight, access to different sources of information, and the ability to juggle many balls at the same time.

Oil dethroned coal in the late nineteenth century, and global oil demand has grown steadily since then, reaching a peak of 65 MBD in 1979. Then the unthinkable happened. For the first time in oil history, demand went into a steady decline, falling to nearly 59 MBD in 1983. A global economic slowdown in the late 1970s and early 1980s and high oil prices negatively affected demand, but the main reason for the decline was the decision by governments in major oil-consuming countries to speed up energy conservation measures to curb demand. These measures included stricter vehicle fuel performance standards, lower speed limits, and energy-efficient building codes. Consuming countries also began switching to other sources of energy, such as nuclear, and coal.

Oil production from non-OPEC countries was also on the rise, mainly from the North Sea (the United Kingdom and Norway), Canada, Alaska, Mexico, and the Soviet Union. As competition grew, some oil companies from these countries and regions began a price war with OPEC, which had been setting production and price levels. The state-owned British National Oil Corporation (BNOC or Britoil), developing North Sea oil, slashed oil prices by $4 per barrel below most OPEC official selling prices (OSPs) in 1982, and by a further $5 the following year. North Sea oil production continued to increase even as global oil prices declined, contrary to what Yamani believed would happen. (A similar phenomenon occurred thirty-five years later when oil minister Ali Al-Naimi misjudged the resilience of U.S. shale and other expensive oil.)

Equally important was the launch of the first oil futures market on the New York Mercantile Exchange (NYMEX) in 1983. Investors were able to buy and sell oil futures contracts months in advance, enabling them to hedge against oil-price volatility and putting financial investors at the heart of the oil market. The dual-price system of fixed OSPs and the parallel spot market price came under growing pressure, and the role of oil producers in fixing and setting prices was reduced. OPEC was no longer managing the oil prices.

From the end of the 1970s to the mid-1980s, OPEC was paralyzed, unable to go beyond the traditional remedies of reducing production and changing the official oil price. Yamani and other OPEC members responded with infighting and finger pointing. "It was a useless and painful exercise."[11] OPEC meetings were characterized by arguments over what official oil prices should be, with squabbles over a $2 differential. The resulting duel-price system, with one price for Saudi Arabia and another for the other OPEC countries, distorted the oil market and pitted Yamani against the rest of OPEC, including traditional Saudi allies such as Kuwait.[12]

Even worse for Saudi Arabia was the two-price system for Saudi crude: the OSP and the spot price. From 1979 to 1982, official prices were lower than spot prices by $1 to $8 per barrel (table 1.1). Petromin marketed at least 60 percent of Saudi crude oil, and the remainder was sold to the four U.S. Aramco shareholders at the official Saudi price, not at the international oil price. This state of play inevitably led to a period of abuse that lasted for about three years. Well-connected Saudis bought Saudi oil through front companies at the official oil price and sold it at the international spot price, making millions of dollars in the process. Aramco's former U.S. shareholders marketed about 40 percent of Saudi oil, and they took advantage of this practice. The windfall revenues were so clear that accounting for them caused the companies considerable trouble with the U.S. Internal Revenue Service, and their case reached the U.S. Supreme Court in 1989.[13]

When the market reversed in 1983 and official Saudi prices rose above spot oil prices, these "artificial" customers disappeared. Even worse, regular buyers of Saudi oil, including the major oil companies who were Aramco's partners, reduced their purchase of Saudi oil, switching to lower-priced

TABLE 1.1
Difference between average official oil price and spot price for Saudi crude oil for selected months, 1979–1982

Month	Official Price ($ Barrel Arab Light)	Spot Price ($ Barrel Arab Light)	Difference ($)
April 1979	14.546	21.25	− 6.740
May 1979	14.546	29.250	− 14.704
June 1979	18.000	35.000	− 17.000
October 1979	18.000	38.000	− 20.000
August 1980	30.000	31.387	− 1.387
June 1981	32.000	31.750	+ 0.250
July 1981	32.000	31.783	+ 0.217
March 1982	29.000	28.470	+ 5.30

Sources: OPEC and Nourah A. al Yousef, "The Role of Saudi Arabia in the World Oil Market" (PhD diss., University of Surrey, April 1998).

sellers or to the spot market and to non-OPEC producers such as the United Kingdom and Norway. In both countries, the government was the owner and operator of the oil company, and they had more flexible pricing systems and sometimes offered discounts. This development made Yamani deeply unhappy, and he blamed these producers for the decline in oil prices, at times suggesting that Western powers were engaged in a well-orchestrated plan against OPEC.[14] But the issue was more complicated than this; it also had domestic elements.

YAMANI, ARAMCO, AND PETROMIN

In January 1976, the Saudi government purchased the remaining stakes still held by the U.S. founding partners in Aramco—Mobil, Exxon, Texaco, and Chevron—making it a fully owned Saudi national oil company. But Yamani kept Aramco's management in the hands of the four original U.S. companies under rolling annual management contracts. The Ministry of Finance wanted to oversee some of the company's financial activities, whereas Yamani wanted it to be fully free and independent. According to Ali Al-Naimi, the first Saudi president of Aramco in 1983, Yamani initially considered placing the company under Petromin's management, but the top Saudi management team threatened to resign so Yamani backed down.[15] Many Aramco and Saudi ministry officials have no recollection of this story.[16]

At the same time, Yamani came under fire over the mismanagement of Petromin, where he served as chairman with director general Abdulhadi Taher, who was Yamani's confidant. Taher was accused of failing to develop and grow the agency in the early 1980s, and there was talk of abuse and mismanagement at all levels of the organization. Petromin had also failed to establish a petrochemical industry, one of its original mandates when it was established in 1962. The government responded by handing over the task of creating a Saudi petrochemicals industry to the Ministry of Industries and the Ministry of Planning. In addition, Petromin had been unable to manage the East-West pipeline designed to carry crude oil from oilfields in the Eastern Province to export terminals on the Red Sea, bypassing choke points in the Arabian Gulf. The government intervened in 1984, taking the responsibility away from Petromin and Mobil Oil and giving it to Aramco.

SWING PRODUCTION AND SWINGING DECISIONS

Between 1980 and 1986, the international oil market was undergoing fundamental changes, and OPEC's decisions, in general, and Saudi Arabia's, in particular, were constantly changing direction, adding to market instability. OPEC ministers were faced with the conundrum of how to maintain high oil prices during a period of declining demand, rising non-OPEC supply, and high oil stocks. The only solution was to cut OPEC production, which they did in 1980, but Yamani ordered an increase in Saudi output even as commercial stocks were rising.

In mid-1982, as the market situation deteriorated, Ali al-Khalifa al-Sabah, the Kuwait oil minister, proposed an official OPEC production ceiling of 18 MBD. In the early months of the following year, the OPEC quota system was adopted to defend a price of $28 a barrel and to balance the market. A similar system had been used by the Texas Railroad Commission in the United States in the 1940s and by the multinational oil companies known as the Seven Sisters in later years. Ali al-Sabah and Yamani were close friends, and the two ministers always coordinated their positions in advance of OPEC meetings. Yamani embraced the new system with enthusiasm and decided to play it his way, if need be, by allowing Saudi Arabia to take on the role of swing producer. Saudi Arabia was allocated a quota of 5 MBD but chose to decrease its production unilaterally to balance the market when needed. Yamani went on to reduce Saudi production for the ensuing three years until it became clear that this policy benefited everyone except Saudi Arabia. Saudi oil production fell from 10.5 MBD in 1980 to 2.2 MBD in March 1985 but took off in the opposite direction in early 1986 when Saudi Arabia increased production to 6 MBD.

Yamani's decision to allow Saudi Arabia to take on the role of a swing producer has been the subject of much debate. It is still being discussed today and most likely will be for many years to come. Within Saudi Arabia, the consensus was that the policy was deeply flawed and that the kingdom should never go down that route again. Thirty years later, during a period of instability in 2014 to 2016, Al-Naimi referred to this period in his argument against a production cut by Saudi Arabia when prices were gradually falling. Yet it should be noted that Saudi Arabia was not the only country to reduce its production. OPEC production dropped from almost 30 MBD in 1979 to less than 14 MBD by 1985. Saudi

Arabia accounted for half of that reduction, but other OPEC members accounted for the other half.

WHY SAUDI ARABIA CHOSE TO BE A SWING PRODUCER

One possible reason Saudi Arabia chose to be a swing producer is that Yamani was persuaded by Ali al-Sabah, his trusted friend and colleague, who believed this would be a temporary situation and that demand and prices would soon recover.[17] Even when oil prices collapsed in 1986, both men tried to convince other OPEC ministers that demand was rising and that they would soon benefit from this increase.[18] But that argument makes little sense. Yamani was too smart to allow others to manipulate him, and it is more likely that the decision was Yamani's. He believed, as a lawyer, that the production level (in this case Saudi Arabia's quota) was exclusively a sovereign issue that should be decided by the country alone and not by a third party such as OPEC.

Other important factors in Yamani's decision-making in the early 1980s can be attributed to his opinion of the international market based on information he was given or the way he interpreted it. Yamani did not pay much attention to numbers and details, and this was reflected in his presentations and press statements at the time. A presentation he made to the Oxford Energy Seminar in September 1982 showed confidence in his sources of information and his ability to predict outcomes.[19] It also came at a critical time. Yamani was at the peak of his powers and prestige as an oil price-setter just before the market and OPEC experienced major challenges that Yamani could not predict or influence.

Indeed, Yamani's predictions were wrong on several counts. In one statement at the Oxford event, Yamani said, "If the price of oil had gone down to $28 per barrel or well below that level, I would then say with confidence that there would be a shortage in the supply of oil and energy in the future—probably even by the end of this decade." Yet just four years later the price of oil fell below $10 and stayed below $20 until the end of next decade. There was no shortage of supply, even following Iraq's invasion of Kuwait in 1990 (when the international market lost a combined four million barrels daily from both countries).

Yamani went on to say, "On the supply side, we all know that some of our fellow members in OPEC will gradually stop being exporters after 1985 and will completely disappear as exporters by 1990." However, this did not happen; only Indonesia stopped being a net exporter, and that was not until twenty years later.

Regarding a price of $28, Yamani remarked, "If we freeze the price of oil until the end of 1983 and probably for part of 1984, then we will encourage demand for oil and reduce consumption of coal and will reach a balanced supply-demand situation sooner than is expected." But if the price goes to $24 per barrel or less, Yamani suggested that "the immediate result would be an immediate shift from coal to oil that would put a stop to any invest-ment in exploration [and] probably some of the oilfields in the North Sea would become marginal and maybe even not profitable." However, North Sea oil production rose from 1.5 MBD in 1982 to 3.3 MBD in 1985, and on to 3.5 MBD in 1990, and the average oil price fluctuated between about $15 and $25 for most of the period.

Being optimistic about the future of the oil market is one thing, but being overconfident and predicting market behavior is quite another. Yamani had an unshakeable belief that lower oil prices ($24–$28 in 1982) would lead to stronger demand growth for OPEC oil because of a shift from coal to oil and lower production from some areas, such as the North Sea. If these assumptions had become facts, then assuming the role of a swing producer might have made sense. What did not make sense, however, was to assume that the other OPEC producers, including Saudi Arabia's allies, would adhere to their quotas while allowing Saudi Arabia alone to increase its production when demand rose.

It did not take long for Yamani to discover that his policy of fixed oil prices and lower production had failed to reverse price falls in a com-petitive market with excess production capacity available to some OPEC members and other producers at a time of declining demand. Inter-national market developments, such as the rise of the futures market, played a major part in the death of OSPs, but it was decisions by OPEC ministers, including Yamani, that hammered the final nail in the coffin. After four years of playing the role of swing producer and cutting pro-duction year after year, Yamani suddenly reversed direction and decided to sell as much oil as he could. This approach was later adopted by Ali al-Sabah in Kuwait and Luis Giusti in Venezuela, and partially by Ali Al-Naimi in Saudi Arabia. Other oil ministers and leaders may adopt this policy in the future.

Yamani ordered Aramco to increase production, which proved to be a challenging task for Saudi Arabia. Recovering lost customers whose requests for crude had been rebuffed over the previous four years was challenging. Following nationalization of their oil assets, many OPEC countries had failed to realize the importance of integration within the oil industry and did not establish professional oil marketing departments to foster a close working relationship with customers. As a result, selling extra crude became very difficult.

First, price differentials within OPEC and the price differential for Saudi oil created multiple distortions in the oil market. Second, the special discount given to customers by some OPEC members and, more important, by non-OPEC countries (such as the United Kingdom and Norway) led to a more competitive market. Third, the nationalization of oil assets was not followed up with the creation of strong national oil companies in all chains of the industry. Finally, emergence of the futures market created a new platform where buyers and sellers could set prices disconnected from the physical spot market and OSPs. Yamani was rapidly losing the battle to control pricing and maintain reasonable production levels.

Apart from the financial problems that Saudi Arabia faced at the time, low oil production had led to a shortage of associated natural gas produced in tandem from the oil fields, which was needed for electricity generation, water desalination, and as feedstock for an emerging petrochemicals industry. The introduction of netback pricing in 1985 dealt the death knell to OSPs. The fully integrated international oil companies (IOCs) had used the netback system for years to price internal transactions. When Yamani asked the IOCs, especially Aramco's partners, to buy more Saudi oil at the OSP, they refused and suggested using netback formulas. He accepted the new system in the hope that Saudi oil production would increase, or even double, without a significant decline in oil prices.

From that moment on, netback pricing became the norm, and neither Yamani nor anyone else, particularly the Ministry of Finance, knew in advance what the price of Saudi crude would be. Crude would be sold to refiners under a fixed formula based on product prices that not only changed daily but also varied from one country to another and, at times, from one refiner to another. The refiners were happy because it gave them a guaranteed margin, and Yamani was satisfied that they were selling a large amount of oil. Saudi production increased from under 3 MBD in 1984 to 6 MBD by the end of 1985.

In the beginning, the Saudis received a reasonable price per barrel and sold larger volumes. However, other producers soon jumped on the net-back bandwagon, which had terrible consequences for all. The oil market collapsed on the back of lower product prices and high crude and product stocks. By 1986, a barrel of crude was down to less than $10 (from about $28 the previous year). Saudi Arabia's net oil revenue fell, even though it was producing much more oil. A low point was reached when a cargo of Saudi crude netted just $3.25 per barrel from a refinery in Brazil. The Saudi economy was struggling, and many in the kingdom, including ministers, intellectuals, academics, and journalists, firmly placed the blame at Yamani's door.

The Saudi government's official budget was further reduced by two major off-budget oil deals. Yamani was involved in both deals, but his reasons were unclear. Was he trying to please some highly influential people within the government to make up for the negative effects of his oil policy on the economy, or was he trying to play some domestic game within the government? Was he forced to go along with these deals, or had he simply lost his influence?[20] The two off-budget deals were the following:

1. The Al Yamamah defense agreement with British Aerospace (BAE), negotiated in 1984 and signed in 1985, was to supply Saudi Arabia's Ministry of Defense and Aviation with a wide range of military equipment, including jet fighters, to be paid for under a barter deal in which Saudi Arabia would deliver about five hundred million barrels of oil daily (an ever-changing number that varied from year to year) over the lifetime of the contract. Aramco would supply the oil to British Petroleum (BP) and Royal/Dutch Shell, which would market the oil internationally for a commission of 10 cents per barrel. The cash was to be deposited in a special account in a British bank over which the UK government would have control, and the government received a special commission (another 10 cents) for overseeing the account. This deal was to continue until 1996.[21]

2. The Saudi Strategic Storage Program (SSSP) was to establish storage facilities for petroleum products in Saudi Arabia to be used in case of emergency. It consisted of underground tanks for gasoline, diesel, and jet fuel in five locations (Riyadh, Jeddah, Abha, al-Medinah, and al-Qassim). The program was

under the control of the Ministry of Defense and Aviation during the construction phase. The construction design was by the British Company Jacobson and Windmark (J&W), and the Swedish Company ABV Rock did the actual construction. Yamani began negotiations with J&W in London in 1986, but he left the ministry before the contract was signed and the work was started. The project was much smaller than originally planned. The deal involved the allocation of about 200,000 barrels daily (the amount varied) to be sold by Aramco, with the money deposited in a special account of the Saudi National Commercial Bank. The Ministry of Defense and Aviation had full control over the account and could spend the money as it saw fit. This arrangement continued until 2005. In 2008, control of the project was transferred to Aramco and became part of its domestic product distribution network.[22]

The total amount of oil allocated to these two projects varied over the years. The project received criticism inside Saudi Arabia, but during attacks on the Abqaiq and Khurais oil facilities in September 2019, it proved to be very useful (chapter 11).

In 1984, when Yamani was asked about the Al Yamamah program, the oil for defense equipment barter deal, and the resulting increase in Saudi oil exports, he defended it and asserted that it would not harm the international oil market. "The barter deal was not used to increase output levels. It was used for internal fiscal reasons because there was no allocation for that in our budget, and therefore we had either to draw on our financial assets, which we are very reluctant to do, or to arrange a barter deal."[23] After leaving office, Yamani told the author of his biography that he opposed the deal when he was a minister because it would, as he said, "lead to 34.5 million barrels of extra oil floating around the market, feeding the glut and helping to depress prices even further."[24]

YAMANI'S RELATIONS WITH OTHERS

During the three years before his departure, Yamani did not have a good working relationship with some fellow ministers. They did not like his working style and disagreed with many of his decisions on petroleum matters because of their negative impact on the Saudi economy. Mohammed Aba al-Khail, the minister of finance who had a high profile both nationally and internationally, disagreed with Yamani over a number of issues.

In particular, he objected to Yamani's policy of keeping billions of dollars as a reserve for both Saudi Aramco and Petromin. Aba al-Khail wanted the funds to be transferred to the government to help deal with the ever-growing financial deficit.

The conflict between the two about these cash reserves continued for more than two years. King Fahd wanted an end to the impasse, and he asked Hisham Nazer, the minister of planning, to arbitrate. Nazer was a close friend of both ministers, and he recommended that the money be transferred to the Ministry of Finance. King Fahd agreed with this recommendation. Yamani was unhappy with this decision and kept a distance from Nazer for some years after the episode despite Nazer's best efforts to explain that his suggestion was the best possible outcome for Yamani.[25] Thereafter, Aba al-Khail, Nazer, and some ministers were not on good terms with Yamani. Within the kingdom, just as in other countries, a high value is placed on having good working relations with your colleagues to achieve the best outcome. Without this relationship, unilateral decisions by one person can damage another minister's chances of reaching the desired goals.

During that time, Yamani also faced growing opposition from the Saudi media and from economic and energy experts. Among his critics was Ali al-Juhani, a young economics professor at the College of Petroleum and Minerals (now King Fahd University). When Yamani gave a lecture about the oil market and OPEC policy at the university in March 1984, al-Juhani was openly critical of him. Yamani said that oil was an important strategic commodity to which economic logic did not necessarily apply. Al-Juhani argued that oil was subject to the law of supply and demand like any other commodity or product. Al-Juhani followed up with an article in *Asharq al-Awsat*, a Saudi-owned newspaper that generally reflected the government's opinion, in which al-Juhani expressed his views.[26]

By the beginning of 1986, Yamani was fighting a losing battle on both the national and international fronts. The attempt to go after market share by raising production and using netback pricing was damaging the Saudi economy, and it offered few if any benefits. The price of oil fell below $10, and government income was at its lowest in years. Yamani conceded that the political power of the Arab world, including Saudi Arabia, was declining because of low oil prices.[27] Yamani was fired in 1986. Saudi Arabia had been expecting this since 1985, but many people in the West were surprised.

YAMANI AND DECISION-MAKING

Yamani's actions and his decision-making style were influenced by his personality traits and the environment in which he operated. The most obvious of his personality traits were his great sense of ego and the excessive care he took in managing his image. Yamani paid special attention to his physical appearance and to the language he used.

The first significant element of Yamani's personality that influenced his decision-making was his reluctance to consult people within the ministry about important issues, such as netback pricing. He had a small circle of friends and advisers on whom he relied for many of his decisions. Well-placed Saudi and Kuwaiti sources recount that Yamani and Ali al-Khalifa al-Sabah decided privately to go after market share and abandon the quota system and OSPs. Yamani did not consult with King Fahd or any members of the cabinet, nor did Ali al-Sabah inform his government.[28] "He used to think that he was bigger than the numbers and bigger than the facts," said Pierre Terzian, a well-known energy analyst.[29]

The second significant element was Yamani's relationship with the Saudi kings. During King Faisal's reign (1964–1975), Yamani had a direct and close relationship with the king, consulting and seeking King Faisal's approval on both small and large national and international issues. King Faisal trusted Yamani and even asked him to undertake diplomatic missions. In 1973, Saudi Arabia established the ministerial-level Supreme Council for Petroleum and Minerals, which was chaired by Crown Prince Fahd (who later became king) with Yamani as vice chairman. The council was to oversee Saudi petroleum policy and approve important decisions.

King Khalid became head of state in 1975, and he asked Crown Prince Fahd to take charge of economic matters, including oil. A new cabinet was formed, and most of the incoming ministers were young and inexperienced, although they typically had master's degrees or PhDs from Western universities. Two ministers kept their posts: Crown Prince Sultan bin Abdulaziz, who was the minister of defense, and Yamani. This was a clear sign of the degree of trust, confidence, and good relations that both King Khalid and Crown Prince Fahd had in Yamani. When Fahd became king in 1982, he too kept Yamani on as oil minister, giving him the same level of confidence and trust previous monarchs had. Their relationship was excellent in the beginning, but King Fahd's confidence in Yamani's management began to sour as oil prices continued to drop. To make matters worse, Yamani kept promising King Fahd and the government that oil demand would soon pick up and that Saudi Arabia would gain from higher oil production and high prices.

Issues related to oil or OPEC were normally dealt with directly by King Fahd and Yamani, but other key petroleum issues related to Aramco and Petromin were subject to debate in the Council of Ministers, the Supreme Council for Petroleum and Minerals, or the follow-up committee at the Ministry of Planning. Yamani did not like the follow-up committee and occasionally would become angry and storm out of meetings. This might have been one reason Yamani did not ask King Fahd for permission to increase production and to adopt a netback pricing system.

A common belief, especially in the West, is that King Fahd did not like Yamani from the start. Although we cannot know King Fahd's real feelings, evidence backed up by Saudi sources before the 1985–1986 petroleum crisis suggests the opposite. King Fahd sought Yamani's advice on many issues, including those not directly related to oil. Even when some OPEC heads of state wanted to discuss oil matters with Saudi leaders, they would be told to talk them over with Yamani. King Fahd stood by Yamani after his departure when Yamani needed medical treatment, and the king supported Yamani's desire to travel abroad without any restrictions. If King Fahd had wanted to fire Yamani, he definitely would have done so. Contrary to what some in the Western media believe, King Fahd did not hesitate to fire ministers he did not like, including his close friend Ghazi al Gosaibi.[30]

The third important element in understanding Yamani and the influences on his decision-making process is the information and analysis that he received and the way he selected and interpreted this information. During the 1970s, oil market information and analysis available to energy ministers was limited to a few sources.

1. **Ministry of the Petroleum Economic Department.** This small group of four people was headed by Farouk al-Husseini, one of the most respected oil economists from the 1970s through the early 1990s, both nationally and internationally. Yamani listened to him but sometimes made decisions without al-Husseini's knowledge or agreement. Yamani also relied on two departments within the ministry when making decisions related to OPEC: the legal and the general accounting departments.

2. **Major international oil companies (especially Aramco partners).** These companies studied all aspects of the oil market, including supply and demand and OPEC behavior. Yamani received their reports, highly valued their opinions, and asked them about certain issues.[31]

3. **OPEC secretariat.** OPEC did not have a research department that could provide in-depth market analysis at that time, so ministers did not have an independent source of information such as they have today. Typically, the OPEC secretary-general or his deputy would provide a verbal report to ministers about the state of the international market before meetings began. Likewise, when representatives from member states met at the Economic Board, they tended to highlight their own country's position rather than provide a good independent assessment of the oil market.

4. **Independent experts and consultants.** Yamani relied on reports published by consultants and referred to them in speeches and press conferences. He had good relationships with a few oil experts, in particular with the Oxford Institute for Energy Studies (OIES), headed by Robert Mabro. Yamani's and Mabro's views on the oil market sometimes mirrored each other.

Yamani also had close personal relationships with some journalists. Most journalists liked him, although he did have some enemies in the media.[32] Yamani was particularly close to *MEES* and to its British editor, Ian Seymour, and gave him exclusive interviews. When speaking to the media, most of the time he was delivering messages to others inside OPEC, as well as to outsiders such as oil companies, other producers, and government officials of consuming countries.

Other factors that influenced Yamani and other oil decision makers included the long-term outlook for oil. In the 1970s and early 1980s, some major government and independent institutes were researching the future of commodities. They believed that the world's available resources could not satisfy future demand. Many predicted that this would lead to a shortage and higher prices, with severe consequences for the world economy and the public, perhaps by the end of the twentieth century. Among those think tanks was the famous Club of Rome, which published a report in the early 1970s titled "Limits to Growth." This was followed by similar analyses, including a U.S. government report predicting an emerging shortage of commodities before the end of the twentieth century, a theory common among economists and scholars at the time. These studies influenced and reinforced the beliefs of some OPEC and non-OPEC decision makers, including Yamani, who tended to use reports that either suited or confirmed his own beliefs (or even his wishful thinking).

Yamani and other Saudi Ministry of Petroleum officials lacked reliable and timely information about the oil market and supply, demand, and commercial stocks. The information that was available was mostly geopolitical, there was no internet, and fax machines had only begun to be used to pass information along quickly.

Yamani tended to mix oil with politics. The decision by King Faisal (in coordination with Egyptian president Anwar el-Sadat) to go ahead with the 1973–1974 oil embargo was political, and Yamani seemed happy to execute the policy without hesitation. This may have been due to the general political mood at the time. Yamani was neither an economist nor a businessman, and he did not appear to have taken into account the possible damage to the relationship between oil producers and consumers or the potential negative behavior of consumers in terms of demand management. He also didn't account for the impact on the public image of oil producers, especially Arabs and OPEC, among and within major consuming nations.

For example, after the 1973 Arab-Israeli war and the oil embargo, Yamani said, "I think what we have as an oil weapon is far greater than what we did, what we did is nothing at all." He added that the cut in production could have been much higher, 20 percent or even 80 percent.[33] Such statements were very harmful, and this is still a major concern in the United States, even with changing energy circumstances and policies. Yamani kept up the rhetoric, even after the death of King Faisal. When President Anwar el-Sadat expressed his willingness in the late 1970s to sign a peace treaty between Egypt and Israel, a move opposed by all Arab countries, Yamani said, "unless the Israelis will realize the facts of life and accept peace, I think they will pay a heavy price, everybody will pay a heavy price and the whole world will suffer."[34] In later years, Yamani continued to mix oil with politics, accusing the United Kingdom and Norway of having political motives when they refused to cooperate with OPEC in 1984.

Yamani was a smart and articulate man who was able to influence events through political maneuvering and media manipulation. During his career, he was loyal to king and country, eager to serve both to the best of his ability, but he wanted to be seen as a star and as a unique figure. He was, in many ways, a victim of his own success. He failed to recognize that his rise to prominence on the world stage was because he was the minister of petroleum of Saudi Arabia, the world's largest oil producer and exporter (with the largest reserves and production capacity) rather than being based on his own merit or because of his role in OPEC.

Yamani's exit from the world stage was as dramatic as his time in office. Yamani heard of his removal on the news, and it was a blow that he had not seen coming. Yamani found the loss of prestige extremely difficult. It was clear that he had wanted and expected to stay on even longer. To many in the West, where he enjoyed celebrity status, his departure was unexpected and not readily accepted.[35] Like other officials who remain in power for a long time, Yamani felt that he was indispensable and irreplaceable and that the office was his. He found it hard to adjust to no longer being in the international spotlight after being on the stage for close to twenty-five years. Even after he had left office, he called some ministers he trusted before or during OPEC meetings to find out what they were discussing and to offer advice. For several months after he left, he remained in close contact with the deputy secretary-general of OPEC, Fadhil Chalabi.

In 1990, Yamani established an energy think tank in London, the Centre for Global Energy Studies (CGES), under the directorship of Fadhil Chalabi. The CGES organized an annual oil conference, to which Yamani would invite oil ministers (mostly his friends) and oil company executives from around the world. Yamani delivered the keynote speech at the conference as if he were still the oil minister, addressing the international oil market, OPEC affairs, and giving his opinion and suggestions as to what oil producers should do. He also spoke to the media, occasionally on the record, with comments on oil prices and his own predictions about future directions. The CGES offices were housed in an office building owned by Yamani in central London, next to a building owned by Petromin. The think tank provided Yamani with a platform, but it was a drain on his finances because it generated little income. Over time Yamani lost his star power, and in 2014, after twenty-four years of Yamani's involvement, CGES closed its doors.

Yamani was the Saudi oil minister during one of the most important and controversial chapters in the history of Saudi Arabia, OPEC, and the international oil market. It was a time when decision-making prowess and an outsized ego combined to make an indelible mark in the world oil market. Yamani was successful in the 1960s and 1970s, but he could not keep pace with the fast-changing oil market of the first half of the 1980s. His relationship with King Fahd and with his colleagues, his advancing age, longevity in office, overconfidence, and the way he dealt with information all contributed to Yamani's eventual downfall.

Chapter Two

HISHAM NAZER

Shifting Interests and Looking Nationally

Ahmed Zaki Yamani was a global energy leader whose fame at times eclipsed that of many OPEC heads of state; King Fahd realized that replacing such a large personality would not be easy. King Fahd decided to place the kingdom's oil policy into the capable hands of Hisham Nazer, who was currently the minister of planning and who had worked under both powerful predecessors, Abdullah al-Tariki and Yamani. Nazer and King Fahd had been close friends for more than twenty years. They saw each other regularly and discussed matters relating to the Saudi economy, social issues, and even sports.

Nazer wanted to bring about changes not only in oil policy but in the entire Saudi oil industry. Nazer was determined to make his mark, and he had the personality, energy, and background to make that happen. He had worked at the Ministry of Petroleum since 1958 in numerous roles and with various responsibilities. As minister of planning, Nazer had supervised development of the Saudi economy, including the energy sector, and in 1970 he drafted the kingdom's first five-year development plan.

Nazer was born in 1932 into a prosperous and distinguished family in Jeddah in the western region of Hejaz. He attended elementary and middle school in Jeddah, but was then sent to Victoria College, a private boarding school in Alexandria, Egypt, that followed the British curriculum and was the Arab world's elite school at that time. Many of Nazer's classmates, including King Hussein of Jordan, would go on to play key roles in the region and beyond. Nazer next went to the United States, where he received both bachelor's and master's degrees in international relations from the University of California at Los Angeles.

Returning home in 1958, one newspaper carried a small news item about Nazer's academic degree that drew the attention of Abdullah al-Tariki, head of the newly created Ministry of Petroleum (previously oil and minerals had been part of the portfolio of the Ministry of Finance). Al-Tariki called Nazer at home and asked him to join the ministry. Al-Tarika had taken a chance on an unknown newcomer, which is perhaps one reason Nazer did not hesitate to hire new people when he later became a minister, a rare trait among managers in the Arab world. In 1960, the ministry moved from Jeddah on the Red Sea coast to the capital of Riyadh, a move that was not easy for Nazer and his family, but he was willing to take on the challenge.

GETTING THE ATTENTION OF KING FAISAL

In the early 1960s, Riyadh was a small city with a population of less than 200,000. It had one international hotel, no cinemas, one modern restaurant, no cafés, two high schools, and a small new university. Nevertheless, it was growing rapidly and was starting to compete with Jeddah as a commercial, cultural, and intellectual city.

Socially, Riyadh was dominated by a small local elite of princes, traders, and intellectuals that included leading members of the ruling Al Saud family, among them Prince Fahd, Prince Abdullah, and Prince Salman bin Abdulaziz—all later became king; and Crown Prince Sultan bin Abdulaziz, the influential minister of defense; and Prince Talal bin Abdulaziz, who became an important figure in the Saudi political system. Other leading members of the capital's elite included educated government officials and business leaders such as Ibrahim al-Angari, Nasser Almanqour, Abdulaziz al-Muammar, and Faisal al-Hejailan. Some of them became ministers and important decision makers within the government, others became professors at the new King Saud University or intellectual leaders, and a few went into exile during the 1960s.

These groups engaged in fervent political debates centered on the prevalent schools of thought at the time—Arab nationalism, socialism, political liberalism, and social conservatism—and these debates and the people involved have played major roles in the formation of modern Saudi Arabia. The future direction of Saudi Arabia as it emerged from a tribal society to a modern one with an oil-fueled economy was hotly debated. This political debate between different power centers within the royal family and society at large was intense during the political upheavals of the late 1950s and early 1960s and led to the replacement of the second King of Saudi Arabia, King Saud, in 1964, when his brother Faisal became king. Some prominent Saudis declared themselves members of the opposition and decided to leave the kingdom. Saudi intellectuals were eager for change, espousing liberal ideas and calling for a constitution and even creation of a constitutional monarchy. Nazer was part of a group that met regularly in the afternoon at a café in the Al Yamama Hotel, the only modern hotel in Riyadh at the time, and on weekends at the home of one of the group's members. Nazer established himself as a progressive thinker on social and economic issues but never sided with any political movement. Nazer was loyal to the royal family and to the Saudi system.

Nazer told me many times that his role in two external events during the 1960s indirectly led to his promotion to the rank of minister. The first event took place in Baghdad in 1967 following the Arab-Israeli war. In response to the Arab defeat, Arab oil ministers discussed possible measures against Western countries that had supported Israel, particularly the United States. Yamani could not, or would not, attend the meeting and sent Nazer, his deputy, as head of the Saudi delegation. During the meeting, the head of the Algerian delegation launched a verbal attack on Saudi Arabia for failing to support the Arab cause. Nazer responded with a strong counterattack, accusing the North African state of having double standards and failing to appreciate what Saudi Arabia had done for Algeria during the war of independence and the support it had given to other Arab issues and causes. Nazer took a major risk in attacking the newly independent Algeria because it had assumed the mantle of leader of the Arab world and was an important player in the Non-Aligned Movement (NAM). Nazer worried that King Faisal would be unhappy with his remarks, and members of the Saudi delegation, mostly from the Saudi embassy, were quick to report Nazer's comments to the royal court. However, Nazer was pleasantly surprised to hear from the royal court that King Faisal was pleased with what he had said.

The second event that drew King Faisal's attention was Nazer's performance during an Arab summit in Khartoum, Sudan, which was called to look at ways to help the defeated Arab countries (Egypt, Syria, and Jordan) after the 1967 Arab-Israeli war. Nazer was a member of the Saudi advance team, representing the Ministry of Petroleum. When King Faisal arrived, he asked if any of the advance team members could brief him on the issues and the position of each country. Nazer was the only one who had notes and a report, which earned him King Faisal's appreciation once again.

In 1968, Nazer was appointed head of the Central Planning Organization, and he quickly got to work on the kingdom's first economic development plan. He consulted international experts from several organizations, including those at the United Nations, and led the key Follow-Up Committee, which had the power to question all ministers about their development plans and evaluate their performance. On one occasion, Yamani was questioned by the committee, seeking assurances that projects included in the national plan were being implemented by his ministry and by Petromin. Yamani stormed out of the committee hearing when it criticized his team for its poor performance.[1]

Nazer became more influential in 1975 when the planning organization became the Ministry of Planning and he was appointed as a member of the Council of Ministers. Over time Nazer developed good working relations with most cabinet ministers and high-ranking members of the royal family, notably Prince Abdullah, head of the National Guard, and Prince Sultan, minister of defense.

Saudi Arabia took a major economic step forward in the mid-1970s with development of a nascent petrochemical industry. Petromin was responsible for developing the petrochemical industry, but it did not do much beyond setting up the Saudi Arabian Fertilizer Company (SAFCO) as a joint government and publicly owned entity in a venture with Occidental Petroleum of the United States. SAFCO was to use natural gas feedstock supplied by Aramco. The company defined itself as Saudi Arabia's first petrochemical company, but after a promising start, it began to struggle financially in the mid-1970s.

Nazer worked to promote the kingdom's petrochemical potential, giving it a key role in his first economic development plan. In October 1975, responsibility for developing the petrochemical industries was taken from Petromin and given to the newly established Ministry of Industry and Electricity, headed by Ghazi al-Gosaibi, an academic from King Saud University who was a close friend of Nazer's. Al-Gosaibi was a young ambitious man, and he played a key role in the kingdom's development and administration during the next forty years, first by moving responsibility for the oil industry from Petromin to the new ministry. "We received tons of files of petrochemical projects from Petromin, but nobody came with the files to explain their content," al-Gosaibi recalled.[2] Most of Petromin's planned projects were subsequently dropped by the new ministry because they were too ambitious.

Development of a Saudi petrochemical industry went hand in hand with creation of the Royal Commission for Jubail and Yanbu, two industrial cities built on the Arabian Gulf coast and the Red Sea coast of Saudi Arabia, respectively. The vision was to create industrial hubs that hosted petrochemical and other energy-intensive industries. The new commission was chaired by Crown Prince Fahd, and Nazer was vice-chairman. The royal commission was responsible for designing, building, and administering the two cities.

As part of its drive to create a major national Saudi petrochemicals company, the Ministry of Industry established Saudi Basic Industries Corporation (SABIC) in 1976 as an independent company (30 percent owned by the public and the rest by the government). Today it is the third largest petrochemical company in the world, with a presence in more than fifty countries.

During the latter half of the 1970s and the first half of the 1980s, Nazer became one of the most important ministers in Saudi Arabia, with responsibility to oversee several economic sectors. The government embarked on ambitious plans covering priority sectors, such as education, transportation, health care, and urban planning, all underpinned by the economic visions of the Ministry of Planning. Nazer's growing prestige was such that one of the most important stops for heads of state and other high-ranking foreign officials visiting Saudi Arabia was the Ministry of Planning to hear a presentation on Saudi economic achievements and the kingdom's future plans. Visitors included India's prime minister Indira Gandhi in 1973, Spain's King Juan Carlos in 1982, and King Carl Gustaf of Sweden in 1984, among others.

Nazer's education and socioeconomic background undoubtedly influenced many of his decisions, but Nazer also had a unique personality. He was open-minded and widely read but was also a religiously devoted man. He believed that Saudi Arabia should adhere to Islamic principles; however, he was liberal on issues such as hiring women for government jobs. Indeed, the Ministry of Planning was one of the first Saudi ministries to employ women. This led to a strong attack against him from religious conservatives, especially during the Gulf War of 1990–1991.[3] Nazer was kind and trusting of others, especially those who worked closely with him, but he turned against those who betrayed his trust. He was cautious yet prone to emotional outbursts, a trait that created problems for him later in his career.

Unlike Yamani, Nazer was shy in large gatherings, especially with the media, and in first impressions people often labeled him as an arrogant man. His command of Arabic and English was perfect, and he wrote poetry in both languages (although mainly in Arabic). Yet when he stood in front of the press or delivered a speech, he would become nervous and make mistakes. On one occasion in London, Nazer's assistant had handed him the pages of his speech in the wrong order. In the middle of the speech, he noticed that the audience was confused and unable to follow him. He tried to remedy the situation, but it was too late.

Important personality traits influenced Nazer's decisions and management style. He was against the status quo and was willing to take risks both with new ideas and with new people. In the history of Saudi Arabia, only a few decision makers have been willing to make such bold decisions, including hiring and firing people within their organizations; al-Tariki, al-Gosaibi, and Nazer were outstanding examples of this style of management.

When Nazer became the minister of petroleum in 1986, he immediately began restructuring the ministry and the organizations and companies in its orbit. The restructuring targeted Aramco and Petromin, and within two years he had successfully managed both. His willingness to make bold decisions was influenced by his background in economic issues, and his decisions were an advantage for the energy industry. His good relationships with key cabinet members, especially the minister of finance, helped him win approval for some of his restructuring goals. Finally, and most important, Nazer had a strong relationship with King Fahd, who trusted him and supported his key initiatives.

Nazer's first goal was to develop capabilities within the ministry. He began to bring in new blood from the Ministry of Planning, the Saudi Royal Commission for Jubail and Yanbu (which he headed), and several Saudi universities. During his twenty-five-year tenure, Yamani hired few people of stature, and it is not clear if Yamani hired Prince Saud al-Faisal because King Faisal asked him to do so or for other reasons. Indeed, most of the top people working with Yamani, including Nazer, had been hired by the previous minister, Abdullah al-Tariki. The young people recruited by Nazer were highly educated; two of them became ministers and members of the Saudi cabinet, and another three have ministerial ranks. These five went on to leave their mark on the petroleum industry at home and internationally.

1. Prince Abdulaziz bin Salman became minister of energy in September 2019 (chapter 11).

2. Prince Faisal bin Turki joined the ministry in 1987 at the age of twenty-four. He had studied industrial management at King Fahd University before working in the United States and was keen to make a difference. He played a leading role in several key restructuring projects in the energy and mining sectors and was closely involved in the establishment of new companies. He was responsible for development of the natural gas sector and contributed to the growth of the petrochemicals industry as well as the reorganization (and eventual closure) of Petromin. He took the leading role on the establishment of Ma'aden (a major Saudi mining company), the Saudi Industrialization and Energy Services Company (TAQA) that provides petroleum and related industrial services, and the Saudi Geological Survey. In addition, he played a leading role in establishing Ras Al Khair, an industrial city on the Arabian Gulf, and Wa'ad Al Shamal, a similar city in the northeast. In 2017, he left the ministry to serve at the royal court as an adviser with the rank of minister.

3. Musaed al-Aiban received his PhD from Harvard University and became a law professor at King Saud University. He worked at the Ministry of Energy as legal adviser from 1991 to 1993. He played a major role in developing Saudi Arabia's policy on climate change and was involved in several international negotiations. He joined the royal court and became a minister of state and a member of the Council of Ministers in 1995 and has had important roles in the Saudi cabinet ever since. He carries out responsibilities at the Saudi Council of Political Affairs and the Council of Economic and Development Affairs. Moreover, in 2017, King Salman appointed him chairman of the National Cybersecurity Authority and, in 2018, chose him to be national security adviser to the king. He is the only current minister to hold his job for more than twenty-five years and to work with three kings (Fahad, Abdullah, and Salman).

4. Majid al-Moneef is a professor of economics at King Saud University who joined the ministry in 1989 as an economic adviser and later became Saudi Arabia's governor to OPEC. When he left the ministry, he became a member of the Consultative Assembly of Saudi Arabia and was a member of the board of Saudi Aramco. He was the secretary-general of Saudi Arabia's Supreme Economic Council and is currently secretary-general of the Supreme Committee on Hydrocarbons Affairs of the Kingdom of Saudi Arabia. He was chairman of the International Advisory Committee of the King Abdullah Petroleum and Research Center (KAPSARC) and is currently chairman of the Saudi Association of Energy Economics. He is also the author of three books on energy and economic issues.

5. Abdurrahman Abdulkareem moved with Nazer from the Ministry of Planning to head Nazer's office and to supervise a number of financial and administrative activities. He worked closely with both Ali Al-Naimi and Khalid al-Falih. He also worked with Prince Abdulaziz bin Salman when he became the minister, until his retirement in 2021.

Recruitment of these figures (and many more) reflects Nazer's personality and his willingness to hire and work with people who were previously unknown to him, based on the recommendations of those he trusted. Prince Abdulaziz bin Salman played a major role in bringing new blood into the ministry. Nazer's open recruitment policy was in contrast to both Yamani before him and Al-Naimi who followed him.[4]

Like al-Tariki, Nazer created a team of qualified people at the ministry, some of whom continue to play key roles in the present day. However, for Nazer, restructuring meant bringing in new qualified people without reorganizing the ministry itself. This unwillingness to tackle the root cause of institutional inefficiencies was undoubtedly one of Nazer's most significant shortcomings. However, he was able to restructure two of the most important institutions under the ministry's influence: Aramco and Petromin.

RESTRUCTURING SAUDI ARAMCO

Once Saudi Arabia had completed the purchase of Aramco and transferred ownership in 1980, Yamani had three options. The first was to merge Aramco with Petromin, an idea he might have favored but that would have been strongly opposed by some Saudi ministers and Aramco. The second option was to create a new Saudi oil company, which he might have wanted to do but could not because of opposition within the government on legal and financial grounds. The third option, which Yamani accepted, was to leave management of Aramco in the hands of the four U.S. oil companies (that had owned Aramco) for a fee and other privileges.

By the time Nazer became oil minister in 1986, Aramco was fully owned by the Saudi government and Ali Al-Naimi was president but not CEO. Most of the senior management was Saudi, although John Kelberer remained chairman and CEO. Legally, Aramco remained an American company incorporated in the State of Delaware, and the four previous shareholders—Chevron, Texaco, Exxon, and Mobil—effectively controlled Aramco's management under the contract signed with the Ministry of Petroleum. The company continued to conduct upstream business, but its crude production was refined and marketed by Petromin and the four U.S. companies.

Restructuring Aramco involved multiple steps. The first task was making Aramco a Saudi-registered company, which required a huge amount of legal work within Saudi Arabia that took two years to complete. Nazer's work was made easier by the good relationship he had with King Fahd, who trusted him, and with other ministers. In 1988, the company became Saudi-registered and was renamed to Saudi Aramco.[5] As minister of petroleum, Nazer became chairman of the newly created board, and Al-Naimi was named CEO and president.

Three major developments contributed to the emergence of Saudi Aramco as an integrated international oil company. First, Saudi Aramco secured the exclusive right to market the kingdom's crude internationally, establishing a new marketing department at the company's headquarters in Dhahran and opening marketing offices in the major consuming regions (New York, London, and Singapore). Second, Saudi Arabia introduced its sophisticated monthly pricing system in the three major marketing areas (United States, Europe, and Asia). Iran, Iraq, and Kuwait were among the countries in the region that adopted the Saudi pricing system (with some adjustments). The kingdom also established Vela International Marine to deliver Saudi oil to customers. Finally, to become an integrated company and secure a market for its crude, Saudi Aramco entered into downstream joint ventures in major consuming nations, expanding the capacity of refineries and developing a product distribution network.

The first deal was sealed in January 1989. Texaco and Saudi Aramco agreed to form a joint venture known as Star Enterprise: Saudi Aramco would own a 50 percent share of Texaco's refining and marketing operations in the eastern United States and on the U.S. Gulf Coast. Similar deals followed in Korea (1993), the Philippines (1994), and Greece (1995). In 1993, Nazer and a small group from the ministry and Saudi Aramco visited China to begin negotiations on a deal to supply Saudi crude to China and set up refining joint ventures. The target of the Saudis was China's domestic market, but China was exporting oil at that time and was not interested in building new refineries other than for exporting purposes.

In its early years as a national oil company, Saudi Aramco crystalized its philosophy, which continues to guide it today. A truly international integrated Saudi energy company needs to operate throughout the entire value chain, from exploration and production to transportation, marketing, refining, and distribution of petroleum products and, more recently, petrochemicals. Saudi Aramco has secured its markets through joint ventures with local partners that use Saudi crude and have local and international distribution networks.

Saudi Aramco has gone through three major transformational stages since 1933. First, government acquisition in the 1970s, and second, becoming a fully integrated national oil company in the late 1980s and 1990s. The third major stage involved floating some of the company's shares in the domestic market in 2019. These three stages reflect the prevailing political and business conditions of the time and highlight the role of decision makers in restructuring the oil industry and the Saudi economy.

RESTRUCTURING PETROMIN

The story of the General Organization of Petroleum and Minerals (Petromin) provides an interesting case study of the role of key decision makers in national industrial development. Petromin was an important government-owned petroleum and minerals organization for more than twenty-five years, the second most important company in Saudi Arabia (after Saudi Aramco) not just in the petroleum and mineral industries but also in the economy. It was brought down by a combination of mismanagement and perceived corruption.

Created in November 1962 in an effort to lessen the control of foreign companies over the petroleum industry, Petromin was a homegrown Saudi national oil company responsible for refining, distributing, and marketing oil products in the kingdom and abroad. It also awarded exploration blocks outside the Aramco concession areas, such as in the Red Sea.

In the 1960s and 1970s, Petromin was relatively successful in building refineries, both in joint ventures and independently, and it established a large distribution network inside Saudi Arabia. It also created the first Saudi Arabian Fertilizer Company (SAFCO) in the 1960s and had ambitious plans to build multiple petrochemical plants. Petromin also oversaw two companies that offered gold mining and petroleum services such as drilling. As Petromin grew, many activities overlapped, and claims of mismanagement were made with increasing frequency. The company also failed to deliver key projects assigned to it by the government: developing the kingdom's petrochemical industry and building the strategically important East-West oil pipeline to link oilfields in the country's east to ports on the Red Sea. The government responded by taking responsibility for these projects away from Petromin (chapter 1).

When Nazer became oil minister in 1986, he was fully familiar with the scale of the problems at Petromin. Nazer formed a special team within the Ministry of Petroleum to work on restructuring the company and hired U.S. management consultants Arthur D. Little to prepare a major study and offer suggestions. As a result, Petromin was split into six core areas of business, down from eighteen, and two new gold mining companies and two oil service companies were created. An international subsidiary, Saudi Petroleum Overseas Ltd., was also established in London.

In addition, Saudi Arabian Marketing and Refining Company (SAMAREC) was created in 1988 to bring Petromin's refining and distribution activities under a single umbrella as a commercial, profit-oriented company. The company got off to a good start and was quickly put to the test during the campaign to liberate Kuwait from Iraq's invasion in 1990–1991. As foreign troops poured into the country, there was an urgent need for timely supplies of oil products for military operations. SAMAREC performed well, delivering supplies for the military while continuing to supply the local market. However, the company struggled to become incorporated, with the Ministry of Commerce finally refusing to register SAMAREC as a company.

More important, however, was that the culture of mismanagement started at Petromin continued, and the company's top management stopped taking orders from the minister.[6] Nazer's decision to select SAMAREC's management from the ranks of Petromin instead of hiring managers from outside proved to be a mistake. By 1992, Nazer was so unhappy with this mismanagement that he moved some important decision-making responsibilities to his office at the ministry in Riyadh to get greater control over the company's activities. However, Nazer did not make the difficult decision to change the top management, and in June 1993, after five years of existence, SAMAREC was dissolved and its oil activities transferred to Saudi Aramco.

When Ali Al-Naimi became minister in 1995, he decided to shut down Petromin, and I was a member of the committee that implemented the dissolution. By 2003, forty-one years after its birth, Petromin was dead. Although Petromin had a mixed record of accomplishment, it is one of the most important stories of the Saudi oil industry and provides insights into the kingdom's industrial development.[7]

KING FAHD AND NAZER

Nazer completed Saudi Arabia's first five-year plan in 1971. However, he was fraught with anxiety and feared that it would not be approved by the Council of Ministers, headed by King Faisal. Nazer decided to present the plan first to Crown Prince Fahd, then minister of the interior and second deputy prime minister. If Prince Fahd endorsed the plan, Nazer thought King Faisal was likely to accept it.[8] From then on, Prince Fahd became Nazer's de facto boss.

The relationship between the two men went beyond government business. Prince Fahd supported al Hilal FC, a Riyadh-based soccer team, and Nazer was a strong supporter of their archrival, the Jeddah-based al Ittihad. Endless banter about football increased the depth of their relationship. When writing about his appointment as acting minister of petroleum following Yamani's sacking in August 1986, Nazer related this conversation:

At eleven o'clock, King Fahd phoned me and talked about many issues including football games. At the end of the phone call, he told me that he would call me at one o'clock in the morning to give me a new assignment.

At one o'clock in the morning during the news bulletin, the newscaster read the announcement that I would be Acting Minister of Petroleum besides my job as Minister of Planning.

> Before I absorbed the great surprise, the King called again and asked me:
> What do you think now?[9]

King Fahd called Nazer to confirm his new appointment and stressed that, like his two brothers Nayef and Salman, he had full trust in Nazer's abilities to perform well in his new assignment.[10]

The high regard in which King Fahd held Nazer was made apparent in July 1994 when Nazer's brother (Abdulfattah) died. King Fahd visited Nazer at his home to offer his condolences. He stayed with Nazer for about two hours and talked about many subjects, including the Iraqi invasion of Kuwait and social integration in Saudi Arabia, while paying tribute to Nazer and his family's distinguished service to their country.[11] King Fahd's gesture was unusual; normal practice was for the king to invite the relatives of a deceased person to his office (where he would extend his condolences).

King Fahd gave Nazer a lot of support on domestic oil policy. On some issues, decisions needed the approval of the Supreme Petroleum Council or the Council of Ministers. However, when it came to the kingdom's international oil policy, especially concerning OPEC, Nazer had to coordinate closely with King Fahd, who typically gave clear instructions regarding the kingdom's oil policy. Before any OPEC meeting, Nazer provided a report to King Fahd that outlined the situation in the oil market, the policy options available to OPEC, the likely position of each member, and recommendations on the kingdom's policy. During OPEC meetings, Nazer regularly consulted with King Fahd over the phone, and once the meeting was over, Nazer immediately called the king to report on the outcome. Nazer also sent a report to the king after the meeting describing what had happened during the conference, with an Arabic translation of the decision and the communiqué.

The extent of King Fahd's involvement in OPEC decision-making during Nazer's tenure was apparent on two occasions. After the Iraqi invasion of Kuwait on August 2, 1990, the international oil market lost more than 4 MBD of crude and products from Iraq and Kuwait, which had to be replaced quickly. Saudi Arabia started working on a plan to unilaterally raise production from 5.4 MBD to 8.5 MBD within three months, but King Fahd refused to give permission for the production increase until the kingdom had OPEC's approval. Saudi Arabia and some of its allies asked for an extraordinary meeting of OPEC ministers as early as possible, but Algeria's oil minister held the presidency of the conference and refused to convene a full meeting, but he agreed to convene what he called "a consultation with interested OPEC oil ministers at the organization's headquarters in Vienna." This meeting turned into an extraordinary ministerial meeting and was able to make binding decisions.

A few days before the meeting, in an effort to put pressure on the group, Nazer declared that Saudi Arabia would increase its production even if it did not have OPEC's approval, but the following day official Saudi sources indicated that Saudi Arabia would not increase its production unilaterally and was waiting for OPEC's decision. This statement was most likely approved by King Fahd and showed the extent to which he valued OPEC and wanted to preserve consensus within the organization.

The second time King Fahd asserted his authority on OPEC matters was in 1993 when the market was awash with oil even though global demand had increased by about 2 MBD since the invasion. OPEC had to reduce supply, adhere to a new production ceiling, and establish new quotas. OPEC had abandoned the quota system more than two years ago, but Kuwait's production had risen to its prewar level and Iraqi production had resumed under the United Nations' oil for food program. In February of 1993, after two days of intensive negotiations in Geneva, the quota for Saudi Arabia was set at 7.89 MBD, lower than their actual production of 8.63 MBD. Nazer informed King Fahd of the initial agreement, but the king insisted that Saudi Arabia should not go a barrel below 8 MBD. Nazer was forced to reopen negotiations with other OPEC ministers to reach a deal based on the new Saudi red line. The idea was to keep the overall ceiling but to lower quotas for one or two countries, and Algeria agreed to a lower quota to accommodate Saudi Arabia. This agreement proved to be beneficial for the kingdom, and its production never went below 8 MBD except during the oil market collapses in 1998 and 2008.

KING FAHD, NAZER, AND OPEC

Nazer witnessed the establishment of OPEC in its early days and was the first Saudi OPEC governor, but by the 1980s OPEC had attracted international attention because of its influence on oil prices and on the global economy. OPEC had also won considerable political importance through key events such as the Arab oil embargo, the Iranian revolution, and the Iraq-Iran war. OPEC was seen as a successful model for the struggle between the developing and the developed countries.

King Fahd had stressed "the importance of ending the mess and disorder in the oil market,"[12] and immediately after being appointed acting minister of petroleum (before his first visit to his new office at the ministry) Nazer started engaging with OPEC. The king also asked Nazer to join him at the upcoming Gulf Cooperation Council summit in Abu Dhabi. On November 2, 1986, immediately upon arriving in Abu Dhabi, Nazer met with Kuwaiti oil minister Ali al-Khalifa al-Sabah, who had played a prominent role in OPEC during much of the 1980s. The meeting turned into a marathon, lasting more than fourteen hours as al-Sabah explained the range of complex issues surrounding OPEC, including oil prices, the price-setting mechanism, the OPEC ceiling, the prevailing political atmosphere, and personal rivalries between ministers.

After the meeting, Nazer wrote a report to King Fahd, who held a meeting in his hotel suite to discuss the situation. King Fahd invited Prince Saud al-Faisal, the minister of foreign affairs, Mohammed Aba al-Khail, the minister of finance, and other senior Saudis to attend alongside Nazer. It was clear that King Fahd wanted to hear a range of views and opinions before reaching a collective decision. With the current instability in the oil market, King Fahd thought consensus would provide to the best way forward for the kingdom's oil policy. The king desired a minimum price floor of $18 a barrel and instructed Nazer to convene the OPEC Ministerial Pricing Committee to discuss a mechanism for achieving this goal.[13] King Fahd, along with Prince Saud al-Faisal, engaged with other OPEC countries to secure the success of the new policy.

King Fahd wrote to the heads of state of OPEC member countries and to some leaders of non-OPEC producers, asking them to support a production cut. On November 14, 1986, OPEC's Ministerial Pricing Committee met in Ecuador and agreed on the $18 price floor and creation of a new basket price for a range of crudes, replacing the previous benchmark made up of Saudi Arab Light, West Texas Intermediate (WTI), and Algerian Sahara Blend. After the meeting in Ecuador, Nazer engaged in whirlwind diplomacy, visiting Algeria and holding many telephone consultations with OPEC ministers.

The OPEC proposal and the new price target were soon fully debated by the Saudi Council of Ministers. During the discussion, Nazer insisted that it would be difficult to achieve the $18 price floor without lowering combined OPEC production by at least 1 MBD to 17 MBD. This would mean a pro rata reduction in Saudi production from 4.353 MBD to 4.133 MBD. But King Fahd continued to hold out for a higher price without the need to cut Saudi production, if possible.

"Therefore, a deep and long discussion took place inside the Council of Ministers, and the decision was to form a committee with Prince Saud, Minister Mohammed Aba al-Khail, and I, to meet and write its recommendation to be presented to the Council of Ministers to take the suitable decision," said Nazer.[14]

Five days later, the cabinet held a special meeting to analyze the committee's report and its recommendations. King Fahd and the other ministers endorsed the five recommendations made by the committee.

1. Saudi Arabia's position during the OPEC ministerial conference (to be held December 11) would focus on the importance of achieving (and maintaining) the $18 target price for two years. If other countries asked for a higher price, Saudi Arabia would be ready to study and examine the request in light of prevailing oil market conditions;
2. Saudi Arabia would seek a transition toward ending netback contracts over the following six weeks to two months;
3. If market studies presented to the OPEC ministerial conference suggested that there was a need to lower oil production, then it should be on a pro rata basis;
4. The minister of petroleum should always be in direct contact with the king during the conference; and
5. If any country violated its quota and price target, Saudi Arabia would no longer be bound by the agreement.[15]

These five points became the official blueprint for Saudi Arabia's OPEC policy for the next two years. Equally important was this new process of oil policy and decision-making. Even though King Fahd respected and trusted Nazer, the king wanted to oversee all international oil policy decisions—big and small—going forward. King Fahd no longer wanted decisions to be taken without his prior knowledge and approval, as had sometimes been the case with Yamani.

On December 9, 1986, Nazer flew to Geneva to attend the twentieth OPEC Ministerial Conference. He spent the first two days in bilateral meetings, where he met other ministers and made new friends, many of whom would become trusted advisers. By the end of the ministerial meeting, Nazer had secured a deal on Saudi terms, as instructed by King Fahd. Throughout his stay in Geneva, Nazer was in direct and continuous contact with the king, informing him of what was going on and suggesting what the next step should be. Shortly after his return to Riyadh, Nazer was appointed minister of petroleum and mineral resources and acting minister of planning.

Nazer aptly described the December OPEC ministerial meeting (which would be a valid description today):

> They are a group of diverse individuals. Each has its own goals, perhaps different goals. They try—each in their own way—to do anything to achieve those goals. Their governments help them in this chaotic task without a clear understanding of the technical elements of the issues under discussion.
>
> After this meeting, it became clear to me that the only way to achieve a working plan with solid goals is to win the battle on two grounds: at home and within OPEC. This responsibility is no doubt long and arduous.[16]

Nazer became a national and international figure in the global oil industry and consolidated his international status, taking a leading role in OPEC much as Yamani had done before him. Nazer actively sought the cooperation of non-OPEC oil producers, visiting the Soviet Union, Norway, and Mexico and holding talks with other non-OPEC producers. Nazer's efforts paid off when the first OPEC/non-OPEC oil producers' ministerial meeting was held in 1988. That meeting did not achieve much, but it started a process of cooperation between the two groups, leading to a positive outcome in 1998, 2016, and 2020.

Nazer and the ministry of petroleum faced a series of challenges when Iraq invaded Kuwait in August 1990. Saudi Arabia needed to increase production as quickly as possible, with output rising from 5.4 MBD to 8.5 MBD within three months thanks to the hard work of Aramco's management and staff and the capacity expansion plans put in place by the ministry and Saudi Aramco eight months earlier. The decision to increase production capacity had been approved by King Fahd in January 1990 on the ministry's recommendation.[17]

Nazer then had to work with allies to ensure oil market stability. For the first time, the ministry embarked on a comprehensive media strategy that included daily briefings. In parallel, a telephone hotline was established with both the U.S. embassy in Riyadh and the Department of Energy in Washington, D.C.[18] The ministry had to ensure that oil products would be available for military operations, both on land and at sea. Some products came from Saudi refineries, but other products were imported to supply a rapidly expanding military operation. This included building up off-shore crude and product storage capacity, especially at Red Sea ports, to help stabilize the market. At the same time, oil spills in the Arabian Gulf during the war were threatening Saudi refineries, marine life, and water desalination plants, and this needed to be contained. The ministry had to mobilize international help, but Saudi Aramco engineers took the lead in coordinating the response. The ministry also played a major role in helping Kuwait extinguish the many oilfield fires that were started by the retreating Iraq army.

One of the most important developments in the international oil arena was the idea of starting a dialogue between oil producers and oil consumers, which led to the first energy ministerial meeting in Paris in the summer of 1991. King Fahd supported this initiative, and Nazer took part in the Paris meeting.[19] In 1992, Nazer went to Rio de Janeiro as the head of the Saudi delegation to the first United Nations Conference on Environment and Development (UNCED), known as the Earth Summit.

Toward the end of his tenure as minister, Nazer faced two major problems of his own making. First, SAMAREC had an ever-increasing negative image within the kingdom, and Nazer did not take the hard (but necessary) decision of changing its management team. In 1993, the government dissolved SAMAREC and let it be taken over by Saudi Aramco. The story made headline news, and the negative image of SAMAREC persisted in Saudi minds for many years and adversely affected the public's perception of Nazer.

The second issue to harm Nazer was a petrochemicals project involving his son, Loay, and his son-in-law, Mohammed Attar. The two men entered into a joint venture with Mobil Oil Corporation to build a Methyl Tert-Butyl Ether (MTBE) plant in Yanbu. MTBE was a promising new environmentally friendly petroleum additive that was considered a more than excellent investment with high potential returns, especially in Saudi Arabia. Nazer believed that his son had the right to make such an investment as long as he followed the rules. However, some inside and outside the kingdom saw the deal as nepotism and a clear conflict of interest because Mobil Oil Corporation had joint-venture refineries in Saudi Arabia. Many Saudi business people wanted to be part of the deal, but they did not have the chance, which made matters worse. The debate came to a head when the *New York Times* published an article about the project. King Fahd responded by ordering termination of the project. Nazer continued his close relationship with King Fahd even during the fallout from this controversial deal. Nazer was left angry and despondent, not because the project was blocked but because the *New York Times* article portrayed him negatively and had been published without giving his office or his son the chance to comment.[20]

NAZER OUT OF THE MINISTRY

The Kuwait war and its aftermath generated a wave of internal debates in Saudi Arabia leading to calls for constitutional and administrative changes. This included creation of a Shura Council (Parliament) and a full cabinet change because some ministers had been in the same posts for more than two decades. People were asking for and expecting a cabinet reshuffle, with growing rumors about who would be out and who would stay. In the morning of August 2, 1995, Nazer was in his office in Jeddah when news came that King Fahd had decided on ministerial changes that would be announced on the regular 2:30 p.m. radio news.

Nazer was not sure if he would be in or out, and he expressed mixed feelings to me and one other close adviser. His big worry was whether the changes would include some of his colleagues and friends. Nazer had feared that he might be singled out, and he was relieved to learn that all the ministers were leaving. After the news, he told me that he did not want to be "a Yamani type" and had no intention of speaking publicly about oil matters, OPEC, or Saudi oil politics. He was happy and relaxed knowing that Ali Al-Naimi, whom he trusted and liked, was replacing him.

In 2003, Nazer was appointed Saudi Arabia's ambassador to Egypt, one of the most influential countries in the Arab world and a close Saudi ally. During his tenure as ambassador, he established a good network of relationships with Egyptian officials, the media, and intellectuals. Egypt was in the grip of a revolution and counterrevolution that began in 2011 with the uprising against President Hosni Mubarak. As the security situation in the country worsened, thousands of Saudis in Egypt sought to escape the country, which led to chaotic scenes at Cairo's airport. Nazer was at the airport to oversee emergency evacuation flights, and a Saudi woman questioned his ability to help the stranded Saudis. He asked her whether she had other solutions. His dismissive riposte was recorded on a smartphone and quickly went viral. Nazer was relieved of his post in 2014, an early casualty of social media.

Upon his return to Saudi Arabia, Nazer spent most of his time in his hometown, Jeddah, with his family. Nazer died in November 2015, and King Salman offered condolences to his family. Some Saudi newspapers published articles about Nazer, but he was largely forgotten—like many other distinguished ministers in the history of the Arab world.[21]

Nazer's legacy in restructuring the Saudi oil industry, including Saudi Aramco, was successful and resulted in exponential growth in the national hydrocarbons sector. Some people he hired are still in the ministry and elsewhere, and their contributions to Saudi Arabia are unquestionable. There is no doubt that Nazer was a bold and strong decision maker who did not mind making mistakes and correcting them later, if needed.

Chapter Three

SADDAM HUSSEIN AND SHEIKH ALI AL-SABAH

Invasion of a Nation

On May 3, 1990, a day after an OPEC Ministerial Committee meeting in Geneva, Switzerland, Kuwaiti oil minister Sheikh Ali al-Khalifa al-Sabah and I had a private talk in the lobby of the Intercontinental Hotel.

"The price of oil in London opened down this morning. It is strange, isn't it?" I asked.

"No, it was expected," the minister said.

"But you signed an agreement last night accepting a quota of 1.5 million barrels daily for Kuwait. This means that your production will go down by about three to four hundred barrels daily."

"Who said I will reduce our production? I will not."

"Then why did you sign the agreement?" I asked him.

"To be nice. Out of respect for Saudi Arabia," he replied.

"If you do not honor OPEC agreements, why do you continue as a member?"

"The decision is not mine; otherwise I would have left OPEC."

"But you know the geopolitics in the region are very intense," I reminded him. "Iraq is accusing you of harming their economic interests by not adhering to your quota."

"I am not worried," the minister quietly told me.

Since February, the political situation in the Arabian Gulf had become increasingly tense because of a simmering dispute over oil prices. Iraq, in particular, was furious about the low prices. The war with Iran had ended in 1988, and Iraq's economy was in poor shape and on the verge of collapse. Iraq was faced with a large international debt, out of control inflation, falling revenues caused by weak oil prices, and mismanagement.

Iraq's president Saddam Hussein believed that he and Iraq and were victims of a conspiracy in which certain countries were intentionally driving down petroleum prices to squeeze Iraq's economy and deliberately weaken the country. He blamed Kuwait and the United Arab Emirates, specifically, and thought that Saudi Arabia and the United States might also be involved. Saddam Hussein played a leading role in establishing the Arab Cooperation Council (ACC) in February 1989, a multistate body comprising Egypt, Jordan, and Yemen as well as Iraq. Many saw this as an attempt to counter the influence of the Gulf Cooperation Council (GCC), established in 1981, a powerful group made up of Saudi Arabia, Kuwait, the United Arab Emirates, Bahrain, Oman, and Qatar. In February 1990, the Iraqi leader sent a letter to both King Fahd of Saudi Arabia and Sheikh Jaber al-Sabah of Kuwait asking them to lower Kuwait's oil production to help raise prices and allow Iraq to attain its desired target of $18 per barrel (this price was desired by Saudi Arabia and the rest of OPEC as well).

The following month, the oil and energy ministers of the three countries met, but they did not agree to cuts in production. OPEC members convened in May, and ministers reached an agreement to curb production but did not make a strong commitment to adhere to quotas. Toward the end of May 1990, Saddam delivered a speech at the Arab heads of state summit in Baghdad condemning Kuwait's oil policy. In hindsight, this speech carried a strong hint that an armed conflict was about to begin.

"Since 1986, we have been going through a difficult time related to the chaos in the oil market because of our brethren that are not adhering to the OPEC agreement," he said. "Sometimes wars are fought using soldiers, and other times using economic tools. I am talking to our friends; this is a type of war against Iraq. If our skin can bear it, we will. But we have reached the point that we cannot bear it any more. We will all benefit from adhering to the OPEC agreement of production and prices." He even quoted an Arab proverb to support his argument, saying: "Cutting incomes is much harsher than cutting throats."[1]

Iraq invaded Kuwait in August 1990, and this speech highlights how politics, oil markets, and personalities are inextricably linked. The conflict is also a prime example of how ineffective communication, misunderstandings, and the misinterpretation of intentions can result in severe consequences, even between neighboring or allied countries. A number of people were involved in the events leading up to Iraq's invasion of Kuwait, but Saddam Hussein and Ali al-Sabah, knowingly or not, had the major decision-making roles throughout the period that led up to the invasion of Kuwait.

But this story had much deeper roots.

IRAQ, KUWAIT, AND OIL

As far as Kuwait was concerned, the modern relationship between the Arab Gulf state and Iraq dates back to the time of the Ottoman Caliphate. Kuwait was then part of the Ottoman province of al-Basra, in southern Iraq, and the province extended south all the way into parts of the eastern Arabian Peninsula. In the late 1800s, the British Empire wanted to expand its presence in the Arabian Gulf region and weaken Ottoman power. They also wanted to expand their overall commercial, political, and military control in the region. To do so, the British offered local tribal leaders protection from the foreign power and semi-sovereign status as independent "emirates" (Arabic for states). In 1899, Kuwait's Sheikh Mubarak al-Sabah signed an agreement with Great Britain, and Kuwait became semi-independent, albeit under British protection.

After collapse of the Ottoman Caliphate at the end of World War I, Great Britain and France signed the secret Sykes-Picot Agreement in 1916, which formed the basis for redrawing the borders and carved up control of the newly created states between the British and the French. Kuwait remained under British protection, and Iraq was placed under a British mandate. The border between Kuwait and Iraq was never clearly established, even when Iraq gained full independence in 1932. When Iraqi oil exports (and subsequent revenues) began to rise sharply, this issue came to the fore.

Relations between Iraq and Kuwait were closely intertwined and defined by economic and oil issues. When Iraqi oil surged and its economy was growing in the 1930s, the ports on Shatt al-Arab and al-Basra were overcrowded with dry cargo. To cope with the high demand for its oil, Iraq needed a third port to manage this growing maritime traffic, and in 1936 the government in Baghdad started planning for a new port on the Arabian Gulf. At first, the Iraqis wanted to build the port on Kuwaiti territory and sought an agreement with Great Britain, but London rejected the proposal. Instead, the British offered to give Iraq the fishing village of Umm Qasr, which was located in an undefined boundary area near Kuwait. Baghdad accepted the offer but demanded that Iraq also be given control of the islands of Warbah and Bubiyan at the mouth of the port. The port was built in 1958, but the British gave Iraq waterway rights to the Gulf.

The border between the two nations was not fully defined even after Kuwait got full independence in 1961.[2] At that time, Baghdad claimed that Kuwait was part of Iraq, and it was willing to use force to take control of it. However, due to Saudi, Arab, and international interventions, the dispute ended peacefully. Both countries then maintained peaceful relations until August 1990, when Saddam Hussein invaded Kuwait and declared it part of Iraq. Although his predecessors in Baghdad may have wanted to do the same, they were unable to do so for a number of political reasons.[3] Saddam's decision to invade Kuwait changed the landscape of both oil and politics in the region, with consequences that would play out for many decades to come.

After the end of the Iraq-Iran war in 1988, Iraq invited a group of Arab journalists to visit the war zone. One of them was Othman al-Omeir, editor-in-chief of *al Sharq al Awsat*, a leading Pan-Arab newspaper, and he asked Saddam this: "Now you won the war with Iran . . . and Iraq and Saudi Arabia have officially signed a border agreement, might it not be the right time to officially recognize the border with Kuwait?" Al-Omeir was sitting in Saddam's villa in the south, close to the border with Iran (where the war took place), and the Iraqi leader replied: "Even Nori al-Said did not recognize the border with Kuwait, and you think I will?"[4]

Nori Al-Said was the prime minister of Iraq from 1950 to 1958. While he was in office, many Iraqis viewed al-Said as a British agent and a traitor—a puppet put in place to defend Britain's interests. Saddam portrayed himself as a patriot devoted to his nation and as the leader of the Pan-Arab nationalist movement (the Ba'ath Party) and believed it was his mission to unify all, or at least parts, of the Arab world. He did not trust the intentions of the West and was skeptical of their allies in the region.

Saddam Hussein ruled Iraq from 1979 to 2003, and he was one of the most ruthless and brutal dictators in the Arab world during the twentieth century. He used fear and terror as tools to stay in power and to fight against his adversaries at home and beyond. Saddam had a highly complex personality, and his personality traits influenced his decision making. He was obsessed with the Iraq-Kuwait relationship and saw conspiracies everywhere.

Saddam understood the history of Iraq and the region and was proud of its long history dating back thousands of years to the days of the Babylonian civilization. He also understood Iraq's complex relationships with its neighbors, especially Iran and Kuwait, and had a thorough knowledge of the evolution of Kuwait as a sovereign state. However, the Iraqi dictator was selective in his choice of historical events—focusing only on events that serve his own interests and reinforced his beliefs. He regularly compared himself to other Iraqi leaders and wanted to achieve more than they had. When negotiating a border treaty with Kuwait, for example, he rejected any solution that did not involve the islands of Bubiyan and Warbah being given to Iraq—a long-standing Iraqi aspiration that previous leaders had failed to achieve.

The Iraqi president often took decisions without first collecting comprehensive background information, undertaking thorough objective analysis, or canvassing expert opinions. Saddam expected his ministers to listen to him and implement his orders directly and without question. A Russian diplomat with long experience in Iraq said that "[within Saddam's inner] circle, the safest course is always to be 100 per cent more hawkish than the chief. . . . You stay out of trouble that way."[5]

The Iraqi leader did not always reveal his plans and decisions even to his closest advisers and consultants. For example, when Saddam ordered the Iraqi army to invade Kuwait, he did so without consulting his minister of defense or top military staff.[6] To make matters worse, he did not change course even when his military strategy began to go wrong. In consultation with Kuwaiti leaders during the war, King Fahd put forth the possibility of renting Iraq the two disputed islands, finding an acceptable solution to the Rumaila oilfield, and forgiving all of Iraq's debt from GCC countries. But Saddam rejected King Fahd's ideas as well as ideas from other Arab leaders and the Soviet Union and refused to withdraw his troops. Had he accepted the offer, he might have been seen as the most influential leader in the Arabian Gulf and the greater Arab world.

The Iraqi president believed that Kuwait, the United Arab Emirates, and perhaps even Saudi Arabia and the United States, were overproducing oil to bring down prices and hurt the Iraqi economy, which relied heavily (and still does to this day) on oil export revenues.[7] Had Saddam been better informed or taken his oil minister and his advisers more seriously, he would have understood how each of the four countries had very different oil policies, goals, and interests.

Saudi Arabia was also suffering from low oil prices at that time, but its leaders had a full understanding of the complexity of these problems. Saudi Arabia was also unhappy with Kuwait's oil policy, and the United Arab Emirates would lose 25 percent of its income even if it cut production by 25 percent to raise prices. The Emirate of Abu Dhabi was bound by the OPEC agreement, so any cut in production would be borne by Abu Dhabi alone. Although an integral part of the United Arab Emirates, the Emirate of Dubai had its own oil policy, and it was producing about 0.4 MBD of oil at the time.

The Iraqi leader was a poor listener. He preferred to do most of the talking himself rather than entertain the ideas of others, and he rejected advice from trusted friends such as King Hussein of Jordan and Egypt's president Hosni Mubarak. Neither did he listen to his own ministers—many of whom were highly capable individuals—although Issam al-Chalabi, the Iraqi minister of oil, said he was able to take a different position and succeeded in changing some decisions. When Saddam sat with foreign officials, he barely paid attention to them and did not take their words seriously.[8] At formal diplomatic meetings and conferences, the Iraqi president was not a clear, direct, or fact-driven communicator. Instead he made general statements with hidden messages and expected others to understand these messages.

To make matters worse, the Iraqi leader thought others used the same passive techniques and hidden messages, which may have influenced his thinking when he met U.S. Ambassador April Glaspie on July 25, 1990— only seven days before Iraqi forces invaded Kuwait. Glaspie and Saddam discussed the growing tensions in the region and Iraq's massive deployment of troops near the border with Kuwait. Acknowledging that Saddam had the right to rebuild his country (after the war with Iran) and grow its economy, Glaspie told the Iraqi president that the United States had "no opinion on your Arab-Arab conflicts, such as your dispute with Kuwait," but was clear that the United States was against the use of force. Nevertheless, Saddam listened selectively and decided that the United States was indifferent to the issue, including the potential for an invasion.[9]

The Iraqi dictator was a reckless political adventurist constantly in conflicts with others, both domestically and internationally, but in particular with Iraq's neighbors. For example, immediately after assuming power in 1978, Saddam entered into a conflict with neighboring Syria, even though both governments were members of the Ba'ath Party. Two years later he entered into a war with Iran with the aim of seizing control of Al-Ahwaz, the Arabic-speaking region in Iran, and the Shatt al-Arab waterway that forms the southern border between the two countries. That war lasted eight years and resulted in heavy losses and huge expenses for both sides. After the war ended, it took Saddam just two years to start another major conflict and invade Kuwait.

Saddam's decisions were invariably determined by his political agenda. He believed oil was a direct gift from God to the Iraqi people and the Arabs and that the region should always enjoy high oil revenues. He thought Arab producers should only sell petroleum at a high price, irrespective of the long-term consequences. It was with this mindset that Saddam invaded Kuwait, thinking that by seizing the emirate and its oil he would be able to exercise more influence. He believed strongly that the result would be greater power for him over world oil production and the ability to dictate OPEC quotas.

Saddam wore a military uniform at many public appearances and considered himself a military leader although he had never served in the armed forces nor had any formal military training. He also ordered all senior government and party officials to wear military uniforms to show Iraqis that a war was on and that they should take it seriously. This is how he commanded fear and loyalty from his subjects. With this combination of personality traits, decision-making style, and mentality coupled with a total lack of checks and balances and transparency, it is hardly surprising that Saddam got himself into major conflicts without considering a way out.

Before the Kuwait invasion, the United States and Saddam had an interesting love-hate relationship. During Iraq's war with Iran, the Iraqi government received some help from the United States that played a role in helping Iraq win the conflict. Later the United States helped rebuild Iraq by providing financial and economic aid along with other support. But Saddam's relationship with the United States also had its rocky side. The United States was irritated by the Iraqi president's attempts to develop a chemical weapons arsenal and by his constant threats against Israel.

Saddam's perception of the United States and oil resonates today in some circles. In the summer of 2018, U.S. president Donald Trump put out a couple of tweets about oil prices, OPEC, and the Arab Gulf states, asking for an increase in oil production to bring down prices. OPEC+ had decided to increase production by 1.2 MBD due to market-related circumstances, but because of the media attention generated by Trump's tweets, some people, especially in the Arab world, believed the U.S. president had dictated OPEC+'s decision to increase production. An old speech by Saddam soon went viral on social media in the Arab world and elsewhere. In this February 1990 speech at a summit meeting of the Arab Cooperation Council, the Iraqi leader was speaking about the Soviet Union's collapse and the rise of U.S. dominance on the world stage:

> If the Arabs are not aware, the Arab Gulf States will be controlled by the United States and its desires. This situation will evolve to the point where the United States will decide the amount of oil being produced and exported. The U.S. will decide the oil price according to a special view related to the U.S. interests, which ignores the interests of others.[10]

SHEIKH ALI AL-SABAH

The other side of the story of the Iraqi invasion of Kuwait can be found in the personalities of Saudi and Kuwaiti decision makers and the roles that they played. Sheikh Ali al-Khalifa al-Sabah (hereafter Sheikh Ali) was one of the most important figures in the history of Kuwait's financial and oil sectors, especially in the 1980s. In fact, his influence made him a key figure in the greater Gulf region and within OPEC. Sheikh Ali was a visionary. He had business ambitions for his country and for the Kuwaiti National Oil Company, but he unwittingly helped lay the groundwork for Saddam's invasion of Kuwait. Let's start with a general look at Sheikh Ali's background.

In 1898, Sheikh Mubarak al-Sabah of Kuwait allegedly killed two of his brothers, one of whom was Ali al-Sabah's grandfather. After the murder, the family went into exile in Iraq and did not return to Kuwait until the 1950s. Ali al-Shabah was born and raised in Iraq, and he studied there as well as in Egypt, the United States, and the United Kingdom.

Sheikh Ali's career in government began in the 1970s when he worked at the Kuwait Ministry of Oil and the Ministry of Finance. His commitment to his work and his competence impressed senior officials at both ministries, and they singled him out for rapid advancement. In 1976, Sheikh Ali became the chairman of Gulf Bank, and two years later he was appointed minister of oil. In 1983, he was named finance minister but left two years later and returned to lead the ministry of oil in 1985. In 1990, he again became the minister of finance, but he had a clear influence on oil policy. Sheikh Ali ended his tenure in government in 1991 after the liberation of Kuwait and went into private business. He was later accused of corruption in Kuwait, but no legal charges were made.

Sheikh Ali wanted to make Kuwait a global hub for oil, business, manufacturing, and finance. During his fifteen years of service in the public sector, Kuwait became a major international powerhouse in both petroleum and finance. His noteworthy achievements both as minister of finance and of oil included expansion of the Kuwait Sovereign Fund in the 1980s, a state-run investment enterprise, as well as multiple investments abroad that included a significant stake in British Petroleum (BP). As the minister of finance, Sheikh Ali was put in charge of the Kuwait Investment Authority, and he undertook a reorganization and expanded its activities to include overseeing most of the country's financial reserves, including the Reserve Fund for Future Generations that received 10 percent of the state's oil revenues. The fund was so successful that Kuwait was the only OPEC member to generate excess revenues in 1986 after the oil price collapse. The Kuwait Sovereign Fund also provided the government with cash when members of the royal family, ministers, and a large number of Kuwaitis went into exile after the Iraqi invasion (the Saudi government provided free housing to the Kuwaitis during the occupation). When Kuwait was liberated after six months of Iraq occupation, the fund provided the money needed to rebuild the country.

In 1980, Sheikh Ali played an important role in establishing an international oil company, Kuwait Petroleum Corporation (KPC), which rapidly expanded via a number of global acquisitions across the energy value chain, including upstream, midstream, and downstream assets and oilfield services. Kuwait was the first OPEC country to create a fully integrated national and international oil company through overseas investments, and it did so eight years before Saudi Arabia and fifteen years before Venezuela.

By the early 1980s, many people viewed Sheikh Ali (along with Yamani) as one of the most important OPEC ministers of their time. The Kuwaiti minister also enjoyed the full confidence of the Kuwaiti government. In fact, Sheikh Ali could make key decisions, such as increasing oil production beyond the quota and ceilings established by OPEC, without prior approval from Sheikh Jaber, the head of the government. Sheikh Ali's real boss was the crown prince and prime minister, Sheikh Sa'ad Abdullah al-Sabah, who some Kuwaitis said adopted and supported Sheikh Ali throughout his career and had his full trust on oil and financial issues.

Sheikh Ali began as a man who cared about OPEC's success, but he became mistrustful of the organization over time and indifferent to its fate. He also shifted his focus from defending oil prices to maintaining market share, a policy that other officials including Saudi Arabia's Ali Al-Naimi and Venezuela's Luis Giusti came to adopt later in their careers (chapter 4). Overall, Sheikh Ali was widely considered to be a global authority on oil and financial matters. However, he could not sense (or care about) the changing geopolitical environment in the region or Iraq's unhappiness with Kuwait's policies. He also did not recognize the intense frustration of other countries (including long-time ally Saudi Arabia) with Kuwait's policy of ignoring its OPEC quota.

When Saddam called Kuwait's ambitious production policy a "War from the South" and an "economic war," Sheikh Ali did not take him seriously. As one Kuwaiti petroleum official put it, Sheikh Ali was "naïve politically."[11] During an OPEC ministerial-level meeting in the late 1980s, the influential Kuwaiti minister publicly promised that his country would adhere to the established quotas and ceilings, but Sheikh Ali had different thoughts in private. When discussing the production numbers that OPEC had set with some of his friends in the media, he would state confidently that it was "the invisible hand that opens the Kuwaiti oil tap."[12]

As the years went by and his influence as an oil policy maker grew, Sheikh Ali began to express his feelings in public. At a press conference in November 1989, Sheikh Ali stated that "perhaps within the next couple of years all this quota business may become irrelevant." When asked if late 1991 "is the time you see the quota system in OPEC coming to an end," Sheikh Ali replied, "I think that is the maximum period where a quota system within OPEC will exist. Possibly even by the end of 1990 there will not be a need for a quota system, but definitely by the end of 1991 there will not be any need for a quota system."[13] But other OPEC members, including Kuwait's allies, did not see the quota system the same way. To make matters worse, oil prices slumped from more than $20 per barrel in early February 1990 to a low of almost $14 per barrel in June, and oil-producing countries saw their oil-dependent revenues decline.

During the first half of the 1990s, the behaviors and statements made by both Saddam and Sheikh Ali created misperceptions and generated tensions that pushed the two countries ever-closer to an escalated conflict, and some officials in OPEC member states were increasingly concerned about the tone of their rhetoric. Were Sheikh Ali's actions partially to blame for Iraq's decision to invade, or were there other considerations? The answer is both yes and no. On the Kuwaiti side, two other issues contributed to the Iraqi invasion.

First, after Kuwait won full independence from the British in 1961, it embarked on an ambitious economic development program. The newly independent state used oil income to become a pioneer in the Arab world in education, culture, intellectual pursuits, and health care, among other fields. Kuwait had a basic democratic system that included an independent and freely elected parliament and a relatively free press, which differed from systems in neighboring states. Despite having a small land mass, Kuwait played an outsized role in the political arena. The late Ahmed Al-Rubei—a Kuwaiti minister, member of parliament, and intellectual—described the situation this way in 2001:

> Kuwait thought in the 1960s and 1970s that it was capable of playing a much bigger role in the geopolitical field than it had previously. Therefore, experienced Arab politicians privately said that there were three major powers in the world: the Soviet Union, the United States, and Kuwait. In light of this unpractical illusion, Kuwait paid a very high price.[14]

By "paying a very high price" he was referencing the Iraqi invasion of 1990 and indirectly referring to the growing regional involvement of the state of Qatar in recent years. The second important factor that led to the Iraqi invasion was the personality of Kuwait's ruler, Sheikh Jaber al-Ahmad al-Sabah, who ruled from 1978 to 2006. He was an amiable and pliant man who lived a simple modest life and was focused on family life. Sheikh Jaber appeared to pay little attention to OPEC and the oil market and did not take Saddam's threats seriously. When Sheikh Jaber made key decisions, he avoided the finer details and trusted the judgment of those around him, and he was led to believe that OPEC quotas were not respected by other countries.

In 1985, the sheikh's popularity rose after he survived an assassination attempt. However, many intellectuals and academics criticized Sheikh Jaber for dissolving Parliament in 1986. Parliament was reconvened in 1992, and lawmakers quickly launched an open debate about petroleum policy before the invasion and Kuwait's relationship with Iraq. They undertook a comprehensive study of the Iraq-Kuwait war in 1990, and summarized their findings as follows: (1) mismanagement on the part of the government, (2) bad policies and policy making, (3) no government transparency and constraints on free media after 1986, and (4) a lack of vision on the part of decision makers.[15]

KING FAHD

King Fahd of Saudi Arabia was doing his best to solve the conflict between Iraq and Kuwait from the start. For much of the twentieth century, Saudi Arabia and Kuwait had a close but delicate multidimensional relationship that included politics, economics, culture, national borders, and more. Their relationship went through some rough periods (sparked by disagreements over historical events and political interests), but they maintained close ties. Both Saudi Arabia and Kuwait are members of the GCC, which was created in response to the growing number of geopolitical challenges facing the Arab Gulf states. In particular, their governments wanted to have a unified foreign policy following the Iranian revolution, the Iraq-Iran war, and the Soviet invasion of Afghanistan.

King Fahd had a cool-headed personality and never made impulsive decisions, especially when responding to major events. When Iraq invaded Kuwait on August 2, 1990, it took the king three days to formulate a Saudi response as he sought to find a peaceful solution. King Fahd tried to call

Saddam Hussein the first day of the invasion but couldn't reach him (to put it another way, Saddam was unwilling to take his call). King Fahd had tried to encourage Saddam to withdraw his troops peacefully, and after the invasion King Fahd was in a state of disbelief. He said "early in the morning before dawn, I will perform an Istikhara Prayer and ask God for guidance."[16] Following a thorough review of information from Saudi government agencies and the U.S. government, and after consultation with others in the Saudi leadership, King Fahd decided to allow U.S. and foreign troops to be stationed in Saudi Arabia as part of an international coalition to liberate Kuwait from Iraq.

In the 1980s, the Saudi and Iraqi leaders had developed a close personal relationship even though they were politically and philosophically on opposite ends of the regional spectrum. King Fahd presided over a religiously conservative state and preferred regional stability and the status quo. Saddam, on the other hand, was a revolutionary Arab nationalist who wanted to unite the countries in the region under his own banner (using force if possible—covert or overt). The two leaders initially found common ground after Iran's Islamic Revolution in 1979 and the new Iranian regime's expansionist mindset. Saudi Arabia threw its full support behind Iraq during the war with Iran, backing Iraq financially, politically, and (indirectly) militarily.

Petroleum policy was a big factor in the Iran-Iraq regional conflict. Syrian president Hafez al-Assad, who had a strong personal conflict with Saddam, supported Iran and decided to close the pipeline that carried Iraqi oil to the Mediterranean through Syria. When Saddam asked for help, King Fahd agreed to build an alternate pipeline that extended from Iraq, through Saudi Arabia, to the Red Sea to avoid disruption of Iraqi exports by Iran. The IPSA I pipeline was completed in late 1985 with the capacity to transport 0.5 MBD, and IPSA II (with a capacity of 1.65 MBD) was inaugurated in late January 1990.

The relationship between King Fahd and Saddam was cemented in the last week of March 1989 when the king visited Baghdad to congratulate the Iraqi leader on winning the war with Iran. During the visit, the two leaders signed a friendship agreement and established guidelines for political and economic cooperation between their two countries. (The border agreement between the two countries was signed in 1981.) Saddam awarded Iraq's highest medal to King Fahd, and the king reciprocated with the highest

Saudi award for the Iraqi president. Their speeches during the week were peppered with affectionate phrases such as brother, friend, and lovely, among others.

In the Arab world, King Fahd was a regional problem solver. One example is the important role he played in ending the Lebanese Civil War by getting the factions together to resolve the conflict. His mediation resulted in the Taif Agreement of 1989, which remains in place today. King Fahd was highly respected by many Arab leaders, whereas the Iraqi leader never played any role in finding a peaceful solution to regional problems.

In mid-1990, Saddam sent Sa'dun Hammadi, Iraq's vice president for economic affairs, to Saudi Arabia to deliver a special message to King Fahd. He asked for an urgent summit meeting between the leaders of Saudi Arabia, Iraq, Kuwait, the United Arab Emirates, and Qatar. The aim of the summit would be to address the lack of adherence by Kuwait and the United Arab Emirates to their OPEC oil-production quotas. King Fahd suggested instead that the issue be discussed at the ministerial level first. King Fahd told the Iraqi president that if the ministers fail to come to an acceptable solution a summit could be held.[17]

Hisham Nazer (the Saudi minister of petroleum) was asked to go to Kuwait, the United Arab Emirates, and Iraq with a clearly defined mission and a letter from King Fahd to the leaders of these states. First, Nazer went to the United Arab Emirates and met Sheikh Zayed al Nahyan, who told Nazer "please tell King Fahd that whatever he wants—I will do it." Sheikh Zayed also gave an assurance that his country was willing to adhere to the oil-production quota of 1.5 MBD even though only the Emirate of Abu Dhabi was bound by OPEC agreements.[18] Nazer next went to Kuwait and spent around six hours discussing the oil market and Kuwaiti oil standing with the Kuwaiti minister of oil, Rasheed al-Amiri (Sheikh Ali's replacement).

Following these exchanges, the Iraqi government informed Saudi Arabia that Saddam was available to meet with the Saudi minister of petroleum on July 1. Nazer went to Baghdad and told the Iraqi president that King Fahd was determined to find a solution to the problem in a manner that would be acceptable to Iraq. He also reiterated that the Saudi king believed strongly that the matter could be resolved. Nazer pointed out that King Fahd believed the oil ministers should be given enough time to handle the situation. According to Nazer, Saddam told him the following:

I will deliver a speech to the Iraqi people on July 17, the anniversary of the Iraqi Revolution (a coup d'état that put the Ba'ath Party in power). If a solution [to the oil-production problem] is not reached by that time, I will tell the Iraqi people that Kuwait and the U.A.E. are stealing the milk from [the Iraqi people's] children.[19]

Nazer replied, "Let us—the ministers—meet, and if we do not solve the problem, then do whatever you like." Saddam agreed to a ministerial-level meeting of five countries, which would be held in Jeddah, Saudi Arabia, two weeks later.

I regret not going with Minister Nazer on his trip to Kuwait and Baghdad. I lost the opportunity to meet Saddam and to receive his gift—a watch with Saddam's portrait as a souvenir. Such was his vanity that he had designed a watch bearing his image on its face to give to visitors. It has since become a collectors' item.

JEDDAH AND OPEC MEETINGS

The Jeddah ministerial meeting was an important event in the history of OPEC and in the Kuwait-Iraq conflict. Among other issues, adherence by Kuwait and the United Arab Emirates to their OPEC production quotas were to be addressed as this was thought to be the root cause of the oil-price decline and the escalating political problem. Kuwait's ruler removed Sheikh Ali from his position as oil minister and appointed him minister of finance because there was a growing belief by some Gulf oil officials that he was part of the problem. He was replaced by a technocrat, Rasheed al-Amiri.

The oil ministers of Iraq, Kuwait, Qatar, Saudi Arabia, and the United Arab Emirates met in Jeddah on the morning of July 10, 1990, and negotiations continued for almost eighteen hours. Al-Amiri, the new Kuwaiti minister, did not grasp the geopolitical landscape and did little to reduce tensions. During one of the breaks, he told reporters that Kuwait would request a higher production quota "later this year." Once the ministers came to an agreement, al-Amiri told the media that the deal met Kuwait's demands by allowing it to raise production in the fourth quarter of 1990. He remarked that "the Jeddah Agreement called for adherence to quotas, but without detailing particular numbers."[20]

Neither of these claims was true, and they gave the Iraqis more reason to believe that Kuwait was not serious about reducing its production. Some Saudi and Kuwaiti officials were also unhappy about what it felt were al-Amiri's ill-advised remarks given the extremely tense political environment. Many years later, Issam al-Chalabi told me that al-Amiri's statement created the impression in Baghdad that the Kuwaitis were not serious about finding a solution to the problem.

The Iranians issued a statement during the Jeddah meeting and made things worse, saying that oil prices should be no less than $35 per barrel of crude oil (BBL). Issam al-Chalabi, the Iraqi minister of oil, explained that Baghdad responded to the proposal without waiting for his return. "While I was still in the air on my way to Baghdad, the minister of information announced that Iraq supports the Iranian initiative."[21] Later on, Saddam asked al-Chalabi to secretly meet with the Iranians to coordinate their oil policy, especially prices, which they did on July 16, 1990. We later learned that the Iraqi leader started to secretly communicate with the Iranian leadership in late April 1990.[22]

When the ministers met in Jeddah, King Fahd was determined to ensure that the meeting produced a successful outcome. King Fahd was in contact with Nazer at all times and offered to intervene directly if needed. Nazer, too, was intent on making sure that the meeting was a success and appeased the Iraqis. In fact, Nazer asked his Iraqi counterpart, al-Chalabi, to write down what he wanted the agreement to include so that the Saudi policy makers could make sure Iraq's demands were met. Notwithstanding al-Amiri's comments, the gathering was more successful than expected with an agreement on the following points:

1. The oil price target was raised from $18/BBL to $21/BBL.
2. Production quotas of 1.5 MBD for both Kuwait and the United Arab Emirates. The heads of state of each country made a clear commitment to respect and abide by the limits that were set.
3. OPEC production would gradually increase once the price reached the targeted level of $21/BBL. The added oil would be distributed pro rata.
4. All participants at the Jeddah meeting accepted the terms of the agreement, and the ministers agreed that it should be on the agenda for the OPEC ministerial meeting in Geneva on July 28.

Most participants were happy with what was achieved at the meeting, but the Iraqi statement supporting Iran's position was a clear sign that the Iraqi oil minister was not in sync with his government's decision makers and had limited authority in these issues. The meeting was so successful that a high-ranking Kuwaiti official told me after the meeting:

> We felt that the meeting had addressed the major Iraqi concerns—and the oil market as a whole—in a way that would satisfy Iraq. They set a new target price that already started to move toward the desired goal before even going to Geneva. We had also received strong commitments regarding quota adherence and established a new mechanism to link the target price level with a ceiling increase. [The Jeddah meeting] was [more successful] than what we expected when we started.[23]

Oil ministers do not act autonomously; many factors in addition to personality and background define a minister's role and authority, including the political system within which they operate and their relationship with their boss (the head of state). The Iraqi oil minister was a smart petroleum engineer who began his career at the National Iraqi Oil Company in the 1970s. He rose up the ranks in both the industry and the government, becoming minister in March 1987 based on his qualifications rather than on his political affiliations. Al-Chalabi was a technocrat and one of the few members of the cabinet who was not a member of the ruling Ba'ath Party. Because he was not part of the ruling party elite (where loyalty and personal relations trumped professionalism), al-Chalabi sometimes had difficulty functioning effectively as oil minister. His undefined authority, weak political links, and limited communication with Saddam exacerbated the situation with Kuwait and other countries.

Al-Chalabi worked hard to achieve Saddam's policy aims but was often undercut by the political regime in Baghdad. Immediately after the Jeddah meeting, Baghdad issued a statement disavowing the accord al-Chalabi had just signed. The news came as a shock to participants, and al-Chalabi told Nazer, "as you see, the decision was not mine, nor did I recommend it."[24] A similar story emerged less than three weeks later during the OPEC meeting on July 28. Before the official meeting, the ministers who had attended the Jeddah meeting had an informal gathering during which al-Chalabi told other ministers that Iraq wanted the target oil price to be raised again, this time to \$25/BBL (\$4/BBL higher than the one established in Jeddah). One minister retorted that "we cannot raise the target price from \$18/BBL (the level set before Jeddah) to \$21/BBL and then again to \$25/BBL all within one month." He added, "You realize that it is impossible to do all of that at the same time." Al-Chalabi explained that he was ordered to demand this new target price by Baghdad. In response, another minister said: "What you are saying is that this is a political price." Al-Chalabi responded yes, which meant that Saddam had decided the new price level.[25]

The Saudi oil minister then asked al-Chalabi to call Saddam and discuss it with him. The Iraqi minister appeared shocked at the suggestion, saying, "I, myself, call the president?" Nazer responded with "do you want me to call him?" It was clear that al-Chalabi was out of his depth, but he told the ministers he would inform Baghdad that it would be best to go with the already established \$21/BBL target price for the time being. The others did not realize that al-Chalabi, who headed Iraq's most important ministry and who was at the center of a major economic and political storm, could not speak directly to his boss.

When it came to many issues related to oil policy, al-Chalabi communicated with Hussein Kamel al-Majid, the powerful Iraqi minister of industries who was a second cousin and son-in-law of Saddam. Many years later al-Chalabi told me that Saddam did not take telephone calls from outside Iraq. Al-Majid was one of the few people the Iraqi president fully trusted, which gave him substantial power and the ability to communicate directly with Saddam on oil issues. Al-Majid oversaw and directed a number of ministries, including oil, but he had no background in oil nor in the international petroleum market and OPEC. (This did not stop him from becoming oil minister when al-Chalabi was fired on October 29, 1990.)

The OPEC meeting on July 28 yielded good results. Not only did both Kuwait and the United Arab Emirates commit to adhere to their quotas, but they immediately reduced their oil production. In addition, OPEC adopted a higher target price and established a clear mechanism for how and when OPEC members could increase their production and prices. Everyone was satisfied, including the Iraqi delegates, who believed they had achieved their president's aims. Saudi Arabia's Nazer felt the meeting had accomplished what was needed to end the crisis. While Nazer was waiting to board his plane for his annual vacation, he told me that "the major problem is over and I am happy with the result [of the meeting]. While I am in California, I am sure that the king will not ask me to come back [from vacation] if the oil issue gets more complicated."[26] The last thing Nazer expected was that war—or a military confrontation—would break out shortly afterward. He was not alone.

In the evening of August 1, 1990, I was having dinner with a group of international and Middle East senior policy analysts, government officials, and prominent journalists in London. None of them expected a full invasion, although a few predicted that a partial occupation would take place (to take the Rumaila oil fields and the two Islands of Bubiyan and Warbah). However, four hours after the dinner ended, Iraqi troops marched into Kuwait and took over the entire country, advancing as far as the Saudi border. The Kuwaiti invasion highlights how the diametrically opposed decision-making processes and mentalities of the leaders of the two countries led to these dramatic consequences:

1. The Kuwaiti government neither expected the invasion nor did it have a plan in place to deal with it, even though the warning signs had been multiplying for more than four months.

2. Saddam Hussein personally planned and ordered the invasion without the knowledge or involvement of senior officials, including his own defense minister and military chief of staff. A fuller account was subsequently published by Saad al-Bazzaz, an Iraqi journalist and government official.[27] Indeed, according to al-Chalabi, only four people knew about the decision, all close relatives to Saddam. It looked like a family decision.

3. Saddam did not have a detailed plan of what he wanted to achieve after the invasion. At first he said Iraqi troops were on the ground to help Kuwaitis start a "new revolution." However, he soon changed that narrative and insisted that Kuwait was an integral part of Iraq. He continued to offer conflicting justifications for the invasion and plans for the future.

4. Many in the close circle of the Iraqi president had a limited understanding of the international oil market. By combining the oil reserves of Iraq and Kuwait (20 percent of the world's total), they thought Baghdad would become a powerful global force on the world stage and have greater protection from external threats. Vice Prime Minister Sa'dun Hammadi believed that Iraq's oil quota would increase by 1.5 MBD once Kuwait became part of Iraq and the country's total oil production would then be 4.5 MBD. He did not recognize that Iraq

would not be able to export a single barrel of oil. He also declared that Iraqi oil reserves would jump from 100 billion barrels to 194.5 billion barrels.[28]

The Iraqi invasion of Kuwait yielded important lessons about the oil market. First is the fact that even though the conflict cost the international markets over four million barrels of crude oil and another half a million of refined products per day (which added up to 7–8 percent of the world's total supply), there were no real shortages in the market and the price increases were limited in terms of length in time and dollar value. Oil prices peaked in late October 1990 at over $40 and steadily declined after the start of the war in February 1991. This was partly because the invasion had already been factored into the oil price by forward-looking assessments and aggressive statements by officials of major producers, especially Saudi Arabia. When the war to liberate Kuwait began a few days later, oil traders anticipated correctly that it would not disrupt the market, and as a result, the oil price collapsed to a level that was much lower than before the invasion.

The global oil markets remained stable following the invasion and the international military buildup in response to it for two fundamental reasons. First, other oil producers increased production. Saudi Arabia alone boosted output from 5.4 MBD to 8.5 MBD. The United Arab Emirates and Venezuela also increased their production. Saudi Arabia had large oil processing facilities equipped to handle even greater production increases. There was a pipeline project in place, gas separation plants, storage units, and export facilities that together could handle up to 14 MBD of oil exports from the Arabian Gulf region alone. Within three months and against all expectations, Aramco mobilized teams that were able to ramp up production to more than 8.5 MBD.[29]

The second reason for the relative stability of the oil market was the close coordination between the officials of the Saudi Ministry of Petroleum and the U.S. Department of Energy. Other agencies in both countries also worked together under the auspices of the Energy Technical Committee, which was created in 1989 between the United States and Saudi Arabia. The committee built personal relationships between officials of the two allies and facilitated communications between both upper- and midlevel government officials immediately after the invasion and the outbreak of war. These personal relationships proved to be very useful. Within a week or two of the invasion, the two governments were exchanging information and ideas daily about energy-related matters, including oil markets and prices. They also issued coordinated statements aimed at bringing down prices and preventing panic in the market and dismissed rumors, speculation, misinterpretations, and other forms of information that could lead to uncontrollably high oil prices.

The oil market, too, was in shock over the sudden loss of 4 MBD of production, a gap that had to be filled urgently. Oil prices more than doubled, surpassing $40 a barrel in October 1990, nearly $25 higher than when the markets had closed the day before the invasion. This was also $15 more than the price the Iraqis had been demanding. However, Iraq could not benefit by a single dollar because the country's oil exports were immediately blocked. Saudi Arabia generated a large increase in oil export revenues because of the combination of higher prices and increased production, but this was more than offset by the cost of the war, payments to the United States for its military involvement, and other ancillary costs. Other countries, especially Iran, benefited greatly from the war in every way, including the ability to increase oil production and generate record revenues.

Modern history shows that major military conflicts or revolutions—particularly wars that involve nations in major oil-producing regions such as the Middle East—have led to structural changes in the oil market. Notable examples include the Arab-Israeli war of 1973, the Iranian revolution, the war between Iran and Iraq, and the Venezuelan oil strike of 2002. These conflicts directly affect oil facilities in some countries and lead to changes in the general petroleum status quo. They also influence the roles of key decision makers such as heads of state and ministers. Examples of these changes following Iraq's invasion of Kuwait include the following:

1. The loss of oil revenues in Iraq because of its inability to produce 3.4 MBD of oil. It took Iraq more than twenty years to regain its lost production capacity. Saddam's goal was to have had Iraqi production similar to that of Saudi Arabia (about 5 MBD at that time).

2. Kuwait lost production of nearly 1.5 MBD of oil, and its overall 2.0 MBD capacity was damaged when oil wells were torched by the retreating Iraqi troops. It took Kuwait about a decade to recover its oil-production capacity.

3. Saddam's decision to invade Kuwait contributed, directly or indirectly, to the U.S.-led invasion of Iraq in 2003, which ended the Iraqi president's hold on power. This created a power vacuum that led to the creation of the Islamic State

of Iraq and Syria (ISIS) and bolstered Iranian influence over Iraq (and later Syria).

4. Ali al-Khalifa al-Sabah lost his job, and his achievements were quickly forgotten. He was placed under investigation following accusations of corruption and was not able to recover his previous stature despite repeated attempts to regain prominence through his own Kuwaiti newspaper and TV channel.

The six months leading to the Iraqi invasion of Kuwait provide a salutary lesson in diplomacy. The events leading to the conflict highlight the important roles of the protagonists in the decision-making process and how their personality traits and their grasp of complex issues (domestic and international) determine policy. These decisions have far-reaching consequences for many years and decades, not just in the oil industry but also for the global economy, war and peace, and geopolitics worldwide.

Chapter Four

LUIS GIUSTI, THE JAKARTA AGREEMENT, AND ITS AFTERMATH

Minister Erwin Arrieta and Luis Giusti Lopez, the heads of the Venezuelan delegation to Jakarta's November 1997 OPEC ministerial meeting, arrived two days late. They gave no reason for the delay. Perhaps they wanted to avoid pressure from other countries about Venezuela's overproduction, but I believe they were sending a message that they just did not care.

In 1994, Luis Giusti Lopez was named chairman and CEO of the Venezuela National Oil Company (PDVSA). The following year, Ali Al-Naimi was appointed minister of petroleum in Saudi Arabia and chairman of its national oil company, Saudi Aramco. Two years later the paths and personalities of these two men would intersect with significant economic and political consequences for both countries and for the international oil market.

The OPEC meeting in 1997 was an important event for both men, and it's important to know the background of these two important players to understand the Jakarta agreement. These two men had much in common. Both were hardworking professional men who had risen from the rank and file of the oil industry, gradually ascending the ladder to leadership positions, and gaining valuable experience along the way. Both were stubborn men who would not change their position once their mind was made up. They also had a common dislike of politics, both local and international, and both men disliked OPEC—or at least some of its members and the way the organization was run.

We also need to look at the global economy, the international oil market at the time, and the information available in the run-up to Jakarta.

LUIS GIUSTI LOPEZ, OIL, AND VENEZUELA

After OPEC's oil production fell in 1986 and oil prices collapsed, a raging debate began in Venezuela at both the political and the expert levels about the government's oil policy, OPEC, and the national oil company. Venezuela was increasingly divided between the conservatives, who wanted to open the country to international oil investment, and the nationalists and socialists, who did not trust "imperialism" and wanted to keep the national wealth and national company for the people.

During the 1990s the conservatives had the upper hand, controlling the government and dictating economic and energy policy and gradually implementing their plans. The new policy was implemented in 1990 when President Carlos Andrés Pérez appointed Andres Sosa-Pietri president of PDVSA. Sosa-Pietri came from a prominent family in Caracas and was a businessman and a former senator.

According to Bernard Mommer, a Venezuelan petroleum scholar and a government official, Sosa-Pietri wanted to break with tradition. Sosa-Pietri did not think the Ministry of Energy and Minerals or OPEC were important players in world petroleum, and he "drew up an ambitious plan to transform PDVSA from a national oil company into a global energy company." Mommer said that Sosa-Pietri believed "OPEC had never been important players in the world of petroleum" and that "the price increase in the 1970s had been coincidental." Moreover, OPEC was nothing but a mythical entity that should be converted into a research center cooperating with the International Energy Agency (IEA). His preference was for Venezuela to leave OPEC and join the IEA, but Venezuela was not a member of the Organization for Economic Cooperation and Development (OECD) and so was not eligible for membership of the IEA.[1]

Luis Giusti Lopez (hereafter Giusti) was a leading figure in the country's petroleum sector, and when he became the chairman and CEO of PDVSA in 1994, he adopted Sosa-Pietri's policy and began to steer the company with a clearer focus and a strong enthusiastic drive. Within three years of appointment, Giusti had achieved good results: international investments had increased and oil production rose. The new policy included the following key objectives:

1. Open the country to international oil companies by offering the most attractive oil investment regime. A number of laws and regulations were gradually amended to facilitate this strategy, including the law of natural resource ownership, free association between PDVSA and private companies including service companies, and changing the fiscal and oil tax system. As a result, private national and international oil companies were given more and more areas to explore and to produce oil. In 1996, ten promising areas for conventional oil, totaling 18,000 square kilometers, were auctioned based on production-sharing agreements, and Venezuelan production increased each year. Giusti told me that "we had been traveling the whole world in search for big money, for new development (because when looking ahead to the future, our production of light/medium oil would only last thirty to forty years)."

2. Increase Venezuela's oil production to the highest possible level. In 1989, the country was producing less than 2 MBD, but by 1998 production had risen to 3.1 MBD. Giusti's declared goal was to double production again to 6.4 MBD by 2007. He did not believe that national or international constraints, and certainly not OPEC, should stop Venezuela from achieving its target. The increase in production came from both PDVSA and international oil companies working in Venezuela.

3. PDVSA should be independent of the government and be an international oil company that pursues overseas acquisitions and investments in downstream projects such as refineries, petrochemicals, and product distribution. It could also be achieved by participating in production-sharing upstream joint ventures in Venezuela.[2]

Giusti focused his efforts on making PDVSA a successful national and international company without government constraints. However, he underestimated the impact of his policy on both the economic and the political conditions within Venezuela. His focus was on the company's success rather than on the political and economic situation in Venezuela. His thinking was to some extent similar to that of Sheik Ali al-Sabah, minister of petroleum for Kuwait in the 1980s. Some ideas never disappear; they travel the world and come back again and again.

PDVSA was gradually becoming more important than the ministry in determining national and international oil policy. Although Venezuelan energy minister Arrieta was close to the president and had been appointed before Giusti, Arrieta was losing his power to set oil policy for a number of reasons. Arrieta had a pleasant personality and a good political background, but he preferred diplomacy to confrontation. Also, his oil policy did not have clearly defined goals, and the ministry did not have the resources to hire the best experts or to produce authoritative studies that could influence the decision-making process.

Giusti was very strong-minded and had a clear vision of what he wanted to achieve for both PDVSA and his country's oil resources. He also had the trust of the president, and in addition he had resources within the company and good international relations within the oil industry, especially in the United States. This gave Giusti the upper hand when it came to oil policy nationally and internationally. He was the only head of a national oil company to attend all OPEC ministerial meetings, although he could not take part in the closed-door ministerial sessions. He also attended other official intergovernmental gatherings and was present at official bilateral meetings.

In the 1980s and 1990s, Giusti was close to some conservative policy makers who disliked both OPEC and any restraints on Venezuelan oil production. Some saw OPEC as a group for developing countries, and they believed Venezuela did not fit in that category. However, OPEC has been deeply rooted in the culture of the Venezuelan public for decades. Together with Abdallah al-Tariki, Venezuelan oil minister Juan Pablo Perez Alfonzo had been one of the founding fathers of OPEC, an organization that was seen as the most successful international institution for defending and promoting the interests of oil producers in developing countries. OPEC put oil-producing countries on the world map, and Venezuela had played a key role in this. Venezuela and many developing Latin American countries had misgivings about what they perceived as the imperialist West, and the United States in particular. Many people saw the success of OPEC during the 1970s and part of the 1980s as a shining example of achievement in their struggle against the West.[3]

In the 1980s and 1990s, Venezuela was going through difficult times on almost all fronts. The collapse of the oil market in 1986 played a role, but most of the issues were related to government mismanagement and conflicts between different groups and interests within the country. These led to military coups and strikes, uncontrolled inflation, a high level of poverty, unemployment, and protests by many segments of society. When President Rafael Caldera introduced economic measures in 1996, including the decision to increase Venezuela's oil production beyond its OPEC quota, these problems intensified. The issues were debated intensely, and the country was sharply divided.[4]

Before the OPEC meeting in Jakarta, Venezuela was split between the right and the left on almost all fronts, including on oil policy. The new economic measures did not do enough to reduce inflation and tackle high unemployment, and the petroleum minister and the president of Venezuela's government oil company were not fully in harmony. Arrieta was willing to reach a compromise with OPEC, but Giusti was intent on raising oil production regardless of OPEC's quotas. PDVSA was becoming international, and the sky was the limit as far as Giusti was concerned. The first challenge came during Jakarta and the year after where the Saudi minister of petroleum, Ali Al-Naimi (who had replaced Nazer in August 1995), was leading a big change that seemed to parallel Giusti's ideas in the beginning. But dreamers have to face reality one day.

ALI AL-NAIMI

Ali Al-Naimi was hardworking and a fast learner. He was highly focused and as dedicated to his work and responsibilities as he was loyal to his king. He was more comfortable executing orders from a higher authority than initiating them, and Al-Naimi attributed his success to "hard work, good fortune and making the boss look good."[5] He began working at Aramco at the age of twelve as a busboy while studying part-time. Over time, he was able to gain the trust of his American boss, who sent him to Lebanon to continue his high school education. He traveled to the United States to complete his undergraduate studies and received a master's degree in geology from Stanford University in 1963.

On his return to Saudi Arabia, Al-Naimi went back to work at Aramco, rising up the corporate ladder and becoming president in the early 1980s and CEO in 1988. Al-Naimi was well known and highly respected not only within the company but also at the national level, within the government, and by the Saudi leadership. Both King Fahd and Crown Prince Abdullah had met him several times, and he had private meetings with King Fahd before he was named a minister.

In 1995, King Fahd formed a new cabinet, removing all ministers except three members of the royal family (the ministers of defense, interior, and foreign affairs). Al-Naimi was not a candidate proposed by the high committee to lead the Ministry of Petroleum, but King Fahd reportedly chose him over the others. Al-Naimi heard of his appointment while on vacation in Alaska, and the news took him by surprise. He had expected to retire from Aramco because he had reached the age of sixty, the official retirement age. Prince Abdulaziz bin Salman told me he persuaded Al-Naimi to take this position without any hesitation.

Al-Naimi flew back to the kingdom immediately to see King Fahd in Jeddah, the summer capital of Saudi Arabia, and he was sworn in as minister. He was received warmly by management and staff at the Ministry of Petroleum and Mineral Resources, where he was known and respected. The national and international media as well as Saudi social circles welcomed his appointment because of his unique personality and background. He was fortunate to have within the ministry a group of highly knowledgeable people who understood domestic politics and international oil markets and, in particular, the inner workings of the government as well as OPEC. He also had access to the financial and expert resources of Aramco, which he could draw on when needed.

Al-Naimi did not like working with the government, especially in Riyadh, where people from other regions did not feel very comfortable, especially those from the east and west coasts (Al-Naimi came from the east), because of cultural differences. Saudis from other regions did not like politics, and Riyadh had too much of it. They thought Riyadh residents behaved as if they were special and more privileged. (This is a feeling many people around the world have about their capital and its people.)[6]

Khalid al-Falih, who became president of Aramco and later minister of energy, said of Al-Naimi's appointment as minister in 1995: "Many people probably never thought it would happen. We had this image of politicians in Riyadh as if they were completely different creatures."[7] During their time as ministers, Al-Naimi and al-Falih rarely spent a weekend in Riyadh, preferring to visit with their families in the East. Even though Nazer's families were situated in Riyadh, he preferred to work in Jeddah when possible.

On November 29, 1995, less than four months after Al-Naimi's appointment, King Fahd suffered a stroke, and Crown Prince Abdullah took charge until King Fahd was able to resume his duties in February 1996. But the king had not recovered fully and had lost interest in overseeing detailed policies and running day-to-day affairs, the most important of which was oil policy. This turn of events had important implications for Al-Naimi. Oil is of paramount importance for Saudi Arabia, and King Fahd, as head of the Higher Council of Petroleum and Minerals since 1973, had developed a deep interest in and a good knowledge of petroleum issues nationally and internationally and became more and more involved over the years.

King Abdullah did not have the same background on OPEC, but he was an excellent listener with a strong desire to obtain as much information and knowledge as possible. To add to this, the institutional depth of the Saudi system—the existence of a strong establishment and a coherent royal family—did not leave space for any power vacuum. As a result, an oversight committee was formed to oversee many government activities and policies. The committee was made up of important figures including Prince Sultan, who was the second deputy prime minister and minister of defense, Prince Nayef bin Abdulaziz, the minister of the interior, and Prince Saud al-Faisal, the minister of foreign affairs, who was overseeing economic and financial issues, including oil.

Al-Naimi had good relations with the committee, sent regular reports on petroleum issues, and debated energy issues using convincing reasoning backed by good information. One problem Al-Naimi grappled with was his inability to adapt to Riyadh's social and political life; he could not change his personality to fit the Riyadh social scene. He was a quiet man who spoke only when he was asked to explain petroleum issues, and he preferred to be the last to speak. Also, dinner parties in Riyadh, including those at the royal court, tended to be long and to end late, which was difficult for Al-Naimi because he usually went to bed at 9 p.m. or 10 p.m., but he used to go to the majority of them.

Al-Naimi did not enjoy politics at any level, nor could he tolerate government bureaucracy, and he often related a story from 1965 when he was first appointed assistant deputy minister for water resources in the ministry of agriculture in Riyadh, with a salary nearly double what he was earning at Aramco. "At the time, working for the government in such a position was considered among the most prestigious jobs a young Saudi man could aspire to," Al-Naimi said.[8] But from day one Al-Naimi was frustrated and realized that he could not continue working for the government. Four days later he went back to Dhahran to resume his work at Aramco. The minister of agriculture accused him of violating the law, an offense for which he could have been sentenced to prison, but Al-Naimi was able to convince the minister that he was not suited for the job and that it was difficult for him to work in a bureaucratic environment. Therefore, it was good for the ministry to let him go.

Al-Naimi had the same negative feeling about international political and energy relations. He did not like OPEC's structure and the endless deliberation of issues during meetings, and he did not trust many OPEC members. When Yamani was minister, OPEC meetings could take weeks; Nazer was able to shorten them to no more than five or six days. Al-Naimi brought further changes in the way OPEC conducted its business, and on one occasion admonished a fellow minister for being late and asked that ministers adhere to a timetable. He succeeded in shortening the time allocated for bilateral discussions preceding the ministerial meeting to one day, and the OPEC secretariat began to prepare the agenda at least one week in advance of the ministerial meeting and scheduled the start time of meetings (the finish line was always problematic because insignificant issues could take up an inordinate amount of time to resolve). Saudi officials continued a practice that began with Nazer of informing the media about the issues and the items on the agenda, without revealing any of the confidential information.

Al-Naimi saw that some ministers did not adhere to their quotas nor cut their production to the agreed levels, and Al-Naimi believed Saudi Arabia should do the same, without necessarily making it known. The behavior of Venezuela and others in 1997–1998 exemplified this behavior. Venezuela was not only overproducing but was making this known publicly. Nigeria, Algeria, and Qatar were also overproducing and followed Venezuela's example. At the time, Venezuela was producing 1 MBD above its quota, a violation of around 30 percent. Saudi Arabia was also producing around 400,000 barrels per day over its 8 MBD quota, a 5 percent violation. Cheating within OPEC was the norm between 1995 and 1998, but most countries did not make this public.

OIL CRISES IN A CHANGING WORLD

Before the Jakarta OPEC meeting, Venezuela's energy and mines minister ordered PDVSA officials not to discuss oil production and said that his country's oil production was around 2.3 MBD, close to the quota. The minister wanted to show that his country was committed to the OPEC agreement, but Giusti said publicly on November 18, 1997, that the Venezuelan National Oil Company was producing more than 3 MBD and that production was set to grow annually by about 5 percent, or 150,000 barrels per day, in coming years, implying that OPEC and political considerations should not restrict their production. The Caldera government and Giusti were fighting off all of their critics in Venezuela and within OPEC in pursuing this policy. In November 1996, Giusti clearly said that OPEC had to "change or disappear."[9] Al-Naimi may have had a similar feeling, but he never said so publicly. Ali al-Sabah, the oil minister of Kuwait, followed the same policy from 1985 to early 1990 and publicly stated that the quota system is irrelevant.

That was the reality as OPEC ministers headed to Jakarta for the ministerial meeting on November 26, 1997. Giusti and his government were silent for two weeks before the meeting, perhaps because they did not want to take the blame if oil prices fell. Meanwhile, Al-Naimi was strongly advocating for a new official ceiling after four years of no change. Al-Naimi and Giusti were both challenging OPEC's quotas and ceiling, but in different ways.

Elsewhere, the Soviet Union had disintegrated and the major Russian republics were striving to become part of the Western-dominated international system. They were liberalizing their economies and opening up to international investors in many sectors, including oil (chapter 10). All in all, from 1993 to 1997 the global economy was growing annually at an average of 3.5 percent, and growth was very strong in the Asian Tiger economies, which included Hong Kong, Taiwan, Singapore, and South Korea. In addition, demand for oil increased by more than 1.5 MBD each year, a level unparalleled since the 1960s. From 1993 to 1999, oil demand increased from about 68 MBD to 75.5 MBD, and supplies increased from both OPEC and non-OPEC countries, such as Mexico and the United Kingdom. By early 1997, oil prices had climbed to around $25 per barrel, which was 15 percent higher than the four-year period from 1992 to 1995. Many experts and government officials were optimistic about economic growth and the rising demand for oil, but good times do not last forever and one or two price spikes do not signify a trend.

Three interrelated events affected the oil market in the last two months of 1997 and in the following year: a slowdown in some Asian economies, overproduction by some OPEC members, and the decisions that had been taken by OPEC in Jakarta. The economic and financial problems came to be known as the Asian financial crisis and began in the second quarter of 1997 in Thailand. By the middle of that year, the country's currency (the baht) had shed about half of its value, and the stock market had lost about 75 percent of its value. The International Monetary Fund, with a bailout package of more than $20 billion, was hoping to contain the problem and stop it from spreading to other countries. However, that did not work. Within a few months, the downturn spread to other Asian countries, first Indonesia, then the Philippines, Hong Kong, the Republic of Korea, and Japan.

The crisis spread beyond Asia to almost all parts of the world. The U.S. economy saw some slowdown, and on October 27, two weeks before the OPEC Jakarta meeting, the Dow Jones Industrial Average was down by 554 points (7.2 percent), the largest one-day drop in the history of this index. Economic conditions determined whether demand for oil would rise or fall, and the Asian financial crisis affected oil demand on fundamental and psychological levels. In early 1997, the IEA had estimated global oil demand growth for the year to be more than 2 MBD. In early November, three weeks before the OPEC meeting, the IEA revised its estimate down to around 1 MBD. Added to that was a shift in market psychology amid growing fears about the health of the global economy. Fear and uncertainty about the future continued into 1998, and that uncertainty negatively affected the price of many commodities, especially oil, in the futures markets. Analysts also believed that bad decisions were made in Jakarta, and the ensuing debate in the aftermath of Jakarta added to this negative sentiment.

Oil supply had been rising month after month from OPEC and non-OPEC producers alike. The last OPEC ceiling had been set in 1993 at 25 MBD, but actual production continued to accelerate. In January 1997, average OPEC oil production was 26.747 MBD, but it had risen to 27.910 MBD by October—3 MBD above the official ceiling. The increase that year came from several countries, with Venezuela the most flagrant overproducer, pumping 1 MBD above its allocation.

An IEA report estimated actual OPEC production in the third quarter of 1997 at 27.3 MBD, while the implied call on OPEC crude was 26.4 MBD. It is interesting to note that in 1996 there was little divergence between the call on OPEC oil at 25.5 MBD and actual production of 25.8 MBD. (The "call on OPEC" means the crude that it should produce to balance supply and demand with no inventory changes.) The oil market was starting to build large commercial stocks, which by the second quarter of 1997 stood at 1.3 MBD, with the same volume added in the third quarter. The IEA was expecting the call on OPEC oil in 1998 to be 26.3 MBD, lower than the preceding year by about 100,000 barrels per day, and lower than actual production by about 700,000 barrels per day for 1997, and 1 MBD for 1998.[10]

OPEC was heading to Jakarta with a lot of negative information: an economic crisis was looming, demand for its oil was slowing, and there was an oversupply and high commercial stocks. Any decision should have taken this negative picture of the oil market and of the global economy into consideration, but that was not the case. The personality and determination of the decision makers dominated over the facts on the ground, and the psychology and perception of the market was not even considered.

OPEC lacked strong leadership, and leading members lacked the will to work together for the benefit of all, which would have required some compromises. Al-Naimi was a relatively new minister, having been in office only two years, and had not yet been tested as an OPEC leader although he was respected as a professional. Because he did not trust many OPEC members, especially Venezuela, Al-Naimi went into the meeting of a mind to impose his will—putting maximum pressure on the Venezuelans and securing a big quota for the kingdom without careful consideration of oil prices.

The Venezuelan minister was weak, and his government had no interest in OPEC quotas and ceilings, let alone in taking on a leadership role. Such was Venezuela's disdain for OPEC that Arrieta arrived three days after the other ministers despite the sensitivity of the situation and the importance of the conference. He even said that the global climate change meeting in Japan was more important than the Jakarta meeting.

The Iranian minister, Bijan Zanganeh, had little OPEC experience. Twenty years later he admitted that "I was new and did not understand the market."[11] Also, his country did not enjoy the trust of the majority of OPEC members, so he had little credibility for taking a leading role. In addition, Iran had no bargaining power because it had no spare production capacity that could be used to pressure others to compromise.

Algeria had taken on a leadership role in the past when needed, but in Jakarta things were different. The Algerian oil minister, Youcef Yousfi, was a professional and not a fighter. He also understood that Venezuela was the problem and that it would not stop raising its production, let alone reduce it if needed. He had been unable to reach a compromise with them beforehand. Moreover, Algeria was producing above its quota by a large margin.

Abdalla el Badri, the head of the Libyan delegation later told me: "We did not have good information at that time, therefore we went along with Al-Naimi."[12] Al-Naimi had made up his mind before the Jakarta meeting: he wanted OPEC to raise the ceiling and increase quotas to reflect actual production.

Having decided what should be done, Al-Naimi had set his goal, at times against the advice of members of his team at the ministry. Some of his advisers were not supportive of the idea of raising the ceiling to a high level because they believed it would shock the market and lead to lower oil prices. Saudi Arabia was producing above its quota by about 300,000 barrels per day, so there was no need for a large increase. Al-Naimi's advisers supported the idea of increasing the ceiling, but they did not advocate it being raised to 27.5 MBD.

Almost one month before the Jakarta meeting, Al-Naimi gave a lengthy exclusive interview to *MEES* that outlined his plan, which to a great extent reflected Saudi opinions. During the interview in Riyadh with *MEES* editor Ian Seymour, Al-Naimi spoke clearly about what he wanted from the Jakarta meeting: "I think we are going to have a very interesting OPEC meeting in Jakarta in late November. And I believe that there will probably be a desire and hopefully an agreement to raise the production ceiling to a more realistic level." When Seymour asked the minister about the amount of the increase in OPEC's production ceiling, the minister said he wanted it to reflect the forecast call on OPEC oil: "I have seen numbers of between 26 MBD and 27 MBD for the call on OPEC crude for the next year. Of course, the experts haven't finished yet. These are very rough numbers but I think it is the range." He added, "This is just the call on OPEC crude supply—this is what there is to be shared."[13]

Al-Naimi went to Jakarta with a clear proposal to change the OPEC official ceiling and quotas based on what was actually being produced. The increase was to be distributed on a pro rata basis. The logic behind this decision was clear. First, the oil market had been absorbing all 27.5 MBD being produced by OPEC without a negative impact on the price. Second, Venezuela was not willing to accept any quota below what it was producing, and it would not be fair for others not to have a higher share. Third, global demand had been very strong. In 1997, overall demand growth was forecast to be about 2 MBD. In 1998, it was forecast to increase further by 1.8 MBD. But forecasters in Paris, Vienna, London, and New York had their own views, and the reality on the ground was something else.

Al-Naimi's argument was logical and clear, but it did not take into account other facts, most important among them being the psychology of the oil market, which you have to guess at by speaking with market participants such as traders, hedge fund managers, and oil analysts. Market sentiment is very important, and even though it is not measurable, you know it when you see it. The Saudi Ministry of Petroleum had good information about oil market fundamentals and understood the importance of market psychology, sometimes using it to Saudi Arabia's advantage by creating uncertainty and then managing it. In Jakarta, the decision was taken without consideration of these factors. The goal was simple and straightforward: challenge Venezuela, legitimize what OPEC was producing, and divide the total increase pro rata. Walid Khadduri, the editor of *MEES* and a highly respected writer and oil analyst said of the decision, "We were sitting in the lobby as journalists and we were all shocked by the decision. I mean really shocked. I remember the face of the oil company people turned when they heard the news."[14]

Market fundamentals did not support such an increase. By the time OPEC met in Jakarta, expected demand growth for the rest of the year was forecast to be lower than existing production. It was also expected to decline further the following year. More important was the build in commercial oil stocks. Equally important was the fact that the decision to raise the ceiling and increase individual quotas did not stop the violation of production allocations. Countries that did not respect their quotas continued to overproduce. For example, Venezuela was given a quota of 2.583 MBD but was producing about 3.3 MBD.

At the time, Iraq's production was a wild card. After the Iraqi invasion of Kuwait, the United Nations imposed full economic sanctions against Iraq, including on its oil exports. In 1995 the United Nations set up the Oil for Food Program, which allowed Iraq to sell oil for humanitarian reasons under strict UN supervision. The UN was seriously considering increasing the amount of oil Iraq would be allowed to export under the program, but the ministers in Jakarta did not take this into account. More important, the UN decision was not based on volume but on the monetary value of the oil, so if prices fell, Iraq could export more oil. The Oil for Food program, which was worth $2 billion every six months, was due to expire at the end of November 1998, and there was talk that it could be renewed for another six months with a possible increase to $3 or $4 billion.

Iraq was exempt from OPEC production restraints, and in the month of the Jakarta meeting, Iraq's estimated production was between 1.6 and 1.7 MBD. OPEC allocated Iraq a quota of only 1.314 MBD, but in 1998 Iraqi production rose and to more than 2.5 MBD in some months. OPEC had definitely underestimated Iraq's production. Information provided by some OPEC members was also distorted. Some countries claimed that they could and did produce more than the estimates by secondary sources. Iran was a good example of this. The secondary sources were estimating Iran's production to be around 3.7 MBD before and after the meeting, and it was allocated a quota of 3.942 MBD in Jakarta. The new numbers became a major problem for OPEC when it tried to find a compromise solution in the following year (chapter 5).

Al-Naimi did not believe in the psychology of the market, and his analysis of the market fundamentals pointed to continuing strong economic growth. He did not see the Asian financial crisis as a major problem, and Al-Naimi was worried "for the sake of the Iraqi people" that the UN program might not be renewed.[15] In other words, he was hoping that the program would be renewed and even improved.

Arriving in Jakarta two days before the meeting, Al-Naimi was determined to increase the OPEC ceiling by 2.5 MBD for the first half of 1998, and he used all means available to him to achieve this. He delivered a strong logical argument, stating that his proposal would increase production to what OPEC countries were actually producing and that this level had been accepted by the market without a negative effect on the oil price. He also had an important message to other OPEC members, which is that Venezuela shouldn't run the show by producing what they want.[16]

At the OPEC economic board meeting in Vienna two weeks before Jakarta, Saudi Arabia pushed strongly for higher numbers for the call of

OPEC oil in 1998. The Saudis were able to persuade several members of the board to agree with their numbers, and they followed up with a campaign using anonymous sources variously referred to in news media as "Gulf sources" or "a Gulf source familiar with Saudi thinking" to try to persuade others to accept the Saudi proposal and the logic behind it. The media campaign continued and even gained momentum during the meeting. I played a large part in this campaign as one of the sources quoted.

The first thing Al-Naimi did was to secure the backing of the Gulf Cooperation Council (GCC) members in OPEC (Kuwait, Qatar, and the United Arab Emirates), who normally coordinate with each other before OPEC meetings and almost always go along with Saudi Arabia. Kuwait and the United Arab Emirates backed the Saudi proposal, but Qatar was more cautious. The heads of state of the GCC countries directed their ministers to work together during international meetings. Venezuela needed no persuasion because the agreement would legitimize some of their production and validate their policy in the eyes of the world and at home. Indonesia was hosting the conference and wanted it to be successful, but the Indonesians did not support a large ceiling increase. However, they do not favor confrontation and normally go along with the consensus. Nigeria did not support this increase either, but it also usually went along with the majority.

Opposition to a production increase came from Algeria, Libya, and Iran. When Al-Naimi arrived in Jakarta, and before meeting with anybody else, he had lunch with the Iranian minister, Bijan Zanganeh, and tried to convince him to back the Saudi proposal. Al-Naimi and Zanganeh had enjoyed a good relationship during the two previous years, and the Saudi crown prince who was in charge at the time had good working relations with the Iranian president Mohammed Khatami. Other factors also might have convinced the Iranians to go along with the Saudi proposal. Iran's quota would go up to 3.9 MBD, a number that they insisted later was their actual production (chapter 5). More than twenty years later, I asked Zanganeh why he went along with the Saudi proposal, and he replied: "At that time I was a new minister with little knowledge and experience."[17]

The Iranians have a habit of voicing their disagreement with most of the proposals before meetings begin, but if the majority seem to be against them, they go along with them. But then Iran proceeds to produce whatever they can regardless of their allocation. The Iranian delegation normally tried to take credit for OPEC decisions if the outcome was positive, even if they had had no influence on the final accord. Their motive was to show Iranians back home that they played an important role in OPEC.

During the Jakarta conference, the Saudi ambassador to Indonesia had a good idea. He invited the Algerian and Libyan ministers to lunch at his beautiful farm in the mountains outside the capital. The ministers, together with Al-Naimi or separately, went for long walks and discussed the proposal to raise the ceiling by 2.5 MBD. They also discussed Venezuela's violation of its quota, which Al-Naimi emphasized clearly and strongly. The overproduction by Venezuela was irritating to everyone (Al-Naimi used the same argument in 2014 against the U.S. shale oil producers, among others; chapter 9). Al-Naimi told the two ministers that this was not fair to Saudi Arabia, which was adhering to its quota even though it had production capacity of 10 MBD. If there was no realistic increase in the OPEC ceiling, Al-Naimi said that Saudi Arabia would have to do what Venezuela was doing. Even though not fully convinced, by the end of the trip, both ministers went along with the Saudi proposal and Algeria was given a higher quota. Their main concern was that oil prices would fall, but Al-Naimi assured them that was unlikely because the demand for OPEC crude the following year would be higher than the new ceiling.

As a result of these long negotiations, an OPEC ceiling of 27.5 MBD was agreed on December 1, 1997, to take effect on January 1, 1998. OPEC had been producing at that level a month earlier, although some put the number at more than 28 MBD. After the meeting and during press interviews, Libya's Abdalla el Badri was very open, telling *MEES* editor Walid Khadduri on November 30, "We heard about the Saudi proposal to raise the production ceiling before we arrived in Jakarta, so we had time to study [it] carefully. . . . [W]e proposed a rollover of the 25.033 MBD production ceiling." He told the conference that increasing the ceiling "would lead to the decline of prices" because it would legitimize the violation and more oil will come to the market. He went on to say that there were other views that estimated demand for OPEC in 1998 at around 29 MBD. "Libya was adamantly opposed to an increase in the ceiling. However, in order to preserve the organization's unity and so that we won't have different and conflicting views; we all agreed to raise the production ceiling and see what would happen during the next six months," he added.[18] El Badri not only liked Al-Naimi but respected and admired him as well. Iran's Zanganeh refused to speak to the media about the OPEC decision and referred questions to the OPEC secretary-general.

The negative consequences for the oil market that followed the Jakarta meeting can be attributed to two factors: personality traits and information. Venezuela's Giusti was determined not to allow OPEC or any other party to constrain his country's increasing production, and Al-Naimi was unhappy that Giusti and Venezuela were running the show. The other important factor was the role of information. Conflicting views were circulating, and the available information was at times vague and confusing. Twenty years later, I asked el Badri why he went along with Al-Naimi's proposal even as the Asian economic slowdown was looming He replied: "At that time we did not have good information."[19] Leonardo Maugeri, the scholar and strategist for Eni, had a good explanation regarding the information issue: "The actual levels of major producers' output capacity were more a matter of careful speculation than empirical certainty. In this situation, the risk of 'missing barrels'—i.e., of underestimating or overestimating demand or supply—was always present. In 1997–1998 the risk materialized."[20]

One year after the Jakarta meeting, the recently appointed Kuwaiti oil minister, Sheikh Saud Nasser al-Sabah, called the decision a "disaster." He added that "the conference legitimized the race among the countries to increase production and to exceed their quotas. . . . What happened in Jakarta was the worst-ever in the history of the Organization."[21]

The experience of the Jakarta meeting illustrates clearly how two hard-headed men, Giusti and Al-Naimi, were able to create a new direction in the international oil market. After Jakarta, the oil price began a steady decline that continued for about eighteen months. Equally important were the political and economic consequences of that decision, which persist to this day in some countries.

On his way home after the Jakarta meeting, Al-Naimi was asked about the conference. He said, "We consider this conference to be the paradigm shift in the history of OPEC."[22] He was right, but not in the way he had expected.

Chapter Five

PRINCE SAUD AL-FAISAL

An Interim Energy Leader

In December 1997, shortly after the Jakarta agreement, the price of oil began to fall, and it continued on a downward trend for more than eighteen months. By the end of February 1998, the price of oil had fallen by around 30 percent. Although global demand growth was slowing, OPEC production was rising above the ceiling agreed upon in Jakarta. In October 1997, a month before the Jakarta agreement, OPEC members were producing about 28 MBD even though the ceiling had been set at 27.5 MBD. By February 1998, average OPEC production was 28.7 MBD; this new level reflected neither the official ceiling nor the demand for OPEC oil and was a clear sign that the Jakarta agreement less than three months earlier was a failure.

Several countries continued to increase production. Venezuela production was at full capacity (3.384 MBD), more than 800 KBD above its OPEC quota allocation. Nigeria and Qatar were both producing above their quotas by a combined 500 KBD. Iraqi oil exports were also higher; Iraq was able to increase sales under the United Nations Oil for Food program due to falling oil prices and because the UN had raised the financial limit that Iraq could generate from oil sales. Oil producers inside and outside OPEC began to feel the pain, and there was concern that these high levels of production might continue or rise even more.

The market needed a big shock to push prices up, just as the Jakarta shock had brought prices down. The longer producers waited, the more complicated the problem became. Commercial stocks continued to build month after month. There was no end in sight.

Saudi Arabia was the largest oil producer and oil exporter, but Ali Al-Naimi was relatively new to domestic and international politics and was not willing to bring the oil producers together with a meaningful proposal to cut oil production and coordinate implementation. Moreover, he did not trust some OPEC members due to their consistent overproduction, especially Venezuela, whose leaders showed no sign of changing their policy. No other minister or country, except Algeria, which often acted as mediator, was prepared to take on a leadership role. Perhaps, as one official put it, "the fight is between big players. Venezuela was increasing its production month after month and did not respect OPEC and its decisions. Saudi Arabia wanted to take more market share and punish Venezuela."[1]

Nevertheless, Youcef Yousfi, the Algerian oil minister, traveled to Caracas March 7, 1998, and then visited Riyadh on March 11 to meet with Al-Naimi. The Algerians were not happy with the Venezuelans and the way Luis Giusti, head of the Venezuelan National Oil Company, was making all the decisions and overruling Erwin Arrieta, the minister of energy and mines. Yousfi's mission did not succeed.

ROBERT MABRO

While the oil-producing countries waited without taking action to stabilize the oil market, Robert Mabro, founder of the Oxford Institute for Energy Studies in the United Kingdom, came up with a new idea and worked hard to implement it. Mabro was a strong believer in the role of OPEC and in the importance of oil market management. He also believed that OPEC and non-OPEC producers should and could cooperate and work together, especially in times of crisis. Mabro was one of the world's most respected intellectuals and oil scholars and was respected equally by oil-producing and oil-consuming nations, as well as by the oil industry.

This is a good example of my thesis that personality matters in the oil decision-making process, even if the person does not have a political role. As Adrian Lajous, former president of Petróleos Mexicanos (Pemex) wrote, "Robert played a key, if unaccredited role in the secret negotiations that brought together these three countries, in an attempt to stabilize oil prices in the first quarter of 1998."[2] Lajous mentions Mexico, Saudi Arabia, and

Venezuela, but in reality it was Mexico, Saudi Arabia, and Norway. Mabro did not have direct communications with Venezuela at that time.

Mabro had a good relationship with Saudi and Mexican officials, including two individuals who could take on leadership roles and bring the parties together to coordinate action. The first was Prince Abdulaziz bin Salman, the current Saudi energy minister. The second was Adrian Lajous, then CEO of Pemex, who was as important as the Mexican minister of energy in the decision-making process. Mabro chose to work with Mexico rather than with the independent oil-producing countries of Norway, Russia, or Oman for a number of reasons. Norway is a member of the Organization for Economic Cooperation and Development (OECD) and has observer status at the International Energy Agency (IEA) and does not like collective action in managing the oil market. In addition, Norway prefers to coordinate action through bilateral efforts, especially with Saudi Arabia, which has enjoyed a good relationship with Norway on many levels for many years. At the time, Russia did not have a clear international oil policy and was unwilling to assume a leading role in the oil market (chapter 10). Oman expressed some willingness to work with others and to participate in any production cut, but it took no action.

Mexico was willing to be a participant and a partner with the other producers for a number of reasons. First, Mexico was producing high-cost heavy oil whose price was lower than that of Brent, the global benchmark, by about $5/BBL and was getting close to if not below the cost of production. Mexico also faced strong competition in the U.S. market from Venezuela, which was increasing its production of heavy oil. Second, the Mexican government received about 20 percent of its income from oil sales, and the price decline was affecting the country's budget. Third, Mexico had a left-leaning government that believed in market control and was sympathetic to developing countries' interests, such as OPEC. Finally, Mexico had a special role within Latin America and was trying to expand its influence, especially before signing the North American Free Trade Agreement (NAFTA) in 2009 between Mexico, the United States, and Canada. Mexico informed the United States of its involvement with OPEC members in the effort to raise oil prices. Mexico was planning to go ahead with this effort regardless of the reaction by the Americans, but the United States had no objection to Mexico's involvement.[3] However, Venezuela did take Mexico's involvement seriously, and Mexico became an important partner in the effort to shore up oil prices and restore them to the level that had prevailed before the Jakarta agreement ($17–$20/BBL).

At the start of the process in early March, Al-Naimi had no interest in a meeting between the three countries. Venezuelan officials publicly blamed Saudi Arabia for the fall in the oil price and insisted that they would continue increasing their production regardless of price. They even spoke of exiting OPEC, and Arrieta went as far as to say that OPEC was "a gathering of Pinocchios."[4] When ministers frustrated Al-Naimi, he declined to work closely with them, even if the whole system could collapse (meaning oil prices). This happened in 1997–1998 and again in 2014–2016 (chapter 9). After a lot of debate within the Ministry of Petroleum, Al-Naimi agreed to meet with the Venezuelan and Mexican oil ministers if it could be kept secret until they reached a successful outcome. He invited them to Riyadh, and Prince Abdulaziz played a major role in the process.

The Venezuelan and Mexican ministers arrived in Riyadh on March 20, 1998. There was no media coverage and their visit remained secret until the end. Both ministers had the heads of their national oil companies as part of their delegations. The Venezuelan oil minister also invited two important figures who were not part of the Caldera government. They were Humberto Calderon Berti, a former Venezuelan energy minister, and Alberto Quiros, a former CEO of Lagoven and Maraven (subsidiaries of PDVSA) and head of Shell Oil in Venezuela. The inclusion of these two men was an indication of the conflict within Venezuela and the government's concern about the collapse in oil prices, the opposition, and public opinion.

During the meeting, Al-Naimi took a strong line with both ministers, accusing Venezuela of overproducing and not respecting its quota. (Venezuela's production in February was about 3.5 MBD, but its allocation was only 2.583 MBD.) "I will take off a barrel of oil," Al-Naimi told both ministers, "and each one of you will take a barrel off."[5] In the end, the three countries agreed to reduce their total production by 600,000 B/D (300,000 B/D for Saudi Arabia, 200,000 B/D for Venezuela, and 100,000 B/D for Mexico). Mexico's reduction was from their exports and not from production.

This agreement became known as the Riyadh Pact. Unlike the Jakarta agreement, which was based on quotas or on the numbers each country claimed as their actual production, the Riyadh Pact was based on the latest estimates published by selected OPEC secondary sources in the media or by consultants. Al-Naimi telephoned OPEC ministers one by one after the meeting to inform them of the agreement and to ask for their participation. They all agreed to reduce their production. The total reduction from the three countries and others was 1.6–2 MBD. Prince Saud al-Faisal was following this process and talking with Al-Naimi, and he was willing to help if needed.

As part of his effort to bring OPEC and non-OPEC producers together to stabilize the market, Mabro spoke with Norwegian officials about being part of the agreement to cut production. His main contact was Jens Stoltenberg, a former minister of energy who was then chair of the Standing Committee on Oil and Energy in Parliament. Mabro and Stoltenberg had a close relationship, and although Stoltenberg faced strong opposition within Parliament, the Norwegian government announced that it would reduce production by 150,000 BPD.

The Mexican delegation had visited Oslo on March 19, when on their way to Riyadh. Lajous said that "the objective was to seek their participation in reducing global oil supply" and "to provide Mexico with some cover with other OECD countries."[6] The Mexicans received some promises, and the Norwegian Parliament eventually agreed to trim oil production.

The Riyadh Pact, Norway's decision to take part in the production cut, and a decision by OPEC in March 1998 to cut its production led to a more than $2/BBL rise in oil prices immediately. But the gains were fleeting, and the price began a steady decline.

Three factors were behind this price fall. First, Al-Naimi and Giusti did not in fact decrease production in their respective countries. Second, other OPEC countries did not lower their production, some even increasing their output. Third, Iraqi oil production was rising and reached about 2 MBD by April 1998 (OPEC had allocated Iraq a 1.3 MBD under the Jakarta agreement). The fundamentals were bad, and market sentiment was much worse. No country or minister was willing to take a leadership role after this latest debacle. However, the 1998 price fall had major repercussions on the countries that contributed to the decline (Saudi Arabia and Venezuela) and on the two key players in the game: Ali Al-Naimi and Luis Giusti.

From early 1998 to early 1999, Saudi Arabia's economy faltered and Al-Naimi himself was in a predicament. Saudi Arabia's oil income declined by about 50 percent (from US$159.985 million to US$79.938 million in 1998). The deficit rose from Saudi riyal 15.772 to 48.452 million.[7] The Saudi riyal was under strong pressure from currency traders who believed that the riyal's value should go down with a possibility of being devalued. The Saudi Central Bank (SAMA) was engaged in a battle against these speculators nearly every day during the summer of 1998. International traders were betting that the Saudi currency would weaken on the Bahrain market, where the Saudi riyal was traded. SAMA was trying hard to defend the riyal by betting against the forward currency traders. "We used to wake up every morning and burn their fingers by buying more Saudi riyals from the market," said Jammaz al Suhaimi, a senior SAMA official.[8] It was rumored that SAMA borrowed $10 billion for this purpose through Saudi Aramco and the United Arab Emirates. However, Saudi officials later denied it, and Hamad al-Sayari, the governor of SAMA from 1985 to 2009, told me that "we did not need any money, and we did not borrow from anyone."[9] Equally important, according to Lieutenant General Abdulrahman al-Banyan, low oil income may have led to the reduction of Saudi government spending, including on national security, with some possible consequences for the safety of the people.[10]

PRINCE SAUD'S INFLUENCE ON SAUDI OIL POLICY

Prince Saud al-Faisal (1938–2015), the son of King Faisal, played a major role in Saudi foreign and economic policy for more than three decades. He was highly educated and deeply knowledgeable about regional and international issues, including the economy and oil. Fluent in Arabic, English, and French, Prince Saud was an excellent public speaker. After graduating from Princeton University in 1965, he worked as an adviser to Ahmed Zaki Yamani and at Petromin and was later appointed deputy minister of petroleum and mineral resources, where he served for nine years. During that time, he came to know the oil industry, oil policy, and international petroleum relations. His national involvement in petroleum policy became more important in 1973 when he was appointed secretary-general of the newly created Petroleum Council. After the collapse of the oil market in 1986, Prince Saud became an important figure on oil issues, especially in the first year after the appointment of Hisham Nazer as oil minister in 1986 (chapter 4).

After the death of King Faisal and the formation of a new government in 1975, Prince Saud was named minister of foreign affairs, a position he held for more than forty years. He was trusted and respected by four kings—Khalid, Fahd, Abdullah, and Salman—as well as by senior princes and other ministers in Saudi Arabia. When Minister Nazer and later Al-Naimi faced a difficult problem, they would ask Prince Saud to intervene, and he would call the foreign ministers or prime ministers if necessary to settle such issues.

King Fahd had a stroke in late 1995, and Prince Saud, along with Prince Sultan (minister of defense) and Prince Nayef (minister of interior), was part of a special committee of influential decision makers who oversaw the government's policies on the economy and oil during this time.[11] Al-Naimi coordinated and consulted with Prince Saud, and when matters could not be resolved at the level of energy ministers, Prince Saud, a consummate diplomat who was highly respected at home and abroad, could make a difference. Occasionally, Prince Saud would suggest a decision and politely ask Al-Naimi to adopt it.[12]

Prince Saud's involvement in setting oil policy was significant, but few people were aware of this. With the collapse of the oil price in 1998, Prince Saud and other government figures grew irritated with countries that had not reduced their production and its effect on the Saudi economy. Two ideas were circulating in the royal court at the time: that Al-Naimi should be replaced or that Prince Saud should oversee Saudi oil policy, and OPEC affairs indirectly. Prince Saud suggested that Al-Naimi become more active with OPEC and non-OPEC countries and assume leadership by visiting non-OPEC oil producers and asking them to join in a production cut. Prince Saud's advisers attended OPEC meetings as outside observers, and the Saudi ambassador in Austria, who was a member of the Saudi delegation to the OPEC meetings, would also related what was being discussed and done.

What made things worse was that some countries, including Venezuela and Saudi Arabia, according to some secondary sources, did not cut their production. Iran claimed to have reduced its output, but the reduction was on numbers that it chose, not the numbers that the market believed.

The Riyadh Pact of March 1998 was followed by an OPEC agreement on March 30 to cut production by 1.5 MBD, but oil prices continued to decline. The market thought the output curbs were not enough in light of the high buildup in commercial stocks and the slow global oil demand growth, and market sentiment turned negative. Negotiations between the Riyadh Pact countries and other producers inside and outside OPEC were led by Al-Naimi. The Riyadh trio met secretly in Amsterdam on June 4,

1998, and announced the Amsterdam Pact: Saudi Arabia promised to cut production by a further 225,000 B/D, Venezuela by 125,000 B/D, and Mexico by 100,000 B/D. In addition, Al-Naimi lobbied other countries for more cuts during the twenty days leading up to the OPEC meeting on June 24. Despite all these efforts, in mid-June oil prices hit a twelve-year low of $10/BBL. It was the worst drop since the price collapse of 1986.

Why were these meetings kept secret, and why was participation limited to only a small number of countries? Again, the personal desires of decision makers are crucial. Al-Naimi represented the most influential oil-producing country, and he did not feel comfortable with some ministers within OPEC. He preferred to dominate the discussion during negotiations without hearing "nonsense" from others. Al-Naimi was not comfortable with the Venezuelans, but he had developed an excellent working and personal relationship with Luis Téllez, Mexico's secretary of energy, and Mabro's arrangement for the three countries continued for a couple of years. A meeting in secret by a small number of countries may have its advantages, but that is debatable, and some oil analysts and the media saw it as a big shift from OPEC. The *Wall Street Journal*'s headline on June 23, 1998, was "How Saudi Arabia, Mexico and Venezuela Sidelined OPEC: Unusual Production Pacts 'Make a Shift of Power' Outside Fading Cartel."[13] Many OPEC members saw this in a negative light. It would not be the last time the media would report on perceived collusion between a few countries and interpret this as meaning that OPEC was being sidelined (chapter 10).

In any case, the Amsterdam Pact resulted in a further cut of 1.5 MBD, making the total cuts from the agreements reached in Riyadh and Amsterdam from both OPEC and non-OPEC producers around 2.5 MBD. This was equal to the increase agreed upon in Jakarta seven months earlier. They were very interesting numbers. But the high commercial stock buildup in 1997 and the first half of 1998, the Iranian issue, the lack of quota adherence by some OPEC countries, and the negative sentiment in the market exerted downward pressure, and prices remained at low levels.

In the eight months following the Amsterdam meeting, the three ministers individually held several bilateral meetings with some non-OPEC countries, including Norway and Russia. OPEC also had a ministerial meeting in November 1998, which was a big failure. The oil price remained low, which was difficult for all producers, and Iraq's oil production almost doubled to about 2.5 MBD (the Jakarta meeting assumed that Iraqi production would be 1.3 MBD). The oil market was not yet convinced that new cuts and adherence to quotas and the ceiling were enough to push the oil price higher.[14]

LOW PRICES AND ECONOMIC CONSEQUENCES

Saudi Arabia's economy and finances were under enormous strain from the collapse in oil prices, but the Venezuelan economy was hit a lot harder. The Venezuelan government was blamed publicly for its policy and management of the economy, the oil market, and the industry. In Saudi Arabia, the criticism was directed at the Ministry of Petroleum. Al-Naimi was criticized within government circles but not publicly. Inside Saudi Arabia, blame for the collapse of the market and weak cooperation among producers was mainly directed at Venezuela, and the opposition blamed Giusti. Unlike PDVSA, Saudi Aramco was not attacked because the company does not intervene in Saudi Arabia's national and international oil policy and is not involved in OPEC decisions. Moreover, the president of Aramco only attended one or two OPEC meetings. According to some media reports, Giusti and Alberto Quiros, the influential special adviser to the Venezuelan oil minister, attacked Saudi Arabia for violating its quota.[15] It looked like OPEC was involved in the blame game rather than trying to find a real solution.

Regardless of the accusation, the situation in Venezuela was critical. John Paul Rathbon described the situation early in June 1998: "A long slump in oil prices has shaved $4 billion from Venezuela's revenues this year. At the same time, looming presidential elections in December have muddied the political waters, stymied reforms and rattled the bolivar currency."[16] Giusti and PDVSA management were not looking beyond the company's immediate concerns and behaved as if they were not part of the political and economic communities of their country or the international oil market. Their ambitions and their vision for the future were above all other considerations, even though 1998 was a presidential election year and oil policy, PDVSA management, and Giusti were under strong attack from the opposition. The Caldera government's oil policy was exploited by the opposition in the election, and Hugo Chavez was elected and brought about a big shift in Venezuelan oil policy (chapter 6).

During the 1980s and the 1990s, Venezuela faced a number of economic, political, and social problems, including high inflation, currency devaluation, a high crime rate, corruption, and military coups. Rafael Caldera was elected president in 1994, and during his term the currency depreciated by more than 80 percent as the economic problems multiplied. Caldera suspended several constitutional rights and imposed currency and price controls. The austerity plans and a $1.4 billion loan from the International Monetary Fund (IMF), as well as an increase in oil production and higher oil prices helped to stabilize the economy by 1997. However, the fall in oil prices in 1998 led to a budget cut, and the economy in general and oil policy in particular became major election issues. The opposition attacked the government on several fronts and Giusti himself came under attack with accusations that he had abused his power in using the company jet for his personal use, which proved to be an incorrect accusation.[17]

Bernard Mommer, the Venezuelan oil expert and former government official, described the situation this way: "Criticism regarding oil is not limited to the squandering of oil revenues, but it also includes the performance of Petroleos de Venezuela (PDV), the national oil company." Venezuela had embraced a new oil policy ten years earlier known as Apertura Petrolera (opening up the oil sector to private investors), and the Ministry of Energy and Minerals (MEM) had been losing out against PDV. The national oil company took over oil policy, shifting it away from a focus on fiscal revenues to one that prioritized the development of the oil industry. To put it differently, "the policy issues were no longer prices but volumes," Mommer said.[18] In other words, the goal was market share and not more income for the government.

After a year of low oil prices, producing countries were having a difficult time and oil producers felt that something had to be done. Al-Naimi again visited other producing countries and made some proposals. Algeria's Youcef Yousfi also played a major role in convincing other countries to commit strongly to their production cuts.

Algeria was a small oil producer and rarely adhered to its OPEC production quota, but it always tried to play a major role in OPEC decision-making for a number of reasons. First, Algeria still had the mentality of a nation struggling against the imperialists of the West, and OPEC was seen as part of this struggle. Second, Algeria was one of the leading countries in the

Non-Aligned Movement and the North-South dialogue, so it was natural for it to defend the interests of developing countries' oil producers. Third, Algeria had been one of the hardliners within OPEC. The members of this group changed over time, and at various times included Venezuela, Libya, and Iraq. But Algeria—and to some extent Iran—had been considered to be the leading member of this group. These countries were so-called hawks who wanted to see higher prices and strict adherence by others to quotas and the OPEC ceiling even though they did not adhered to their own quotas as much as others did. Fourth, for domestic and international political reasons, Algeria wanted to be seen as being active in the global arena, particularly in the oil market, and had hosted more ministerial meetings on oil policy than any other oil-exporting country. It hosted the first OPEC summit in 1975.

Finally, the Algerian oil minister, Youcef Yousfi, was highly educated and well informed not only about oil issues but also about national and global economies. He had previously worked at the World Bank in Washington, D.C., and he had a good relationship with Abdelaziz Bouteflika, Algeria's president. Equally important, Yousfi was respected by other OPEC oil ministers, and he had a special personal and working relationship with Al-Naimi, who had more respect for him than for any other Algerian oil minister.

Despite the hard work by Algeria and the Riyadh Pact countries, 1998 ended with low oil prices and no clear direction for the future. The desire to do more work, including more cuts, was getting stronger, and there were more visits and exchanges of ideas among oil ministers. The pressure on the oil ministers from their leaders was increasing because of the hard economic, political, and social problems low oil prices caused for many of the oil-producing countries both in OPEC and beyond, as well as problems for the industry at large. Prince Saud was also pushing Al-Naimi to solve any outstanding problems, and the Iranian dilemma in 1999 is an excellent example that highlights Prince Saud's role in this process.

THE IRANIAN DILEMMA

Iran mixed politics with oil policy to a greater degree than any other OPEC members, weighing domestic politics and the reaction of the Iranian Parliament against the economic benefits of OPEC decisions, which created problems for OPEC decision-making and decision makers (i.e., ministers). Even though the Iranians were losing billions of dollars, they were not willing to compromise, and a rational decision-making model could not easily be applied to them. This created a big problem for OPEC and the oil market.

The Iranian government wanted to be seen as an influential player in OPEC even though Iran had nothing tangible to offer regarding production capacity or cuts, and this attitude persisted even while Iran was under sanctions. Iran believed that the United States and Saudi Arabia conspired in setting oil-production quotas as well as oil prices. At OPEC meetings, Iranian oil ministers tried to take credit for any successful results, even if they had made no contribution, and members of the Iranian Parliament, including some religious figures, often attended OPEC meetings. One of the major problems was that Iran did not provide transparent information on their actual production, capacity, or export level, and Iran did not accept the system of production estimates by secondary sources, even though all OPEC members accepted these numbers.

During the Riyadh Pact of March 22, 1998, and the OPEC conference on March 30, the ministers agreed that production cuts should be made from actual production and not from the official quotas that had been created by the Jakarta agreement. The new allocations would be calculated on the basis of secondary source estimates of production, which were used by the OPEC secretariat. Both OPEC and non-OPEC oil-producing countries agreed to this methodology, but Iran did not, claiming that the secondary source numbers were wrong and unacceptable. The Iranians insisted on using their numbers and not numbers from secondary sources.

The Jakarta agreement assigned production quotas on a pro rata basis regardless of actual production capacities, and Iran's quota was set at 3.942 MBD. However, reductions were based on secondary source numbers for March 1998, and those sources estimated Iran's production at 3.567 MBD, which was the level from which the cut should be applied. The Iranians probably felt that the Jakarta agreement and the Riyadh Pact unfairly disadvantaged them, and they may have suspected that the system was designed to hurt them.[19] Iran pledged to cut 140 KBD starting April 1, 1998, and pledged a higher cut of 100 KBD at the OPEC meeting in June, so their production cut during the second half of 1998 should have been 240 KBD. Under the new system of allocations, Iran's production quota should be around 3.20 MBD, but Iran reported its April production as 3.78 MBD and did not give any number for May. The Iranians announced their cut without specifying the level from which the cut was made, and they insisted that the secondary sources were wrong by about 200 KBD. These cuts were all announced on paper—but no actual cuts took place.

Saudi Arabia had good diplomatic and economic relations with Iran, and Crown Prince Abdullah and President Mohammed Khatami of Iran were acquainted with each other. They had held many meetings and visited each other to discuss various issues. Prince Saud and the Iranian foreign minister, Kamal Kharazi, communicated on oil issues and talked about the difference between Iran's actual figure and the figure presented by secondary sources. Iran wanted OPEC to accept their numbers, but other countries would then make up their own numbers and demand the same, making it impossible to reach an agreement. However, Prince Saud had a solution.

In the afternoon of March 7, 1999, Prince Saud invited Al-Naimi and Suleiman al-Herbish, the Saudi governor of OPEC, to his home. Prince Saud asked Al-Naimi how the problem with Iran might be resolved. Al-Naimi answered with an attack on Iran, explaining that Iran would not accept the system of secondary production estimates. Prince Saud told Al-Naimi that he had discussed an idea to resolve this dilemma with the Iranian foreign minister, who had accepted it. The difference between Iran's official numbers and the secondary source numbers was about 200 KBD, and Prince Saud told Al-Naimi that Saudi Arabia would reduce its quota by 100 KBD and that Kuwait and the United Arab Emirates would each reduce their quotas by 50 KBD. Prince Saud said that he would speak with the foreign ministers of both countries and was sure they would accept this proposal. Al-Naimi tried to resist this idea, but Prince Saud argued politely, "We need the extra income, Ali."

Prince Saud also told Al-Naimi that the Iranian oil minister would soon come to Riyadh, and the ministers would announce the agreement together. Zanganeh came to Riyadh on March 9, and the two sides agreed to work together to determine a new Iranian production level and for other producers to take a deeper cut. After two days of discussions at the Algerian embassy in The Hague, on March 11–12 the ministers announced a new oil cut of 2.1 MBD, which was higher than the 2.0 MBD agreed to earlier in

Riyadh and in Amsterdam. The Algerian oil minister, who was also president of the OPEC conference, stated:

> we set about trying to solve the two major issues: one of them with Iran and
> the other with Venezuela. With regard to the latter, it was clear that nothing
> could be done before the change of government in Venezuela. . . . a number
> of meetings [took place] between Saudi Arabia and Iran at which a solution
> was eventually arrived at. After this agreement was reached between Saudi
> Arabia and Iran, this meant that the two major issues had been solved and
> then it became possible to make progress towards an accord.[20]

That was the beginning of higher oil prices, a trend that would continue for
about nine years. Market fundamentals were also helping; the end of the
Asian economic downturn, the decline in U.S. investment and production
of high-cost stripper wells, and the stabilization of Iraq's exports signaled
the return of strong oil demand growth and lower inventory levels.

But the market needed a shock. The cut had to be large enough to surprise the market. After several rounds of talks, a small number of countries decided to meet secretly in the Netherlands. Iran also became part
of this small group of five, along with Saudi Arabia, Mexico, Algeria, and
Venezuela. Algeria held the OPEC presidency at the time and played a
part in bringing these countries together. Iran wanted to be included in
the group so it would be seen as an important player. Others wanted to
show the market that the dilemma regarding Iran's quota and production,
which had generated bad feelings in the market for more than fourteen
months, was over.

The total OPEC and non-OPEC reductions were more than 5 MBD
below what OPEC was producing before the Jakarta decision. Venezuelan
production fell by about 525 KBD, which was what it was producing one
year before Jakarta. Equally important, Saudi Arabia's production fell by
more than 1 MBD (to 7.5 MBD). Both countries lost volume and income
for more than one year. The consequences of Jakarta were difficult for Saudi
Arabia and Al-Naimi, but the negative impact was limited to a year and a
half. After that, things improved for Saudi Arabia and Al-Naimi. The consequences for Venezuela were more damaging. The Caldera government
lost the election, PDVSA was back to it levels ten years earlier, and Giusti
resigned before Chavez officially became president. The new government

appeared to be off to a good start but later went off track because of its political and economic agendas (chapter 6).

PRINCE SAUD AND THE SAUDI GAS INITIATIVE

Saudi Arabia was grappling with the oil price dilemma when Crown Prince Abdullah, who was then the de facto ruler of Saudi Arabia, launched his oil initiative during an official visit to Washington, D.C. in 1998. He invited seven major U.S. oil companies to invest in Saudi Arabia's petroleum sector. The invitations were made during a meeting that was organized without Al-Naimi's prior knowledge, and he sat in the second row and did not participate in the discussion. Prince Saud and Prince Bandar bin Sultan, the Saudi ambassador in Washington, knew about it in advance, and they led the discussions.

According to Nathaniel Kern, energy consultant and founder and editor of the Washington-based *Foreign Report*, Rehab Masoud, who was an adviser to and close confidante of Prince Bander, was asked in 1997 about some ideas for strengthening Saudi-American relations. One of the ideas was allowing American oil companies to invest in exploration and production in Saudi Arabia. Ten days before Crown Prince Abdullah's visit, the idea came back and Kern was asked to consolidate it in the oil sector. Masoud and Kern agreed on the seven American oil companies selected to meet Crown Prince Abdullah to discuss the idea. Two hours before their meeting, Prince Saud meet with the oil companies and explained Saudi Arabia's vision and expectations.

During the meeting, the companies focused solely on investing in the oil sector. Perhaps they thought Saudi Arabia was desperate for money, but at the end of the meeting Crown Prince Abdullah asked them to consider gas investments.[21] The initiative proved to be more difficult to promote than many had thought. European companies and others who were not invited complained through their governments about being excluded. In response, the Saudi government opened the initiative to other major European companies, such as British Petroleum (BP), Total, Eni, and Repsol of Spain.

Initially the heads of the oil companies met with Crown Prince Abdullah personally and presented their proposals. Later on a ministerial committee was formed, headed by Prince Saud, and the committee included the minister of petroleum, the minister of finance, the minister of planning, and the minister of trade and industry as well as some others. Committee members were asked to make a decision and present a recommendation to Crown Prince Abdullah. Several meetings and discussions followed, but the committee could not reach agreement. Prince Saud wanted to open the upstream to international investment, but Al-Naimi was against this, especially in Saudi Aramco operating areas.

Major American oil companies were lobbying as hard as they could, and the U.S government also lobbied on behalf of the U.S. companies. Bill Richardson, the secretary of energy in the Bill Clinton administration, visited Saudi Arabia twice. Lee Raymond, Exxon's CEO, and Al-Naimi got into open conflict at one point. Raymond wanted Exxon to take control of some of Aramco's areas, such as the giant Ghawar oil field. In return, Exxon would provide money for the Saudis to build electricity and water desalination facilities. In one intense discussion, Al-Naimi cited the American actor Danny DeVito "playing with other people's money." Raymond responded by saying "Ali, you are giving me a Rolls Royce with a Volkswagen engine!"

Al-Naimi was supported by a strong and capable team from the ministry and Saudi Aramco and headed by Prince Faisal bin Turki. The ministry was able to change the focus, and the oil initiative became the gas initiative and excluded Saudi Aramco areas. Khalid al-Falih came from Aramco to head the technical team of the gas initiative. Prince Saud decided to get out of it, but the Ministry of Foreign Affairs continued to have a representative on the Technical Committee.

Negotiations between the Saudis and the international oil companies took a long time, around four years from the start of the initiative. Crown Prince Abdullah was unhappy with the process and the time it had taken. He asked his confidant Ghazi al-Gosaibi, minister of water and electricity, for advice. Al-Gosaibi said, "If you want good bread, give the dough to the baker," by which he meant that Al-Naimi, the minister of petroleum, should handle the matter, and that is what happened in March 2003.[22]

Al-Naimi was lucky for two reasons. First, oil prices were rising in the second half of 1999, surpassing $25 and moving higher the following year. The Saudi government was happy with the increase, and Al-Naimi was given credit for it. Second, Al-Naimi was gaining the confidence and trust of Crown Prince Abdullah, whose power was gradually increasing. In the following years, Al-Naimi undertook projects close to King Abdullah's heart, the most important being establishment of the King Abdullah

University for Science and Technology (KAUST) on the Red Sea and building the second largest football stadium in Saudi Arabia in Jeddah.

In July 2003, the Saudi Ministry of Petroleum held a road show in London, where it provided a full and detailed presentation to fifty companies from around the world, followed by a bidding round in Riyadh in September 2003. Three major oil companies from Russia, China, and Spain were awarded large exploration areas, and Shell was awarded a far larger area even though it didn't participate in the bid round. Only one U.S. company, Chevron, submitted a bid that lost. Gas was found in three of the concession areas, but the location, the cost of development and low domestic gas prices did not allow for commercial development and the companies left.

Prince Saud was one of the most diplomatically adept leaders in the history of Saudi Arabia. He had a unique personality and very effective communication skills. Prince Saud was also influential in the arenas of economics and energy policy. He believed that oil should service the economic and public interests of Saudi Arabia and its development, and he played an important role in petroleum policy for fifty years. Prince Saud wanted Saudi Arabia to expand its role beyond OPEC, such as organizing energy meetings, holding conferences, and conducting or supporting energy studies. He also contributed to the idea of creating the secretariat of the International Energy Forum (IEF) in Riyadh. Prince Saud was a strong believer in the importance of international oil management and believed that Saudi Arabia should have a major role in the process. He also took a close interest in the impact of market psychology and sentiment but would usually withdraw from involvement in oil issues once the petroleum or political crisis had passed.[23]

Chapter Six

HUGO CHAVEZ

The Rise of a Man and the Decline of a Nation

U.S. elections usually capture international attention and are watched around the world with anticipation and excitement because of the importance of the United States in the global community—politically, economically, and militarily. Elections in other countries occasionally receive international attention, but elections in developing countries rarely do. The Venezuelan election of 1998 was an exception. There was deep polarization among the competing parties and oil producers, and OPEC and non-OPEC countries were watching the Venezuelan race with great interest. They could see an outcome that would have an impact on the oil market, oil prices, and cooperation among oil producers both nationally and internationally. These concerns, including the status of Venezuela's national oil company, were major issues during the election for both the Venezuelan elite and the public at large. Bernard Mommer, a Venezuelan oil expert and former government official, explained Chavez's success this way:

> Hugo Chavez was a candidate, although the opinion polls give him only a few percentage points. However, Chavez moved inexorably upwards in the opinion as world petroleum prices moved downwards. He was supported by a small political group which had been opposed to PDV's liberal oil policy. This led to his victory at the end of the year.[1]

When Chavez was declared the winner on December 6, 1998, there was a sense of relief in many OPEC countries and other oil-producing states.

On February 2, 1999, president-elect Hugo Chavez delivered a lengthy and wide-ranging inauguration speech in Caracas to an enthusiastic audience that included heads of state, officials, and dignitaries from all over the world. Bill Richardson, the U.S. secretary of energy, headed the U.S. delegation, and Saudi Arabia's oil minister, Ali Al-Naimi, represented King Fahd and led the Saudi delegation. Al-Naimi was to deliver a letter of congratulations from King Fahd to the new Venezuelan president. We all listened to the speech by Chavez, which touched on major energy issues, including OPEC, the Venezuelan National Oil Company (PDVSA), and oil, but the speech was largely directed at the national audience and focused on domestic issues. Al-Naimi sat next to Richardson at the inauguration, either by chance or by design, and Al-Naimi asked Richardson, "Bill, why are you not using a headphone for translation?" Richardson replied, "I speak Spanish."

There is no doubt that Chavez had a huge impact on Venezuela in almost all aspects of life, and the repercussions of his policies continue even after his death in 2013. Chavez also had a direct impact on the Venezuelan oil industry, the international oil market, and on OPEC policy for about five years. Chavez is a good example of my thesis that the personality of the leader matters in bringing about policy changes, and this applies to the oil sector as much as any other. The policy changes began immediately after the election of Chavez and will most likely be felt for some years to come. The damage to Venezuela's oil industry since 2002 can be seen in the numbers: oil-production capacity declined from 3.5 MBD in 2000 to less than 1 MBD in 2021. Experts believe it may take at least a decade to rebuild Venezuela's oil industry, if circumstances allow.

VENEZUELA AND OIL

Venezuela was one of the most important Latin American countries politically and economically during the nineteenth and twentieth centuries. Venezuela had many natural resources, including minerals and agricultural land, a well-educated and culturally diverse population, and successful industries in shipbuilding, tourism, and coffee. Oil was discovered in Venezuela in the early twentieth century. In 1926, oil replaced coffee as the leading export and became the dominant contributor to the national economy. By 1935, Venezuela was the number one oil exporter in the world, and its oil reserves, production, and exports grew rapidly—but at the expense of other industries.

Some major developments in oil policy are worth mentioning. First, Venezuela's minister of hydrocarbons, Juan Pablo Alfonzo, together with the minister of petroleum of Saudi Arabia, Abdullah al-Tariki, had a vision that led to the birth of OPEC in 1960. OPEC was established to defend the interests of and coordinate the policy of major oil producers. This was an important factor in shaping Venezuela's idea of its place on the world stage as well as guiding its political and economic interests.

The second major development was nationalization of the oil industry and creation of PDVSA in 1976, a government-owned oil company. Other OPEC countries as well as some other oil producers followed this trend, but it was a significant development for Venezuela because of its importance politically and economically. In comparison with most other OPEC countries, Venezuela enjoyed a high level of political freedom and transparency.

The third development was opening the country to international investment in 1986, known as *la apertura petrolera*. Foreign investors were invited to participate in oil exploration and production in Venezuela, a process that was accelerated when Luis Giusti became the head of PDVSA in 1994. The nationalists and the leftists were strongly against this policy, and the decision to increase oil production regardless of oil prices and OPEC quotas—even talk of leaving OPEC—became part of the new policy. This led to a fight with Saudi Arabia and other oil producers that contributed to the collapse of the oil market in 1998.

The fourth major development happened after Chavez came into power. Chavez took full control of PDVSA and the oil industry in Venezuela, and he decided that he would be an important international player in world oil politics, especially within OPEC.

The fifth development was the collapse of the Venezuelan oil industry, a process that was instigated by the opposition in 2002 in their attempt to cripple Venezuela's economy and the Chavez government.

Oil has been the most important sector of Venezuela's economy and had influenced its social and political systems since the 1930s. The contribution of the oil sector to GDP, the budget, and the balance of payments varied from one year to the next and depended on oil prices and production. Since the 1970s, oil's contribution to Venezuela's GDP and state income was never less than 50 percent, and its contribution to the balance of payments was about 70 percent, which was similar to, if not better than, the majority of OPEC countries.

The relationships between the three main players in the country—the president, the Ministry of Hydrocarbons, and the national oil company—changed from time to time largely because of the personalities of their leaders. In most OPEC countries, the Ministry of Energy oversees the national oil company. That is the case in Algeria, Saudi Arabia, Iraq, Iran, Kuwait, and the United Arab Emirates, and the lines of authority are very clear. The exception was Libya under Muammar Gaddafi; the relationship between the ministry and the national oil company was never clear and changed according to the personal mood of Gaddafi.[2]

During the 1990s, PDVSA was independent. It made its own policy regarding production, investment inside and outside the country, partnerships with foreign oil investors, taxes, royalties, employment, and social programs. The Ministry of Hydrocarbons did not have much authority over PDVSA, and the company could object to some ministry-planned international policies, especially regarding OPEC, such as quotas and limiting oil production. The president of PDVSA was the only head of a national oil company who attended all OPEC meetings and other bilateral meetings with oil-producing countries, both OPEC and non-OPEC, and he had a major say in any decision. In 1998, the Algerian oil minister visited Caracas for talks with his Venezuelan counterpart. The two ministers reached an initial agreement about quotas and an overall ceiling to be submitted to the OPEC conference. The president of PDVSA arrived late to the meeting, and he not only objected to the agreement but also ripped up the draft proposal.[3]

Ministry officials did not participate in nor were they consulted on PDVSA's commercial negotiations with others. That included, for example, the purchase of overseas refining interests such as CITGO Petroleum Corporation, a U.S. company that owned four refineries with a total capacity of 370 KBD. In addition, the apertura initiative was undertaken by PDVSA alone.

CHAVEZ AND OIL

Countries are run either by individuals working collectively or alone or by organized and well-established institutions or by a few loyal and obedient officials. These individuals are influenced by their background, personality, beliefs, and experiences and by the information available to them. Chavez is one of the most interesting personalities of modern times. A charming man with good communication skills and use of language, Chavez was powerful and determined to achieve his goals. He faced challenge after challenge and was prepared to take on those who dared to challenge him, including some of his colleagues, his second wife, and his once great ally and savior, General Raúl Isaías Baduel.

In 1992, Chavez led a military coup to overthrow an elected and civilian government, a clear sign of his lack of respect for the constitution and the rule of law. He was jailed for two years and became a celebrity once he was freed. He ran and won the election of 1998 by forming a coalition with the leftist and nationalist parties who were not happy with the existing two parties that had ruled Venezuela for more than forty years. As president, Chavez introduced legislation calling for a new constitution, which led to a new election in 2000. He faced strong opposition but gained more votes than he had in the previous election.

In 2002, Chavez faced another major challenge. The opposition parties regrouped under the leadership of Chavez's erstwhile friend General Guaicaipuro Lameda. When the group marched to the presidential palace on April 11, 2002, they were met with gunfire, and nineteen people died. Chavez briefly surrendered power but was reinstated a few days later. The opposition then organized general strikes, especially in the banking and oil sectors, with the goal of crippling the economy in the hope that it would bring about the downfall of Chavez's government.

On December 2, 2002, the labor federation of PDVSA declared a national work stoppage. "It soon became obvious that the strike leaders aimed to shut down oil production, deny government income, and once again try to force Chavez's resignation," wrote Miguel Tinker Salas.[4] In reality, it was not a strike in the normal sense but more an act of political sabotage because the opposition forced workers not to report to work. The managers and engineers at PDVSA had other reasons for supporting the strike.

During the 1990s the company had become an elitist and privileged club, and Chavez's view (and he was not alone) was that PDVSA had become a state within a state, or even a state above the state politically and economically.[5] Chavez's goal was to manage the company from above, and he convened a meeting of the PDVSA board in his office on March 29, 1999.

It was the first board meeting to be held outside PDVSA's headquarters, and Chavez declared that the company "cannot go on acting like the Sovereign Republic of PDVSA." His new minister of energy and mines described the company as "an elephant in a swimming pool. Because it has such weight, any movement it makes immediately produces an effect in the whole of the national economy."[6]

Chavez appointed Ali Rodriguez Araque, one of his closest political allies, minister of energy and mines. Rodriguez was an intellectual, a revolutionary, and an urban guerrilla fighter during the 1960s. He later became an active political figure and was elected to Parliament, where he headed the Energy Committee. He was against opening the oil sector to foreign investments and against the general policies of PDVSA in almost all its aspects. He was also a strong supporter of OPEC and its role in managing the international oil market through production adjustments and setting target oil prices. He believed that the policies adopted by Giusti and the previous government—increasing production regardless of OPEC's ceiling and quotas—were wrong and damaging to the interests of Venezuela.

Along with Rodriguez, in October 2000 Chavez appointed another friend and ally, Guaicaipuro Lameda, to head PDVSA. Lameda was a former general with no background in petroleum, but he was good with numbers, which enabled him to uncover the accounting tricks and legal ruses PDVSA had used to divert some profits away from the previous government. Lameda was a soldier and had sworn loyalty to his commander in chief.[7]

Chavez also reversed all the old systems and processes. He first gave the Ministry of Hydrocarbons full authority on international policy issues, especially regarding OPEC. The new president of PDVSA no longer took part in OPEC ministerial meetings. If there was an OPEC decision to cut production, the company had only to implement it fully, as was the case in most of the other oil-producing countries.

Chavez's desires and the impact of his policies went beyond national borders. He wanted to be a Latin American hero, an oil king, and an international leader. He wanted to become one of the great leaders like Gamal Abdel Nasser of Egypt and General Tito of Yugoslavia, and of course Castro of Cuba, who was Chavez's hero and a close friend.

To be a regional or an international distinguished leader is a common desire among elected and nonelected heads of state, such as Saddam Hussein of Iraq, Muammar Gaddafi of Libya, and even the head of a small state like Qatar. What Chavez did not realize was that the world had changed. Yugoslavia had disintegrated, Egypt was no longer an important global power, and China and India were concentrating on their national interests and were an integrated part of the new world system beyond the old divisions of North-South and the developed and developing countries, which was common in the sixties and the seventies.

Chavez was also a believer in an old Latin American school of thought labeled "dependency," the idea that the lack of development, particularly in Latin America, was due to the domination and control of external powers—a reference to the United States (the domination of the center over the peripheries).[8] The new president decided to make his mark on the international oil map and to be the new "oil king" by bringing OPEC heads of state together in Venezuela after many years of disarray, conflict, distrust, and an unstable oil market. He was encouraged by the rise in oil prices and by the welcome and letters of congratulations he had received after his election in 1999 from leaders of OPEC states and other oil-producing countries. An OPEC summit was the best choice for Chavez to present himself as an international leader.

The first OPEC summit had been held in 1975 in Algeria when OPEC was at its peak. No doubt Chavez had that in mind. At that time, the oil price was high, and OPEC was in control of the market because it was able to decide the price of oil. OPEC was also feared by the industrialized West and highly respected by other countries, especially in the developing world. OPEC was perceived as a very successful organization in the struggle between developed and developing countries, or the North and the South.

Relationships within OPEC countries during the 1970s were relatively good. When Algeria issued invitations to the 1975 summit, Algeria was an important leader among the developing countries and was very active within OPEC, and attendance by heads of state was high. All countries attending that meeting brought their senior representatives. Mohammed Reza Shah Pahlavi of Iran and Iraqi president Saddam Hussein not only attended the meeting but managed to use the occasion to resolve their border disputes, including issues over the Shatt al-Arab waterway. Crown Prince Fahd (later king) was very powerful, and he represented Saudi Arabia.

The situation in 2000 was roughly similar. The oil price was rising following the slump of 1998–1999, and OPEC was back in control after a few difficult years. The new government in Venezuela under the leadership of Chavez was gaining respect within OPEC and beyond, a refreshing change from the confusing policies of the previous government and its anti-OPEC agenda. Equally important, with the exception of Iraq, which was under United Nations sanctions, all OPEC countries were on good terms with each other. Some OPEC leaders, above all Crown Prince Abdullah of Saudi Arabia, liked and respected Chavez. The same could be said about the president of Iran, Mohammed Khatami, and Algerian president Abdelaziz Bouteflika. President Chavez visited all OPEC countries in early 2000 and invited them to the OPEC summit to be held in Caracas in September of 2000.

The summit was a successful event and a clear indication of Chavez's leadership and highly respected status internationally, especially among OPEC countries. Chavez was the star, but two other stars at the summit—Crown Prince Abdullah and President Khatami—also contributed to the success of the summit.

Crown Prince Abdullah put a lot of effort into creating a positive image of Saudi Arabia and forging close international relationships with all countries. Some Western media tried to paint a different image of Crown Prince Abdullah as a hard-core, anti-West Arab nationalist who wanted higher oil prices and possibly was willing to use oil for political gain. He was an Arab nationalist, but the image depicted by Western media was wrong. He was a liberal and a rational thinker with an open mind. Saudi Arabia came first for Crown Prince Abdullah, and the Arab and Islamic world came second. He cared about justice and wanted to establish an excellent relationship with all countries. In 1998, Crown Prince Abdullah went on a world tour, visiting the United States, Japan, Korea, and Pakistan. In 2000, before the OPEC summit in Caracas, he headed the Saudi delegation to the United Nations, and after that he visited Brazil and Argentina.

Khatami became the fifth president of Iran in August 1997. He was highly educated, a philosopher, a theologian, and an Islamic and Iranian scholar. A reformist politician and a liberal within the Iranian clerical regime, Khatami tried to make major changes to Iran's domestic and international policies. He was elected by a large margin (about 70 percent), with strong support from liberals and from the young and women voters. But the conservatives dominated the Islamic state's powerful organizations as well the religious establishment and preferred to maintain the status quo.

They opposed Khatami's reformist policies and did whatever they could to weaken his support and block his agenda. Khatami was respected internationally, and he established good relationships with a number of world leaders and was the first Iranian president to visit Saudi Arabia, where he was well received by King Fahd, Crown Prince Abdullah, and other dignitaries. Ali Al-Naimi, then minister of petroleum, highlighted the importance of Khatami's visit and the close relations between the two countries on the petroleum side, which helped improve understanding between the two countries and led to successful agreements both within OPEC and with other producers. Al-Naimi pointed to the Riyadh Pact and the agreements reached in Amsterdam and The Hague as examples of that cooperation.

The participation of Crown Prince Abdullah and President Khatami at the Caracas OPEC summit was an important measure of success, and it was a vote of confidence in Chavez. He was lucky that the most controversial OPEC heads of state—Saddam Hussein of Iraq and Muammar Gaddafi of Libya—did not attend (even though they were invited). The development of close personal relationships at the head of state, ministerial, professional, and expert levels was an important development at the time. The positive relationship between the ministers of petroleum of Venezuela and Saudi Arabia lasted for two years and had a clear impact, not only on the ties between the two countries but also within OPEC and beyond.

ALI AND ALI

The first time Ali Al-Naimi and Ali Rodriguez met was during the OPEC conference in late 1998. Rodriguez was not yet a minister but was part of the Venezuelan delegation. Al-Naimi and Rodriguez had both been briefed by their advisers on each other's background, but the chemistry came later. Al-Naimi told me that "at the start I did not feel comfortable with Rodriguez. But as we met again and again, I discovered his high qualities and we became close friends."[9] The two men were almost the same age, and they both believed that OPEC should take a leading role in managing the oil market. They also agreed that the national oil companies, such as Saudi Aramco and PDVSA, should be strong and in charge of national hydrocarbon resources in their respective countries. Interestingly, both were strongly against opening upstream oil to international investors, but they favored foreign investment in the gas sector and in refineries and petrochemicals.

It was with this mindset that Al-Naimi opposed the oil initiative in favor of allowing foreign participation in upstream gas projects. Al-Naimi advised Rodriguez and other ministers to make their national oil companies strong and allow them to control oil exploration and production. He tried to persuade both Iraq, after the fall of Saddam Hussein, and Libya, after the fall of Gaddafi, to do the same, offering Saudi help if needed (he believed strongly in the Saudi model).

During his long tenure as minister, Al-Naimi came to know a succession of oil ministers in OPEC countries and considered some to be close friends, including Rodriguez. The two often dined alone or with their delegations, or went fishing and hiking. Once when Al-Naimi was on an official visit to Venezuela, he and Rodriguez disappeared for two days. It later transpired that they had gone to the mountains and visited the famous waterfall—Angel Falls. During their excursion, they discussed OPEC and international issues as well as the new secretary-general of OPEC. Al-Naimi was able to persuade Rodriguez to be the one to lead the organization. This special relationship helped OPEC work with more harmony and facilitated major decisions during the first decade of the twenty-first century. It also helped OPEC achieve a good price for oil-producing countries. For the first time, OPEC agreed to establish a target of $25 and a price range of $22–$28, which remained in effect from 2002 to 2004.

In 2000, OPEC had difficulty selecting a new secretary-general because of a deadlock between Saudi Arabia and Iran; both countries had proposed candidates for the job. Saudi Arabia had put forward its OPEC governor Suleiman al-Herbish, and Iran selected Hossein Kazempour Ardebili, a former ambassador and Iranian OPEC governor. Al-Naimi was able to convince Rodriguez to accept this position as a compromise candidate. Rodriguez held the position from January 2001 to July 2002 but was called home to take over as president of PDVSA and to deal with the general strike of 2002 that had crippled the country's oil production and exports. Rodriguez was able to restore some order but only after firing more than twenty thousand employees (approximately half of the company's employees). It is interesting that a hard-core socialist was willing to dismiss so many workers, but when you are a decision maker, your beliefs come second to your obligations.

The close relationship between Al-Naimi and Rodriguez became strained when Venezuela insisted on keeping the position of OPEC secretary-general after Rodriguez left, as if it was a national privilege. Venezuela proposed a man who was weak on oil issues and spoke hardly any English. Saudi Arabia accepted the Venezuelan nomination but only for the remaining term of Rodriguez. The relationship between Al-Naimi and Rodriguez ended in November 2004 when Rodriguez became foreign minister, but their respect for each other, their good memories, and their appreciation of one another continued for many years.

When Rodriguez died in 2019, OPEC said in a statement, "It is with great sadness that OPEC has learnt of the passing of one of the organization's and Venezuela's most respected and distinguished leaders, His Excellency Ali Rodriguez Araque. . . . Rodriguez was an OPEC legend, a true believer in the goals of the Organization and a great disciple of the values inherent in cooperation."[10] Al-Naimi sent his personal condolences separately.

CHAVEZ: THE KING OF OPEC LOSES HIS THRONE

The early years of Chavez's rule were good for the president and for Venezuela. Oil prices were on the rise, which helped the Venezuelan economy. Politically, Venezuela became a major international player. Chavez met U.S. president Bill Clinton at the White House in January 1999, and he addressed the United Nations General Assembly in New York on September 20, 2006. Chavez established close relationships with other Latin American leaders, including Luiz Inacio Lula of Brazil, who was also an important regional and international figure. Chavez was seen as one of the respected leaders who helped OPEC regain its importance after years of failure, doubt, and uncertainty.

On the national level, events began to move in a different direction in Venezuela in 2002. The opposition, which proved to be more rigid and more militant than was normal in democratic countries, was determined to oust Chavez. On December 2, 2002, the opposition organized a national work stoppage in almost all economic activities, and especially in the oil industry. If the economy collapsed, the opposition thought that the Chavez government would fall. Simple thinking maybe, but they did not realize what a strong and resilient fighter Chavez was. Indeed, this strategy made Chavez and his party stronger and weakened the opposition, and their action cost the country a lot. The effect of the strikes and the sacking of PDVSA staff damaged the oil industry, and the loss of qualified petroleum engineers and managers had huge consequences.

The strike in the oil sector and the way it was quashed in the first three months led to a slump in production. Oil exports came to a complete halt, and Chavez had to ask his newly elected friend in Brazil, President Luiz Lula, to send crude oil to be refined in Venezuela to avoid a domestic products shortage. President Chavez and Rodriguez convinced more than half of PDVSA's workers to obey an ultimatum to return to work, and production and exports began to rise gradually in 2003. But the damage was done, and its repercussions are being felt even now.

One outcome in Chavez's favor was that the opposition lost a trump card in their fight with Chavez. Most of PDVSA's top managers and engineers, who had opposed Chavez's oil policy, lost their jobs and their influence. Chavez and his supporters assumed full control of the oil industry with little or no resistance. PDVSA lost its independence in all operational matters, including control of its spending, selection of top managers, and marketing oil internationally. Chavez appointed loyal friends and supporters to PDVSA's board and management and started giving discounts on oil sold to certain countries in the Caribbean.

Venezuela lost much of its production capacity in 1999 and 2000 because of adherence to OPEC agreements. This left Venezuela with a spare production capacity of at least 0.7 MBD before the strike, but it lost about 1 MBD of production capacity after the strike, and its production has been lower than its OPEC quota since 2003.[11] Spare production capacity is important for OPEC oil producers and for the international oil market at large. It helps countries manage production effectively and is a source of power within OPEC.

For example, Saudi Arabia is the most influential country in the international oil market largely because it holds the bulk of global spare production capacity. The United States and Russia have higher production outputs but little or no spare capacity cushion. Spare production capacity can be used to deal with any shortage of oil supply or at times of high or low oil prices. It can also be used as a bargaining tool during negotiations with OPEC and non-OPEC producers as well as with major consuming nations. That is why some countries, such as Iran, always claim to have excess production capacity even though they do not. When Venezuela lost its production capacity, it became less important in the oil decision-making process.

A major asset of oil companies are their qualified petroleum managers and engineers, and they cannot be replaced easily if lost. After the strike and the mass sacking of PDVSA's staff, a large number of highly qualified petroleum engineers and managers left the company and the country. They went to the United States, Canada, and Saudi Arabia, among others. Losing such highly qualified people can cripple the oil industry for years and make it difficult to rebuild. It takes decades to select, hire, and train new staff, and PDVSA has not replaced the people they lost to this day. Chavez and Rodriguez, who did not have real energy backgrounds, did not understand the importance of keeping a qualified oil workforce. Failure to replace the lost workers was a very damaging decision for PDVSA and for the Venezuelan oil industry. The damage could have been limited to a couple of years, but it became permanent. PDVSA faced three major problems during the Chavez era that persist to this day: mismanagement, corruption, and excessive government intervention.

Chavez's thoughts were largely limited to political and social issues. He did not understand the economy or business, nor was he willing to let others independently manage different parts of the economy, particularly the oil and financial sectors. One of the architects of Chavez's oil policy described Chavez this way: "He doesn't understand economics. Sadly, no one took twenty minutes to explain macroeconomics to him with a pen and paper. Chavez does not know how to manage. As a manager he's a disaster."[12]

When he first became president, Chavez was willing to give private businesses more opportunities, and he was ready to open all sectors of the economy to international investors. He enacted a new oil law that relaxed government control of the sector, and he welcomed international investments in natural gas, production of extra heavy oil (Orimulsion), and downstream activities. These policies were likely put forward by Rodriguez, who may have been influenced by his friend Al-Naimi.

By 2003–2004, Chavez's approach had changed completely. His confidence was high, and he believed himself to be a great leader who had defeated all his enemies, had large popular support, and was an international figure and perhaps a hero to some people in Venezuela and Latin America. He had brought OPEC together at the Caracas summit, and in his mind he had contributed to the increase in oil prices and therefore to his country's income. But in reality other factors contributed to the oil price increase. The oil strike in Venezuela and the decline of both production and exports, the U.S.-led invasion of Iraq in 2003, and the Nigeria oil workers' strikes all happened during a time of strong global oil demand.

Venezuela began to see healthy economic growth and a better distribution of wealth, which had not happened since the 1970s, but the respite
was short-lived. Within four years, Venezuela was even worse off than it
had been before Chavez, in part because of Chavez himself: his personality, his knowledge, his belief system, his interpretation of information, his
understanding of the issues, and his selection of people to run the industry
and the government.

First came increasing corruption and mismanagement of the oil industry. Corruption does not necessarily mean bribery or embezzlement. It
can be simply having the wrong people in important positions or selecting
managers based more on their loyalty than on their qualifications. Many
Latin American countries, including Venezuela, give people with personal
connections important positions in government. The practice is part of the
management process in Latin America, and indeed in many developing
countries. It is a way to ensure loyalty and to exert control. Chavez was no
exception, although he took it to extremes.

During the election and his first year in office, Chavez spoke of social
justice and spending oil income to improve education, health care, and
housing, especially for the poor. However, when revenues increased as oil
prices moved higher, Chavez began to behave differently. Some of his policies were designed to help the poor and underprivileged, but he wasted a
lot of money to further his own interests at the national and international
levels without due process of law.

The "Dutch disease" theory states that natural wealth, such as an abundance of oil, discourages advancement in other sectors of the economy,
and this was the case for Venezuela during Chavez's time. It is equally
important that political and administrative systems, culture, and leadership determine how this wealth is to be used and, indeed, abused. Oil-rich
countries have taken different paths. Norway, Malaysia, Indonesia, Saudi
Arabia, and the United Arab Emirates use oil income to build their economies and increase income from other economic activities. Iran uses oil to
strengthen its military power and regional political influence. Chavez followed a path somewhat similar to the one taken by Saddam Hussein of Iraq
and Muammar Gaddafi of Libya. They both used oil income for personal
interest, privilege, and power on the national, regional, and international
levels. Chavez moved farther along this path after he defeated the opposition and consolidated his personal power.

Some believe that the problem was not in the personality of the president but in the behavior of his opponents. Rory Carroll stated that "Chavez's initial pragmatism in fostering a private and state enterprise meant Venezuela could have thrived and built a broad-based, sustainable economy. But the 2002 coup and strike changed that. He was radicalized by the private sector's repeated betrayals."[13]

Chavez was indeed radicalized in almost everything. The military coups, the strike, and the behavior of the private sector may have contributed to Chavez's changing behavior, but there is no doubt that his personal traits and his belief that he was right contributed to his actions as a dictator with absolute power. Chavez wanted to hold onto power for as long as possible and to transfer it after his death to his close and loyal friend. He used oil money and propaganda for personal gain and to fulfill his own agenda, and there are many examples that illustrate his lust for power.

In the middle of the first decade of the twenty-first century, Chavez created a special fund that he could spend any way he pleased; this fund was beyond public knowledge and outside the official budget. When the oil price moved higher and reached $40/BBL, the government used a price of $35/BBL in setting the national budget, and the difference was deposited into Chavez's special fund rather than being counted as a budget surplus as other countries do. Carroll explained that "in the run-up to elections, the Palace supplemented this with raids on PDVSA funds—Rafael Ramirez always obliged—and plopped another few billion into the kitty."[14]

Financial mismanagement can also be seen in irrational decision-making. For example, Chavez decided to help some South American and Caribbean countries, such as his close ally Cuba, by giving them either free of charge or discounted oil. Providing poor countries with some type of assistance can be helpful, but discounting the oil price or giving another country oil for free is damaging to both sides. No known OPEC leaders ever discounted oil to others, although countries may have provided oil to allies in the form of financial assistance. Saudi Arabia provided oil to Pakistan and Jordan when they faced economic or financial problems and provided Egypt with oil products during energy shortages in 2015. This aid was available under special circumstances and for a short time and was given directly by the Ministry of Finance as part of the budget. OPEC countries prefer to provide financial assistance to friendly or poor countries through existing national, regional, and international funds such as the OPEC Fund for International Development.

The most interesting example of Chavez's illogical oil behavior occurred in the winter of 2007 when he decided to give free heating oil to the residents of twenty-three northeastern U.S. states when heating oil prices were high. Chavez received no direct or indirect benefits from distributing heating oil to the poor in the United States, the richest country in the world. The U.S. government did not object and may have welcomed the gesture, but neither Chavez nor Venezuela saw any benefit from this act of benevolence.

Despite mismanagement and waste, Chavez's popularity was higher than ever in 2006 thanks to the high price of oil. Oil prices were above $60/BBL, and Chavez tried to take credit for this rise. Chavez's charismatic personality helped him win the 2006 election with 63 percent of the vote, the widest margin in the history of Venezuela, but the good times did not last: "The Chavez of 2006 is nothing compared with the Chavez of 2011. He made a series of errors," said Peru's former prime minister Yehude Simon.[15]

Internationally, and especially on the oil front and within OPEC, Chavez began to lose his status. Venezuela was no longer the special leader of OPEC, and Chavez began making alliances with radical groups within OPEC, such as Libya's Gaddafi. He also forged a close relationship with the radical leader of Iran, Mahmoud Ahmadinejad, who had replaced the moderate Khatami in 2004. Equally important, Venezuela began to lose its close energy relationship with Saudi Arabia, the Arab Gulf states, and other OPEC and non-OPEC countries such as Mexico. Chavez gained little but lost plenty.

Another factor that weakened Venezuela's position was its loss of production capacity, a crucial asset in terms of bargaining power within OPEC. Equally important within OPEC is the willingness and the ability to maintain a good record of compliance with quotas. Countries that do not have a sound production management policy or respect for their quotas become marginalized and lose their bargaining power. Nigeria, Angola, and Indonesia recognized these facts, but Iran tried to assume a larger role using faulty claims of spare production capacity.

By adopting such postures, these countries created noise through the media, but in the end good agreements are made and endorsed by those who have production capacity and good adherence behavior. After the oil strike of 2002, Venezuela had planned several projects to raise its production capacity, but these projects failed largely because of bad management and lack of investments.

Chavez visited Iran and met with President Ahmadinejad, one of the most hardline Iranian presidents since the 1979 revolution, to coordinate policy ahead of the OPEC Riyadh summit in 2007. During the summit it became apparent that the other leaders were not comfortable with Chavez's style. He was guided by his dreams and not by reality. He did not respect the hosts of the conference or its schedules and wanted to do things his own way. Chavez and Ahmadinejad tried to steer the summit away from oil matters to suit their political agenda. They wanted to discuss the falling value of the U.S. dollar and demanded that it be replaced with a new oil pricing system. Chavez said at the time, "The dollar is in free fall, everyone should be worried about it. . . . The fall of the dollar is not the fall of the dollar—It is the fall of the American empire." Ahmadinejad went further, declaring that "the U.S. dollar has no economic value."[16]

By the end of the summit, it was clear that Chavez had lost his oil crown; he had lost his oil production capacity and potential and consorted with extremist leaders. Chavez was no longer the self-proclaimed king of OPEC. When the oil price was skyrocketing in early 2008 and Saudi Arabia called for an international conference of oil producers and consumers, Chavez did not attend, and his absence was not noticed. When the oil market collapsed in the second half of 2008, Venezuela had little to do with efforts to restore market balance.

Chavez's rise was as dramatic as his fall. While in power, Chavez's policies had a significant impact on the oil market, on OPEC, and on the Venezuelan economy. But his aspirations exceeded his competence. During his years in office (1999–2013), Chavez failed to create a good structural process within the government at large or at the Oil Ministry, in particular. He inherited a weak system, and he made it even weaker. Chavez passed away on March 5, 2013, and his death went unnoticed by the oil market and by OPEC.

Chapter Seven

KING ABDULLAH, GEORGE W. BUSH, AND GORDON BROWN

The Shadows of 2008

On May 14, 2008, Ali Al-Naimi, arrived in South Korea on an official visit. The nine-hour flight was uneventful, and he was looking forward to receiving an honorary PhD from the University of Seoul and meeting Korean officials, including the president. Upon arrival Al-Naimi received an urgent phone call from the Saudi royal court, telling him that King Abdullah wanted him to return at once. U.S. president George W. Bush was to visit Saudi Arabia on May 16, and the state of the oil market would be at the top of his agenda. We sent a full report about the oil market and the ministry's point of view to the royal court, and Al-Naimi left Korea for home the following day (with his new PhD).

In 2007, oil prices were rising, and this upward movement accelerated in the first months of 2008. By the time President Bush arrived in Saudi Arabia, the price of crude had risen to around $120/BBL, and there was a fair chance that it might rise higher. Just over a year earlier, the price had been $60/BBL. The International Energy Agency (EIA) reported that the average gasoline price in the United States for the week of May 14 had reached $3.40 per gallon and was expected to top $4.00 per gallon in June—a record that remains unbroken—and U.S politicians were alarmed. The Bush administration was worried that high prices would have a negative impact on global economic growth and on the U.S. economy in particular, and signs of trouble were already arising. Gasoline prices are a very sensitive issue during U.S. elections, and Bush was under pressure from the Republican Party to ask the Saudis to do something about the oil supply to bring prices down.

Returning to Saudi Arabia, Al-Naimi immediately headed to the meeting with the U.S. president. King Abdullah asked Al-Naimi to talk to the president about the oil market and Saudi oil policy. Al-Naimi spoke in English, which was easier for both of them than speaking in Arabic and using translators (oil, like other commodities, has its own vocabulary). Among the causes for the increase in the oil price, Al-Naimi named geopolitics, speculation, and negative information and assumptions about production capacity and the peak oil supply theory that was trending at the time. Whether Bush was fully convinced by Al-Naimi's explanation was unclear, but Al-Naimi assured the president that Saudi Arabia was meeting all requests from its customers and was willing and able to increase production if asked. Saudi Arabia promised to move more oil into the market, by up to one million barrels daily, provided there was customer demand for it.

Saudi Arabia's policy was to make sure oil prices did not get out of control, and the kingdom was committed to doing what it could to bring prices down. This policy serves Saudi Arabia's long-term interests as well as its relationships with customers and political allies such as the United States. OPEC had a similar policy and monitored oil prices to avoid harm to the global economy. Bush was focused on oil prices and U.S. politics during an election year. The following weeks saw a further increase in the price of oil despite higher Saudi production and the many positive statements coming from Riyadh and other oil-producing countries.

The Republican administration in the White House, where neo-conservatives were a dominant force, was not in favor of coordinated international actions unless they had no other choice. The United States wanted to be seen to lead on international issues so they could turn them to their advantage. The United States and the United Kingdom regularly exchanged information, coordinated their efforts, and consulted each other, and they were the leading members of a then top secret international organization referred to as the Five Eyes, which included Canada, Australia, and New Zealand. These countries exchanged information and coordinated policies, and discussion probably took place among them after President Bush's visit to Riyadh because the price of oil continued to rise and worries over the health of the global economy intensified. U.S. officials rarely openly discuss the oil market and oil prices with other countries, so the responsibility for doing something about rising oil prices shifted from Washington to London.

British prime minister Gordon Brown sought an international role, but he had domestic concerns as well. In 2000, lorry drivers angry about higher oil prices and taxes had staged protests, including go-slow driving on some highways. This dispute had caused major problems for the British government and the economy, and Brown was worried about another such protest. At the time, similar oil product-related protests were sweeping Western Europe, and government taxes on gasoline and diesel were very high across Europe, including in the United Kingdom. Brown was the leader of a Labour government and had previously served as Chancellor of the Exchequer, and he believed his role extended beyond British domestic issues. Andrew Rawnsley, a British journalist and author, called him the "Chancellor of the world."[1] He wanted to be recognized as an important international leader as was his predecessor, Tony Blair.

The British psyche was equally important. The United Kingdom had the fifth largest global economy in 2020 and had been an oil-producing and oil-exporting country for at least thirty-five years. It was home to two of the largest international oil companies (BP and Shell), and both paid large sums in taxes to the UK Exchequer. Other important oil and gas companies and related manufacturers and services were also based in the United Kingdom, and London is home to the second most important oil futures trading exchange. UK oil consumption was ranked number ten among nations, which reflected the state of its economy and the benefits from high taxation on oil products, and high oil prices did not hurt their economy as they did many other countries such as Japan, Korea, Germany, and China. Indeed, as a producer, the United Kingdom stood to benefit from higher crude oil prices.

Great Britain has long held onto the memory of its colonial past when it ruled one of the most important empires of modern times. Even as its status as a world power has waned, the United Kingdom has often punched above its weight on the international stage, sometimes in cooperation with a few close allies. By far its most important alliance is with the United States, and the two countries have coordinated foreign, military, and economic policies in recent decades. The most obvious example was the U.S. invasion of Iraq in 2003, which the United Kingdom backed wholeheartedly, contributing a large number of troops to the U.S.-led coalition.

It is perhaps this mindset that led Gordon Brown to suggest holding an oil summit of oil producers and oil consumers in London in June 2008. Brown called King Abdullah in early June, proposing to invite heads of state of the most important oil-consuming and oil-producing nations to a meeting as early as possible. Brown knew that no successful oil action could be taken without the full support of Saudi Arabia, and the two countries had enjoyed close and friendly relations at government and personal levels for many decades (including the king of Saudi Arabia, the queen of the United Kingdom, her family, and various prime ministers).

King Abdullah told Brown that Saudi Arabia would do whatever it could to stabilize the market and prevent an uncontrolled rise of oil prices that might harm the global economy. The king told Brown that such a leadership summit had his the full support and his personal blessing too, but King Abdullah proposed that Saudi Arabia host the meeting. He also told Brown that he would let Al-Naimi and the Ministry of Petroleum decide the best option in terms of timing, agenda, location, and level of participation and suggested that Brown consult with the Ministry of Petroleum directly. Al-Naimi formed a committee headed by Prince Abdulaziz bin Salman, the current energy minister, to prepare for the meeting.

Following consultations with the British government, it was decided to hold the conference on June 22 in the city of Jeddah. It was also decided that both King Abdullah and the British prime minister would officially open the conference. Other recommendations from the committee included the following:

1. The meeting should be at the ministerial level because of the short notice and the desire to have participation from as many countries, oil companies, and related institutes as possible. A summit of heads of state would create high expectations that might be difficult to meet.

2. The newly created secretariat of the International Energy Forum (IEF) should take a leading role in this process, together with the International Energy Agency (IEA) and OPEC.

3. Saudi Arabia did not believe that higher oil prices were related to the fundamentals (supply, demand, and commercial stocks), as some countries claimed. Rather, they had more to do with talk about the idea of peak oil supply, which was common at the time in many circles, especially in the United States. In addition, Saudi Arabia believed that regional geopolitical tensions (such as

suspicions that Israel might attack Iran) had given rise to fears that an attack would affect the oil supply and push prices even higher.

4. The claim that oil production capacity was limited and that there were no plans to raise capacity in many oil-producing countries, including Saudi Arabia, to meet growing demand was mentioned as an important reason for higher oil prices.

The Saudi team believed that Saudi Arabia should reassure the market that Saudi Arabia's current production capacity was definitely 11.3 MBD, which left it with spare capacity of 1.5 MBD. Furthermore, it was willing to meet the request of all customers for more oil if asked. Saudi Arabia would also provide reassurance that in light of expectations of growing demand it had plans in place to increase production capacity by 2.5 MBD the following year, and later reach 15 MBD. Saudi Arabia had detailed data regarding the oil fields, the types of crude that would be produced, and the dates of production once the plan was implemented. Saudi Arabia wanted to show the world that it cared about the stability of the market, that it was a reliable supplier of oil, and that it has the capability to increase production.

In Saudi Arabia, the committee coordinated closely with the UK government and with the IEF, IEA, and OPEC secretariats. The committee was responsible for preparing the list of invited ministers, presidents of major oil companies, and heads of energy and economic organizations such as the International Monetary Fund (IMF) and the World Bank. The committee was also responsible for developing a program for the conference, scheduling speakers and the topics to be discussed. More important, the Saudis decided to commission joint comprehensive studies about oil prices and the situation of the international oil market to be presented during the meeting. Writing the final communiqué would be the responsibility of the committee in coordination with the British delegation, the IEF, the IEA, and OPEC.

In recognition of the important role of Brown and the British government, it was suggested that London host a second conference before the end of the year to follow up on the Jeddah meeting. A Joint Technical Committee between the two countries would be set up to ensure that the London meeting was a success.

The response to the invitation to the Jeddah meeting was overwhelming. More than thirty-five countries, twenty-five oil companies, and seven heads of international organizations were represented at the meeting, as well as hundreds of journalists from around the world. The vice president of the People's Republic of China, Xi Jinping, was visiting Saudi Arabia, and he took part in the opening ceremony alongside both the Saudi king and the British prime minister. This gave the conference added international value because China was then the second largest oil importer in the world with the highest energy consumption growth. The reason for holding the conference was mainly to discuss the oil market in terms of supply, demand, commercial stocks, and prices. But discussions went beyond oil market balances and covered issues such as energy poverty, climate change, and helping energy-poor nations, especially in Africa. A number of important bilateral meetings were also held on the sidelines, and two of these meetings merit special mention.

The first was a meeting between Al-Naimi and the U.S. secretary of energy Samuel Bodman, who was a close friend and an admirer of Al-Naimi. Bodman insisted that the high oil price was due to fundamentals and not to speculation, and that the financial market had nothing to do with it. Bodman and the U.S. delegation also asked that Saudi Arabia do more to bring down oil prices even if it was against its oil policy and marketing procedures. For example, some wanted Saudi Aramco to push extra oil onto the market at a discount even if there were no buyers. The Saudis explained that Aramco's marketing strategy could not be changed overnight, and that they should not and could not differentiate between more than eighty customers. Moreover, even if it pushed extra oil, Saudi Arabia did not believe that oil prices would necessarily fall because the reasons for the rising oil price were not related entirely to fundamentals. Some in the U.S. delegation were partially convinced by the Saudi arguments, but they said what they had to say—it was all politics as usual.

The second interesting meeting was with Nobuo Tanaka, the executive director of the IEA. Saudi oil officials disagreed with the IEA's estimate of Saudi's production capacity. The IEA claimed it was only 10 MBD, but the Saudis insisted it was 11.3 MBD. The Saudis believed that reports casting doubt on its production capacity were partially to blame for the higher oil prices, and their argument was very simple: "We have no reason to lie." The Saudis argued that their estimate was done by highly respected petroleum engineers, mostly educated in the United States and trained by Saudi Aramco, and that their work had been tested in 1990 in more difficult times when Iraq invaded Kuwait. Energy analysts and organizations in Paris,

Vienna, New York, and London could not have better estimates because they were not directly involved in the assessment of Saudi production capacity. The Saudis also asked why the IEA continued to publish numbers it was not 100 percent sure were accurate that were not good for market stability and contributed to higher oil prices. The IEA stated that its analysts had good sources and that they had a different definition of production capacity.

The general feeling of participants at the Jeddah meeting and the international media was positive, and the meeting was considered a success. It was a good faith attempt to calm the market, and it provided a framework for cooperation among oil producers, oil consumers, oil companies, and international energy and economic organizations. Everybody was happy with the outcome of the conference, especially the media. *Time Magazine* quoted me as saying that "our goal is to bring back stability to the oil market."[2] This was a direct statement of the positive role Saudi Arabia played during the Jeddah meeting.

The British presented one of the most interesting proposals to Saudi Arabia, suggesting an oil price band jointly between oil producers, oil consumers, and the oil companies. The lowest price would be set at $60 and the highest at $90, with a mechanism designed to keep the price within this band. The Saudis did not accept this proposal because preserving it would place a heavy burden on Saudi Arabia and it would be difficult to implement, as was the case with the OPEC price band of $22–$28 in the early part of the decade. The Saudis instead asked countries to endorse King Abdullah's price target of $75–$80. Neither suggestion made it to the general discussions in Jeddah, and Brown made another interesting proposal.

A close look at the arguments of the decision makers who participated as well as some analysts revealed deep-rooted differences regarding the causes of oil price movements and on how to tackle this and other market-related issues. Officials from the United States, the United Kingdom, and some Western countries considered fundamentals to be the main reason for the oil price rise. They blamed OPEC in general and Saudi Arabia in particular for not increasing production; I heard one official say, "You are not doing enough." These same countries ignored or played down the role of speculation on oil prices by hedge funds, banks, and other traders in the futures market, but during the financial crisis two months later they began to recognize the negative role of speculators on the futures market and tried to regulate it.

They also ignored the impact of geopolitical tensions on the oil market. The main factor was the Israeli threat to attack Iran. A few weeks before the Jeddah meeting, the Israeli transport minister and deputy prime minister Shaul Mofaz said that attacking Iran to stop its nuclear program was unavoidable. As a result, oil prices increased in a single day by $11. One commentator said, "The fact is Brown prefers to ignore geopolitical factors impacting on the oil market because instead of traveling to Jeddah, he would have to fly to Washington and Tel Aviv so as to tone down the rhetoric after first muting his own."[3] OPEC members highlighted other factors, mainly speculators, the falling U.S. dollar, geopolitics, and the policy of some consuming countries for not having enough refining capacity.

Inside each country, the reasons behind the rise in oil prices often reflected domestic issues. It was an election year in the United States, and the oil market became a hot topic that both parties tried to use to their benefit. John McCain, the Republican candidate for president, concentrated his attack on the U.S. reliance on imported oil and argued that it was important to open up deep sea and federal lands for oil investments. Barack Obama, the Democratic candidate, attacked the financial speculators and the relaxation of financial regulations by the Bush administration as major causes of the oil price increase, and he demanded regulation of their attempts to manipulate the market. Chuck Schumer, a leading Democrat in the Senate, directed his attacks at OPEC and Saudi Arabia, blaming them for the high price of oil because they refused to increase production.[4] Even today Schumer tends to attack Saudi Arabia on many issues related to the oil market and the Middle East.

Inside OPEC another conflict arose that also was related to politics and national interests. Iran, Libya, and Venezuela were against giving in to the American and British demands to increase production and believed that Saudi Arabia should not act unilaterally without a collective OPEC agreement. Some members of the Kuwait Parliament were against increasing oil production, believing that the oil should be preserved for future generations and that consuming countries should concentrate instead on reducing their consumption and taxation. Some even went so far as to suggest a conspiracy by the United States to require OPEC members to increase their production while disallowing exploration and production in some U.S. areas, such as the deep sea.[5]

Inside Saudi Arabia, one of the widely read critics of the Jeddah meeting was a well-known Saudi columnist, Abdullah al Fozan, who wrote:

> Are we in need of all of this huge production which has now reached more than nine million barrels daily, and we are planning to increase it to twelve million barrels daily? The answer in my opinion is clear. We do not need this, because we transfer a large part of this daily production to dollar reserve, which stays in Western banks.
>
> We are being polite with oil consumers and speculators against the future interest of our children and grandchildren.
>
> Why do we not re-examine our own production policy by concentrating on our interest as producers of other commodities do?
>
> Why do we give away the interests of our children and grandchildren in order to be nice to those consumers, who do not respect our sacrifices?[6]

OIL PRICE ZIGZAGGING

Sometimes market sentiment plays a larger role than policy makers, speculators, and analysts because the oil market has its own logic. At other times, the market moves in response to an unexpected development unrelated to current policy conflicts. For example, as the Jeddah meeting was reassuring the market and Saudi Arabia agreed to increase production and production capacity, an attack on Nigerian oil facilities led to a 300,000 B/D fall in production. Within three weeks of the Jeddah meeting, the price of U.S. West Texas Intermediate crude oil shot up, hitting a record high of $147 on July 11, 2008, and a well-known financial institution predicted that the price could rise to $200 or even higher, which stoked market fears.

Instead, however, the rise above $140 was the beginning of a free fall. The global economy faced one of the most significant financial and economic crises in eighty years, and this affected both the fundamentals and the psychology of the oil market. The subprime mortgage crisis began in the United States in 2007, but nobody took any notice at first. The collapse of Lehman Brothers, a major U.S. investment bank, on September 15, 2008, created shock waves in the financial system including in the oil market. Some banks, the U.S. auto industry, and other major industries came very close to collapse, and the U.S. government had to intervene to save banks and industries either through bailouts or asset purchases.

The contagion spread to the rest of the U.S. economy and then to the global economy, which began shrinking in a big way. The recession was unprecedented. The U.S. government, other Western countries, and some international financial institutions admitted that speculation and weak financial regulations were responsible for many of the problems in the economy, including the price of commodities such as oil.

One of the most important international developments that resulted from the 2008 financial crisis was the call for heads of state of the G20 nations, comprised of nineteen countries and the European Union, to take action. It was an indirect admission that the IMF, the World Bank, and the World Trade Organization, along with the G7, were not capable of managing major international economic problems. The first G20 heads of state meeting was held in Washington, D.C. in mid-November 2008. As a major oil producer, Saudi Arabia was invited to be part of the group. It was a clear admission of the importance of Saudi Arabia's role in stabilizing the oil market and the global economy.

The oil market was facing major problems simultaneously. Sentiment was negative, fundamentals were clearly bad, and the future looked bleak. After Bush's visit and the Jeddah meeting, total OPEC production increased by one million barrels daily in the first half of 2008. Commercial inventories were building gradually, but demand was falling. For the first time since 1982, global demand for oil fell in 2008 and 2009. The decrease was more than 1.5 MBD from the 2007 level. Equally bad was the release of mistaken information about the oil market from important sources such as the IEA. One report stated that the increase in Chinese imports was going into storage and did not point to a real rise in consumption. This proved to be wrong, but the short-term impact took time to correct. The market psychology during 2008 was another important factor, which Daniel Yergin described in the *Financial Times*:

> Certainly, oil prices were also driven up throughout July 2008 by psychology; what professor Robert Shiller of Yale describes as "Contagious excitement about investment prospects." It was almost like bets in a poker game, with a $200 prediction being raised by a $250 prediction, which would in turn be raised by a $500 prediction. It was all self-reinforcing, creating its own reality.[7]

The same psychological factors again affected falling prices at the end of July. The slump in the second half of 2008 was faster and deeper than the increase in the first half of the year had been. The price of oil fell to about $30 in December 2008, with some predictions that it could fall even lower.

FROM STEEP RISE TO FREE FALL

At first, OPEC did not think the financial meltdown was that serious, and when OPEC ministers met in September 2008, they decided to lower production by just 1.5 MBD, returning to precrisis production levels. However, that reduction proved insufficient, and OPEC held an extraordinary meeting in October and agreed to a further cut of 0.5 MBD. Again, it was not enough to rebalance the market and stop oil prices from sliding further. It was a reminder of what had happened in 1998—many cuts with no results. By December 2008, the oil prices were down by 70 percent from their peak in July 2008.

In times of crisis, a person with a strong personality from an important country is usually needed to provide leadership and deliver a shock to the market. In coordination with Algerian oil minister Chakib Khelil, Al-Naimi decided to take on this responsibility. After a lot of coordination within OPEC and with some non-OPEC producers, the ministers convened a joint meeting in Oran, Algeria, on December 17, 2008, to agree on meaningful production cuts larger than those OPEC had instituted earlier that year. King Abdullah was closely following oil market developments, and Al-Naimi kept the king informed regarding these developments and discussions.

Without a doubt, the Oran conference was one of the most important meetings in the history of OPEC. Al-Naimi was the undeclared leader of OPEC, not only because he was minister of the largest oil-producing and oil-exporting country in the world but also because of his knowledge, personality, and the great respect he enjoyed internationally. Al-Naimi was at the peak of his career nationally and internationally and had the determination, the time, and the willingness to work hard and take a leading role in promoting the necessary actions. Al-Naimi thought that OPEC could and should take bold actions to shock the market. He did not demand, nor did he care a lot about, the participation of non-OPEC countries.

In Oran, OPEC decided to lower production by 2.2 MBD, the largest reduction in the history of the organization at that time, bringing the total reduction since September 2008 to 4.2 MBD. No OPEC country was exempted, and no objections to the methodology for calculating the reductions were allowed. In Oran, cuts were made on a pro rata basis for everybody and according to secondary source production estimates. This rare harmony was possible because all of the producers were eager to see oil prices rise to the high levels they had become used to in the previous eight years. This time, even the Iranians, the Venezuelans, and the Libyans were on board, and Al-Naimi proved that he had the leadership qualities to deliver a good agreement.

Another important market factor that influenced OPEC's decision was the quality of data and market information provided. Good information is important to understanding oil market conditions in terms of supply, demand, commercial stocks, and available spare production capacity. When oil prices was rising in the first half of 2008, the producers felt positive about the future. Most of the published information from organizations and consultants predicted a tight market, high demand, and insufficient spare capacity. Two interesting incidents occurred during the meeting that influenced Al-Naimi's feelings toward Algeria and Russia and the way he dealt with both countries in the ensuing eight years he remained in office.

The night before the joint meeting, Al-Naimi met with Igor Sechin, the head of the Russian delegation. Sechin was then Russia's deputy prime minister and chairman of Rosneft Oil Company (state owned) and a close friend and confidant of Russian president Vladimir Putin. (Russia's oil policy and its relationship with OPEC and Saudi Arabia is discussed in chapter 10.) Al-Naimi asked Sechin to join OPEC in the effort to restore oil prices and cut Russian production. Sechin promised to do so and pledged a cut of 300,000 B/D. Al-Naimi asked him to announce the agreement the following morning before or during the official meeting, but Sechin did not keep that promise, which made Al-Naimi extremely unhappy. It was the third time the Russians had promised cuts only to renege on their promise.[8]

The second incident occurred on the morning of the meeting. After having had breakfast with other OPEC ministers at the hotel, Al-Naimi took the stairs instead of the elevator to return to his suite, which was two levels up. President Abdelaziz Bouteflika of Algeria was already in the hotel for the official opening of the conference, and the hotel was packed with security personnel. As Al-Naimi climbed the stairs, a security man stopped him from proceeding further. Al-Naimi explained that he was the minister of petroleum of Saudi Arabia and needed to get to his room. After an intense argument, the security man reached for his gun and told Al-Naimi to turn back immediately.

Al-Naimi was livid and asked for a meeting with the Saudi delegates, including Prince Abdulaziz and the Saudi ambassador to Algeria. He told them what had happened and said he would not attend the official opening. Everybody in the conference hall was waiting for Al-Naimi, and information leaked that Al-Naimi would not be attending the official opening ceremony. The oil minister of Algeria, together with the head of security, immediately went to Al-Naimi's suite and offered an official apology from the Algerian side. Al-Naimi agreed to attend the ceremony and greeted the Algerian president, but he harbored hard feelings for a long time. OPEC did not meet in Algeria again until after Al-Naimi left office.

FROM JEDDAH TO LONDON

Even though oil prices had started to fall by mid-July 2008, a London meeting had been agreed to in Jeddah as a courtesy to Gordon Brown, who had asked to host it. Immediately after the Oran meeting of December 17, many OPEC and non-OPEC ministers headed directly to London for this meeting on December 19. Saudi Arabia and the United Kingdom are close allies on several fronts, and the Saudis wanted to accommodate Brown, who had played a constructive role in the success of the Jeddah meeting.

Gordon Brown's opening speech in London had a completely different focus from his Jeddah presentation. This time he spoke in generalities about oil market stability, transparency, cooperation between producers and consumers, and oil price fluctuations:

> Wild fluctuations in the market price harm nations all around the world. They damage consumers and producers alike. . . . oil producers particularly those with the lowest crossed reserves will continue to need to invest in capacity. But at the same time volatile prices make that investment less certain, sowing the seed for future volatility.

Brown's change of tone sounded more like that of an OPEC official. He also referred to the negative role of speculation and the role of some financial institutions in the problems that faced the oil market. It was not only the issue of fundamentals of supply and demand and spare production capacity, he explained:

> Our analysis of the oil price developments over the past year—which we are publishing today—shows clearly the interaction between the physical and the financial market for oil. So in reviewing global financial governance arrangements, it is only right that we consider the adequacy of the current regulatory approach of global commodity markets. And I therefore welcome the creation by the International Organization of Securities Commission of a new global task force to examine the existing framework.

He went on to praise the exercise of political power in the oil market, saying, "At a time of visionary internationalism, all across the world we are seeing the power of political will to deliver global action" to stabilize the market.[9]

Brown and other Western energy officials were echoing what Hisham Nazer, Al-Naimi, and other Saudi officials had been saying for about three decades. In Jeddah there were clear differences between Saudi Arabia and the United Kingdom and the United States about the causes behind high oil prices and what to do about them. In London, there was a convergence of opinions on these issues. Developments in the financial and oil markets in earlier months had led some Western leaders to recognize the possible negative role that speculators played in the oil market.

Brown wanted to take credit for managing the oil market, and he made some suggestions during the London meeting and in subsequent months. First, he wanted more similar meetings. The British asked South Africa to invite the participating countries for a third meeting the following year, but this idea was rejected not only because of changing market circumstances but because it would overlap with the ministerial meeting of the IEF. The second suggestion was to create action groups to look at the best way to reduce oil price volatility and help to bring more stability and predictability to the market. This was generally supported by all and was linked to strengthening the IEF. It was suggested that creation of a high-level steering group supported by independent experts be discussed at the IEF ministerial meeting in Cancun, Mexico, in 2010. Overall, the London meeting ended smoothly and provided an opportunity for discussion and dissemination of some useful studies.

LESSONS FROM 2008

What happened in 2008 in the oil and financial markets and in the at-large global economy had not occurred in more than eighty years. The oil price went from below $100 at the beginning of the year, to a high of $147 on July 11, and sank to a low of nearly $30 by year's end. It is important that we learn from these experiences so similar crises do not arise in the future.

First, global leadership is important to correct mistakes and to change course, and creative ideas and new initiatives may be needed, including new institutions. In the oil market, King Abdullah of Saudi Arabia and Gordon Brown of Great Britain came up with the idea of calling for the Jeddah meeting and a follow-up meeting in London to calm the market and find a solution to the high oil price. In the global economy at large, the U.S. president George W. Bush called for a G20 summit in 2008 to establish a new framework of international cooperation to deal with economic issues, including oil.

Second, information and the way it is interpreted is crucial. Knowledge of facts can help decision makers and can influence market direction. Although the role of information had been clear for many decades, its importance was never as obvious as it was in 2008. Information about the oil markets came from more than fifty sources: major banks, oil companies, think tanks, consultants, and energy and nonenergy international organizations. The governments of some oil-producing and oil-consuming nations had their own data. In the United States, more than five federal government departments collected their own information but did not necessarily coordinate with each other. In the oil market, the most quoted information comes from the IEA, OPEC, and the EIA, but major banks such as J. P. Morgan, Citibank, and Goldman Sachs sometimes have an impact on market direction.[10]

How good are they? That is anybody's guess. Certainly, they borrow from each other and compare notes. They may have an economic/statistics model of supply and demand, including their base of prediction, but they rarely have new original information. For example, for a couple of months in 2010, Saudi's actual production was higher by about one million barrels daily than what the secondary sources had noted.[11] Nobody, including OPEC, the IEA, and the EIA, seemed to notice this or change the supply balance. Equally as important is the interpretation of data, which is not a purely mathematical exercise; an element of personal bias or political and economic interests are often inserted. Before the financial crises and the collapse of oil prices, many U.S. and British officials, and even some oil analysts and journalists, were blaming fundamentals for the higher oil price and dismissing the role of speculators and hedge funds. Within a few months, their opinions had shifted.

The market moves based on both fundamentals and sentiment. At times of crises and uncertainty, sentiment overshadows fundamentals and influences the behavior of financial investors in the oil market. Information and the way it is interpreted is responsible to a great degree for creating positive or negative sentiment. These facts were clear in 2008. At the beginning of the crisis, for example, all the talk was about production capacity and declining Saudi and global production and reserves. Also, international banks are buyers and sellers of oil futures contracts for themselves or for their clients, and they have commercial interests in the oil market unrelated to the fundamentals.

Third, the role of governments and international governmental cooperation are crucial in times of economic and oil market crises. When the oil price went above $120, the governments of major oil-consuming and oil-producing countries worked together to stop the market from spinning out of control. When the oil price collapsed, the oil-producing countries, especially OPEC, worked to rebalance the market by cutting oil production, and this was done with the blessing of major oil-consuming countries. When the global financial market collapsed in the middle of 2008, the G20 group of major economies had their first heads of state summit to coordinate policy and restore stability to the financial markets. There are those who do not want government intervention in the oil markets, but the experiences of 2008 proved them wrong.[12]

Fourth, acknowledge the strong convergence between oil markets and the global economy. Many factors pushed up the oil price in 2007 and the first half of 2008, but a major factor was strong global economic growth and the expectation that it would continue. Economic growth brings with it a strong demand for oil and creates positive economic sentiment. When the global economy faced major financial and economic crises in 2008 and 2009 and some economies were shrinking, the oil market collapsed. Part of this collapse was the direct result of economic problems, but part of it was due to expectations of continued positive global economic growth. There is also a linkage between the price of oil and the strength of the U.S. dollar. Oil is priced in dollars, and the weak dollar was one of the reasons oil prices increased in 2007 and the first half of 2008.

The shadow of 2008 lingered for many years, and it affected the oil market for two years. In 2009, demand was still on the downward trend that had started in 2008. Nearly all countries experienced negative economic growth, with the exception of some OPEC producing states, China, and a few Asian countries. Had it not been for courage, leadership, and a clear initiative with a strong follow-up on the part of OPEC, the oil price slump might have persisted for many more years. Credit should go to Al-Naimi and two OPEC ministers, Chakib Khelil of Algeria and Abdullah bin Hamad al-Attiyah of Qatar. Both had good relationships with Al-Naimi and trusted him enough to work with him to achieve the desired results. They also had good working relationships with the OPEC secretary-general Abdalla el Badri of Libya.

Some OPEC ministers stayed on the margins during that period. They included the Venezuelans, the Iranians, and the Iraqis. Their standing in OPEC was weakened because of their extreme policies and their lack of excess production capacity. In addition, Iran and Iraq did not fully adhere to their quotas, which did not help the effort to balance the market. The president of Iran at that time was Mahmoud Ahmadinejad, who was the most radical and extreme nationalist leader since the Iranian revolution of 1979. The prime minister of Iraq was Nouri al-Maliki, who was part of the Shiite Dawa Party, which has close ties to the Iranian religious and political establishment. Both presidents had poor working relationships with other OPEC countries, except Venezuela. Venezuela's quota at the time was much higher than its actual production because of its declining production capacity.

For 2009, OPEC was able to reduce its actual production from 2008. The successive cuts agreed on by OPEC that year totaled 4.2 MBD. According to OPEC secondary sources, the percentage of reduction varied from one country to another. Iraq was the only member to increase its production. Reductions from Iran were 3.3 percent. The cuts were around 10 percent for Kuwait, Saudi Arabia, and the United Arab Emirates. The highest cuts were 12 percent for Algeria and Libya. Production declines also occurred in some non-OPEC countries for a variety of reasons.

By the middle of 2009, the oil price began a gradual recovery. In November 2009, I was with Minister Al-Naimi on an official visit to China, a major buyer of Saudi Arabian crude oil. During that visit, it became clear that the IEA's data and other sources on China had been incorrect.[13] With the growth in China's consumption and demand for energy, and with oil prices recovering, Al-Naimi asked Aramco to increase its production quietly and gradually. By mid-2010, Saudi production reached 9 MBD, although some secondary estimates were around 8.2–8.3 MBD. Saudi Arabia's policy has been to make sure that there was no shortage in the global market and to meet its customers' demand provided it did not have a negative impact on the international oil market.

The experiences of 2008–2009 in the oil market illustrates the importance of having good decision makers ready to deal with major crises. President Bush tried to find a solution to rising oil prices in 2008, but his efforts failed because he thought it could be dealt with by the United States and Saudi Arabia alone, even though the problem was international. King Abdullah and Prime Minister Brown looked at the oil crisis in clearer terms—as an international crisis that required collective action. The Jeddah meeting was on the right track, but when oil prices collapsed in the second half of 2008, it was the work of some OPEC oil ministers that brought the oil market back to stability through prompt action to create a big shock to the market.

Chapter Eight

BARACK OBAMA, DONALD TRUMP, AND JOE BIDEN

A Revolving U.S. Energy Policy

The year 2012 was an election year in the United States, and President Barack Obama was running for a second term. The price of oil was rising for a number of reasons: market fundamentals, Iranian sanctions, and a Libyan outage. In the first quarter of the year, the price of oil reached $128/BBL. More important in the United States was the cost of gasoline, which was as high as $4.50 per gallon in Chicago, the largest city in Illinois, Obama's home state. In the United States, gasoline prices are posted in foot-high numbers on signs at the stations, and the average American driver, including every elected member of Congress, is sensitive to any change in price because higher prices hit household budgets and affect voting behavior. Obama was aware of this fact and was worried about its impact on his chances of being reelected.

In March 2012, President Obama phoned King Abdullah of Saudi Arabia asking for Saudi Arabia's help in lowering oil prices by increasing production or through other means.[1] King Abdullah responded positively and told Obama that he would do his best. This request was strictly confidential between the two leaders and a very small number of their advisers, although it later became known to many people in both countries. (In his memoir, former president Obama also talked about cooperation between the two countries on energy-related matters, including oil prices.) The Ministry of Petroleum had been worried about increasing oil prices since 2011 and did not want a recurrence of what happened in the middle of 2008, when prices reached $147. Such high prices were against Saudi oil policy and not in its interests, especially in the long term. Therefore, Obama's request fit in well with Saudi Arabia's interests and oil policy, and King Abdullah personally favored lowering oil prices because it showed the world that Saudi Arabia cares about its customers and the stability of the world economy. King Abdullah was especially concerned for the interests of developing countries and often emphasized this concern.

The following day, King Abdullah told Minister Ali Al-Naimi about his conversation with Obama and the promise he had given him. He wanted Al-Naimi to fulfill this promise. Al-Naimi asked for a few days to think about it and said that he would then come back to the king with a plan. Early in the morning on the following day, Al-Naimi asked me to come to his office. He told me about the issue, and we discussed what we could do about it. He added that it was strictly confidential for the time being and cautioned that "few people know about it and no other person should know about it, at least until the mission is accomplished." I felt this was one of the biggest challenges I had faced since I joined the ministry in 1989. It required a lot of thinking, and because it was a secret I had to think about it alone, which made it an even more difficult task.

The following day I told Al-Naimi that we had to have a plan in two parts. The first part of the plan was tangible and related to market fundamentals. Saudi Arabia would continue to increase supply to the market, a process that had begun a couple of months earlier and, if possible, add more oil supply over the next few months. Saudi production had been rising based on an appeal by some customers because a disruption of supply in the previous year had led to relatively strong demands for oil. The market was generally well supplied and well balanced, but geopolitical factors, especially Israel's threat to take action against Iran over its nuclear program, were affecting the oil market. Some experts were talking about limited or nonexistent production capacity, but it was not fundamentals that were driving prices higher.

The second part of the plan was related to market psychology or sentiment. An international campaign was needed to convince the market that the oil price was very high (a policy referred to as talking the market down). This suggestion was based on the belief that perception and the psychology of the market are important factors, and occasionally are more important than the fundamentals. The market was in a negative mood about almost everything, which was pushing prices higher, and changing the mood to a positive one could lead to lower oil prices.

In my opinion, six important players are able to influence market direction, one way or another:

1. International business media, particularly specialized energy publications. It is not only what is reported but also the way events are reported, such as the people who are quoted, the news headlines, and news alerts.[2]
2. Oil experts and analysts, whether independent or part of a large organization. IHS Markit and PIRA Energy Group, for example, interpret events and information and predict the direction of the oil market and oil prices, which influences the futures market.
3. International energy organizations, especially the International Energy Agency (IEA) and OPEC. These information warehouses publish monthly reports about the international oil market that are widely quoted, and their estimates on supply and demand and commercial stocks influence the oil market and its behavior.
4. Hedge funds and commercial banks. These players take positions in the oil futures market (long and short), expecting high or low oil prices. Their positions are based on their own in-house information and analysis as well as information from public and private oil officials and experts.
5. Government officials from major oil-producing and oil-consuming countries. Whether speaking publicly or privately, what they say can, and does, have a strong influence on the direction of oil prices, especially when inside information or new policy trends are discussed.
6. Major oil companies (national or international), including oil trading companies. Most of these companies have extensive internal analyses but do not like to discuss the oil market publicly. They don't want to be quoted, nor do they typically reveal their information, expectations, and position in the market. Nevertheless, when their information is leaked or given to a limited number of people in a confidential way, they can influence the market and its direction.

All six of these players influence each other by exchanging information, interpretation, and opinion, directly or indirectly. Therefore, if a large number of these players can be convinced, the market at large will move. That was our thinking in the Ministry of Petroleum.

We formed a small team of highly qualified people who understood the market and had good relationships with various players in the international oil market. They were respected, and their information and analysis was trusted by large segments of the market (including the six players mentioned previously). Al-Naimi explained that their mission was to help stabilize the oil market and to bring oil prices down. They accepted their mission because they believed that high and uncontrolled oil prices were not good for Saudi Arabia, especially in the long term. (Saudi Arabia's reserves could continue to produce oil for at least another eighty years at current production levels.) Production could be disrupted either because of very high prices or because customers decided to adopt measures to reduce their oil consumption, as they did in the late 1970s and early 1980s. This is one of the pillars of the first Saudi Energy Strategy, which was written by the ministry and approved by the leadership in 2000.

The international campaign kicked off in London and New York, true capitals of the oil market, with two dominant oil futures exchanges (ICE and NYMEX) and home to major hedge funds and banks that trade in oil on a global scale. Major financial and energy media outlets as well as influential oil research centers (commercial and noncommercial) also reside in these two cities. Price formation and movements are largely concentrated in these two cities even though some think the market takes its daily direction from morning trade in Asia or that OPEC is the major mover of markets.

The message from the Saudi team was clear: (1) The market is well balanced; (2) commercial stocks are high and going even higher; (3) Saudi Arabia has increased production and might increase it further; and (4) Saudi Arabia has the ability to increase production capacity if there is a shortage or a strong growth in demand. The goal was clear: Saudi Arabia is committed to bringing oil prices down, which is in the interest of the oil industry and the global economy.

Several meetings with highly influential people were also held in Riyadh, London, and New York. The Saudi team was well-prepared, and these meetings were held quietly, either individually or with small groups of experts or media, sometimes over lunch or dinner. Representatives from the media, analysts, hedge funds, banks, and oil companies were carefully selected to ensure quality, credibility, and respect within the market. The majority began to understand that oil prices were artificially high and not supported by the fundamentals, and beliefs between the Saudi team and the international groups began to converge. Analysts and journalists who tended to publish exaggerated reports or mix their political opinions with oil (not neutral) or make sensational statements were not invited. Even without any direct contact, those journalists also ended up delivering the same messages.[3]

The Saudi team also undertook two important projects. The first project was to prepare a carefully written newspaper opinion piece containing a clear message by Ali Al-Naimi. The article, published in the *Financial Times* in March 2012, clearly stated that "high international oil prices are bad news. Bad for Europe, bad for the U.S., bad for emerging economies and bad for the world's poorest nations. A period of prolonged high prices is bad for all oil producing nations, including Saudi Arabia, and they are bad news for the energy industry more widely." Al-Naimi went on to say the following:

> The bottom line is that Saudi Arabia would like to see a lower price. It would like to see a fair and reasonable price that will not hurt the global economic recovery, especially in emerging and developing countries, that will generate a good return for producing nations, and that will attract greater investment in the oil industry.
>
> It is clear that geopolitical tensions in the region, and concerns over supply, are helping to keep prices high.
>
> It is the perceived potential shortage of oil keeping prices high—not the reality on the ground. There is no lack of supply. There is no demand that cannot be met.
>
> [Oil] has transformed our lives and will continue to power the global economy for many decades to come. It will only do so if prices reach a more reasonable level—so it is in all our interests to do what we can to achieve this aim.[4]

The article was widely quoted all over the world. It was well received in many of the world's capitals, and the White House also indirectly expressed its pleasure.

The second project was the launch of a bimonthly eight-page newsletter, *Gulf Oil Review* (GOR), that would include solid analysis of the oil market, interviews, data, information, and more. The first issue had an exclusive interview with Al-Naimi that was widely quoted and was published on

June 11, 2012 (figure 8.1), three days before the OPEC ministerial meeting in Vienna on June 14. Al-Naimi indicated that OPEC would increase the official ceiling for the second half of the year, and he gave assurances that the market would be adequately supplied and explained that "the Kingdom's actions had helped moderate oil prices."

The newsletter was distributed free to selected influential institutions and people on a trial basis and received positive comments on its in-depth oil market analysis. The market analysis on the front page contained solid information and strong logic and explained that the oil market was well supplied, balanced, and commercial stocks were rising. It also explained that high oil prices were not supported by fundamentals and should be around $100 per barrel, the preferred price for Saudi Arabia, the Arab Gulf states, and many other producers. The United States and other industrialized countries indicated unofficially that $100 was acceptable. GOR also included some news items about Gulf countries. The last page had carefully selected data.

The campaign was successful and helped bring oil prices down. Abdulrahman H. Al-Saeed, a former adviser in the royal court, told me he felt that King Abdullah was very pleased with the campaign and its outcome.[5]

11 June 2012

Issue 1, Volume 1

Gulf Oil Review

In this issue:

• GOR Market insight: Seeing is believing
• Interview with Saudi Arabia's Minister of Petroleum Ali Naimi
• US oil independence: a boost to global supply
• Of note: energy speeches and research
• Gulf energy data

GOR market insight: Seeing is believing

• Macroeconomic worries bear down on prices
• Gulf-led OPEC output surge loosens market as stocks build
• OPEC to take wait-and-see approach

Concerns about sovereign debt in the Eurozone and global macroeconomic headwinds continue to weigh down on market sentiment and oil prices. From its peak of above $126 a barrel on 13 March, the ICE Brent crude-oil front-month contract settled at $99.47/b on 8 June. The price drop in May was particularly sharp with the front-month Brent falling by more than $17/b. The first week of June saw further declines in the oil price, ending a prolonged period of above $100/b, with front-month Brent reaching intra-day lows close to $95/b.

FIGURE 8.1. The first issue of *Gulf Oil Review*, an international publication launched by Saudi Arabia, with an interview of Ali Al-Naimi, whose goal was to moderate oil prices in part to help President Obama win his second term election.

Another factor that helped stabilize the markets in mid-2012 was the growth of shale oil production in the United States, which was beating expectations. After remaining steady near 5.5 MBD during each of the first three quarters of 2011, the EIA reported that U.S. crude oil production had surpassed 6 MBD during the first quarter of 2012. The EIA noted that the last time U.S. quarterly oil production was above 6 MBD was in 1998. (For more about shale oil and OPEC, see chapter 9.)

For Obama, one of the important developments in mid-2012 was that the price of gasoline was starting to fall, which increased his chances of being reelected. The Saudis achieved four goals in one action: helping Obama; increasing Saudi production; maintaining an image of being a responsible country whose petroleum policy takes producers and consumers alike into consideration; and bringing oil prices to Saudi Arabia's desired level (at that time) of $100 per barrel. They achieved all of this despite the political, military, and petroleum tension in the region, especially with Iran.

We can draw four major lessons from these events. First, Saudi Arabia is the most important oil country, not only in terms of its production/export level but also because it has credibility and is respected and trusted by others (energy experts, the media, and government officials). Second, sentiment plays an important role in the direction of the oil market. Third, the interpretation of information about fundamentals is critically important. Finally, cooperation and understanding between major oil countries, such as the United States and Saudi Arabia, can influence the oil market's direction.

THE IRANIAN FACTOR

In 2005, the Iranians elected a radical president, Mahmoud Ahmadinejad. He had ambitions to expand Iranian influence and what he called "Iranian culture" in the region (figure 8.2). Iran was also working to develop medium- and long-range missiles as well as nuclear technology and facilities that might lead to building weapons capabilities. Tehran was resisting international demands to stop its development of nuclear power, which might lead to manufacturing nuclear weapons. An important development in 2012 for the world oil market was the imposition of economic and energy sanctions against Iran. With international support, especially from Western countries, the UN Security Council enacted economic sanctions on oil

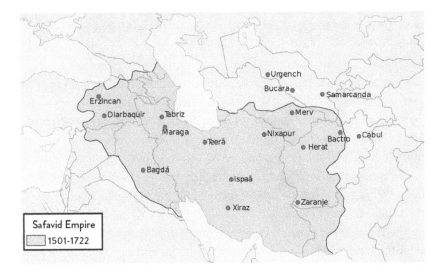

FIGURE 8.2. The Safavid Empire: Ahmadinejad called it a part of Iranian culture (by which he meant influence). *Source: Foreign Reports Bulletin*, October 19, 2010, 3.

investment and exports. In 2011, Iran's average production was about 3.6 MBD. The United States wanted to reduce Iran's oil exports significantly, but U.S. officials did not define "significantly" in concrete numbers.

The United States was lobbying oil consumers to completely stop, or to "significantly" reduce, oil purchases from Iran, and at the same time was urging oil producers to increase their production. To meet any possible supply shortage, Saudi Arabia, Kuwait, Iraq, Angola, Libya, and the United Arab Emirates increased their production. Saudi Arabia, as a general policy, had done so not to replace the Iranian oil (or anybody else's) but to satisfy market needs regardless of the reason for the shortage. Saudi Arabia had increased production at other times, such as from 2003 to 2005 because of shortages in supply caused by the U.S. invasion of Iraq, crises in Venezuela and Nigeria, and the impact of Hurricane Katrina in the United States. Saudi officials made it clear in each instance that the increase was not politically motivated. The aim of the increase was to meet demand from buyers of Saudi crude and to prevent a shortage on the global market.[6]

The Iranians, under pressure from the loss of revenue, fought back on a number of fronts, offering some of their customers deferred payments or other attractive payment methods such as barter deals and discounts. Iran also resorted to spreading lies and threatening attacks against operations at Saudi oil facilities. Their goal was to make the sanctions costly either through shortages of oil, higher oil prices, or both—a situation that would be repeated in 2019 when the United States put new sanctions in place.

On March first 2012, one Iranian media outlet reported explosions in oil pipelines in Saudi Arabia. The report was widely quoted by international media, and as a result, the price of oil rose the following day by about $7. The Ministry of Interior, the Ministry of Petroleum, and Saudi Aramco officials all denied the report, but the oil price did not drop by much once the facts became known and it became clear that the Iranian reports were false. This is an interesting case of the relationship between the oil market, the media, and sentiment.

The Iranians were also threatening, directly or indirectly, to forcefully close the Strait of Hormuz through which about 30 percent of the world's oil is exported. They also stepped up their military activities close to Saudi offshore oil fields. On August 15, 2012, the major computer system of Saudi Aramco was attacked, and 35,000 personal computers, as well as some department computers, were knocked out. Luckily the production, oil storage, pipelines, and export systems were independent of the company's main computer system, and the cyberattack did not affect operations, as had been intended. Investigations by Saudi Aramco and others found that an Iranian of U.S. nationality based in France was behind the cyberattack.

There is no doubt that the Iranians, in their attempt to fight the sanctions, were contributing to higher oil prices by creating a negative perception in many circles. But Iran was not able to affect the actual flow of oil nor its supply to the world market.

THE UNITED STATES AND OIL PRICES

The United States is a petroleum country par excellence. Since commercialization of oil in the mid-nineteenth century, the United States has been the largest oil producer and, at times, exporter and has been the center of the international oil industry for more than 150 years. Oil has made a significant contribution to U.S. economic growth and to its status as an international power. The United States is the center of innovation in oil and energy and home to the largest international petroleum companies, energy sector services firms, investment banks, and other financial institutions that are leaders in global oil and energy investment and trading.

The oil futures market was created in the United States. Currently, the New York Mercantile Exchange (NYMEX), where oil futures contracts are traded, is the world's largest. U.S. hedge funds and banks are major players in this market. Furthermore, oil is traded in U.S. dollars and that is unlikely to be challenged in the near future, despite many attempts to do so. When the oil price goes up, the majority of oil-producing states, such as the Arab Gulf states, invest a large part of their income in the U.S. markets. The amounts deposited are often much higher than their earnings from oil sales to the United States and normally involve both financial and physical assets: the purchase of U.S. government bonds, military hardware, and other commercial and noncommercial activities.

Conflicting priorities can be found at each level of government in the United States: the federal government, oil-producing states, non-oil-producing states, and consumers of energy products. The federal government looks at the overall impact of oil prices on economic growth, the balance of payments, inflation, and the environment. The oil states—Texas, Oklahoma, Alaska, New Mexico, and North Dakota—benefit from higher production and higher prices, and they lobby for lower government regulation and lower taxes on oil production. States that do not produce oil, such as Maine, New York, Massachusetts, and Vermont, tend to be unhappy about higher crude prices. And the American public does not like higher gasoline or heating oil prices, especially in states where gasoline taxes are very high.

Through different types of taxes, local counties, the states, and the federal government benefit greatly from the oil industry, oil trading, and oil consumption. This extends to the activities of U.S. companies around the world that have global operations and related manufacturers and service and trading companies, among many other businesses. In the tenth century, the Islamic Abbasid Empire covered a large part of the world from India in the East to West Africa. Caliph Harun al-Rashid was the fifth caliph of the empire and ruled from his capital in Baghdad. It is said that he looked up at the clouds in the sky and stated that "you can rain wherever you desire, but in the end the taxes from the income you generate will end in my treasury." This is true today to some degree of Washington and the oil industry, even though government officials and intellectuals do not like to admit it.

Petroleum and American politics are tightly intertwined. On a public level, the oil industry is largely seen in negative terms, which differs from the attitude in many countries, including those that must import 100 percent of their oil needs, such as Japan and Korea. Americans' negative picture of the oil industry began to develop in the twentieth century with John D. Rockefeller and his company Standard Oil, followed by the Seven Sisters (the big seven international oil companies), OPEC, and recent increasing concerns about climate change.

During the five decades following World War II, many people in the U.S. oil business had a strong influence on the political establishment, at both national and state levels, especially in the oil-producing states. This kind of power is natural in a free democratic country, but the public viewed their influence in a negative way; it was generally believed that the industry was corrupt and was able to manipulate political power. The 1980s television series *Dallas*, about a fictional Texas oil dynasty, served to reinforce this image of the oil business as corrupt and greedy. *Dallas* was one of the most widely watched series in the history of U.S. television.

On the international political level, the turning point for the American public, politicians, and the media took place in 1973 with the Arab-Israeli war and the Arab oil embargo. These events were blamed for the long lines at gas stations (regardless of the true reason) and increases in the price of gasoline and heating oil. Crude oil prices increased more than fivefold in a short time period, from $3.00 in 1972 to $17 in 1976. Price increases affected the average American consumer, but what was more damaging was the feeling that it had touched upon the dignity of the United States. The U.S. government, the media, and a large section of the public sided with Israel against the Arabs. In addition, Ahmed Zaki Yamani, the Saudi minister of petroleum at the time, and other Arab officials were publicly threatening the West with the possibility of a further cut in Saudi production and exports. The 1973 Arab oil embargo created a lasting impression among many Americans of a worrisome dependence on Middle Eastern oil. President Richard Nixon launched Project Independence, and subsequent U.S. presidents have made reducing dependence on imported oil a top priority, especially oil from the Middle East.

Equally important to the American image of oil was the Iranian revolution of 1978–1979, which reduced Iran's production from almost 6 MBD in 1976 to about 3 MBD in 1979 and to less than 1.3 MBD in 1981. The price of oil more than doubled from 1977, reaching more than $35/BBL by 1979, and taking U.S. diplomats hostage inside the American embassy in Tehran was a major political issue for the U.S. political establishment and the public at large.

Another development during the 1970s and after was the steady decline in U.S. crude oil production, from its peak of nearly 10 MBD in 1970 to 5 MBD in 2008. At the same time, U.S. net oil imports were steadily increasing, from 2 MBD in 1970 to more than 10 MBD in 2005. Security of the oil supply and dependency on imported oil became common political narratives, but these two concepts have little meaning within the oil market, especially after the dissociation between upstream and downstream in the international oil market and the expanded use of the futures oil market. When there is a shortage of international oil supply and higher prices, poor importing countries are affected more significantly than are rich countries like the U.S. When oil prices go up in free economies without price controls, everyone feels the pain equally, even if the country is an oil exporter such as the United States (currently), Norway, Canada, and the United Kingdom.

In addition, during the 1970s the assumption in the United States and worldwide was that the world was running out of oil and other natural resources. A report by the Club of Rome titled "Limits to Growth" was widely circulated, and it pointed in that direction as did other reports and studies (some of which were from U.S. government agencies). No wonder every movement of crude oil and gasoline prices became a domestic political issue during election years. American politicians, as well as some activists and writers, developed slogans based more on political rhetoric than on reality:

1. "American addiction to foreign oil," as if oil was a drug, harmful and being used without any benefits.
2. "Growing thirst for foreign oil," as if the people of the United States were different from the rest of the world in their need for oil.
3. "Reduce dependence on imported oil," without explaining how, or what the consequences would be.
4. "Reduce dependence on oil imports from the Middle East or from unstable nations," as if these countries were forcing American oil companies to buy oil from them absent economic or business considerations. Imagine what the reaction would be if these countries actually decided to stop or reduce their exports to the United States.

George W. Bush came up with a new slogan for public consumption during the 2006 midterm election: "Some of the nations we rely on for oil have unstable governments or fundamental differences with the United States. . . . It creates a national security issue when we're held hostage for energy by foreign nations that may not like us."[7] It is interesting to note that Iraq was under United States occupation at that time and the other Arab Gulf states were very stable and were close allies of the United States.

President Donald J. Trump sent conflicting signals on oil matters to OPEC and the Arab Gulf states during the midterm elections in 2018. Although the U.S. alliance with Saudi Arabia and the Arab Gulf states was a key plank of his Middle Eastern policy, Trump made it known that oil and gas issues were no longer important to the United States because its own oil production has soared in recent years. After the attacks against Saudi oil facilities at Abqaiq and Khurais on September 14, 2019, Trump declared that the United States stood ready to help Saudi Arabia defend its oil installations but added that it was not about needing Saudi oil. "We don't need Middle Eastern oil and gas and, in fact, we have very few tankers there, but will help our allies," he tweeted.

It is important to differentiate between political rhetoric, conspiracies, and facts when discussing oil and U.S. politics. Beliefs in *conspiracy* are commonplace in the United States, in the Arab world, and beyond. There is a general belief in the Arab world, at the public level and even among some intellectuals and policy makers, that the United States dictates oil prices and production levels to Saudi Arabia, Kuwait, and the United Arab Emirates, among others. Officials in Iran and in some other countries believe in these conspiracies and consider them to be facts.[8]

Furthermore, some high-ranking U.S. government officials and journalists have claimed that there is a U.S.-Saudi oil conspiracy against Russia and Iran, among others. In the 1980s, Caspar Weinberger, U.S. secretary of defense during the Reagan administration, attempted to give the administration credit for the collapse of the Soviet Union. Weinberger claimed that Reagan and King Fahd engineered the oil price collapse in the mid-1980s to weaken the Soviet Union, which earned its hard currency from oil sales at that time. Weinberger was not alone, many Americans, and indeed even Russians, claimed this as a fact.[9]

This simple conspiracy idea lacks any truth or understanding of the oil market or Saudi oil policy and behavior during that period. To keep oil prices from falling, Saudi Arabia reduced oil production from about 10 MBD in 1980 to 2.5 MBD some time in 1985. When Saudi Arabia tried to regain part of its market share, it adopted a system of netback pricing, increasing production to about 5 MBD some months into 1985 without causing the oil price to collapse. In fact, the price collapsed because other OPEC producers adopted the same marking system and increased their production. King Fahd fired Minister Yamani because this policy led to the collapse in oil prices; he might not have done so if there was a conspiracy (chapter 1).

Another conspiracy theory that was common in the United States in the 1980s contradicts the previous one. It stated that when the price of oil fell below $10 in 1986, President Reagan sent Vice President George H. W. Bush to Saudi Arabia to discuss bringing the price up. Before he left the United States, Bush spoke of the importance of oil "price stability." This was interpreted as the United States wanting higher oil prices and that Bush would pressure the Saudis to take action. Some linked the visit to the newly suggested price of $18/BBL, which would help American oil companies and petroleum-producing states (such as Texas, Bush's home state). Hisham Nazer, the minister of planning at the time, told me more than once that he accompanied Bush during his visit from the day of his arrival to the day of his departure. He also attended all the meetings with Bush and wrote a report to King Fahd about the visit and the meetings. Nazer made it clear many times that Bush never discussed the oil price with King Fahd or with any other Saudi official.[10]

Conspiracies aside, an important aspect of the relationship between U.S. politics and oil is linked to domestic prices of heating oil and gasoline. U.S. secretary of energy Bill Richardson visited Saudi Arabia in February of 2000 when oil prices were beginning to rise above the level of the previous five years. One topic of discussion was the U.S. government's plan to release oil from the strategic petroleum reserve to bring prices down. Richardson admitted to Prince Saud al-Faisal, minister of foreign affairs at the time, that it had to do with the U.S. election. Vice President Al Gore was running against the Republican candidate George W. Bush, and Bush was critical of the idea of using energy prices and the market for political purposes.[11] However, Bush used oil prices during his second term presidential campaign as discussed previously.

During the midterm election in 2018, President Trump pushed for lower oil prices—meaning gasoline—and he succeeded, but he used completely different methods. In the middle of June 2018, the oil price was about $75 and the gasoline price in the United States was more than $3.50 in some states. Trump was worried that the Republican Party might lose the majority in both houses of Congress. To deliver his messages to OPEC, Trump used Twitter many times instead of direct and confidential communications (as other presidents had). He even used undiplomatic and forceful words against OPEC and some of its members. For example, on April 20 he said, "Looks like OPEC is at it again . . . Oil prices are artificially Very High! No good and will not be accepted!" And on July 4 he tweeted this: "The OPEC Monopoly must remember that gas prices are up . . . they are driving prices higher as the United States defends many of their members for very little $'s. This must be a two-way street. REDUCE PRICING NOW!"

Other important reasons led to production increases in the second half of 2018, including high oil prices, a tight oil market, and expectations of demand growth. More important, however, was Trump's intention to force Iranian oil exports down "to zero." The OPEC+ group, led by Saudi Arabia and Russia, decided in June 2018 to increase their production by 1.2 MBD. Saudi Arabian production in November rose to more than 11.3 MBD, its highest ever. OPEC+ later found out that oil supply was larger than demand, commercial stocks were growing, and oil prices almost collapsed (going below $50, the lowest in two years). The information decision makers based their decision on had been inaccurate or misleading, and misinterpreting this information led to making bad judgments. Trump's tweets and his declared intention to force Iranian oil exports down to zero did not materialize after the United States granted exemptions to eight countries. Iranian production fell, but not even close to zero.

When Trump first began tweeting about OPEC and oil prices in 2018, the market took his statements seriously. Prices fell by as much as $8 in one day after one of his tweets. However, by the end of 2018 and in 2019 the market no longer took him seriously.[12] Trump changed his tone toward the end of 2018 and began to use more diplomatic language in tweets directed at Saudi Arabia and OPEC. On November 12, 2018, Trump said, "Hopefully Saudi Arabia and OPEC will not be cutting oil production. Oil prices should be much lower based on supply!" In another tweet, Trump said, "Hopefully OPEC will be keeping oil flow as is, not restricted." Later in his presidency Trump stopped tweeting and spoke discreetly with Crown Prince Mohammed bin Salman about the oil market.

Since the early 1970s, almost all U.S. presidents have used oil as an election card for their own benefit or the benefit of their party. But basic oil policy, espoused by the Department of Energy and the State Department, among others, is always consistent with long-term U.S. interests, such as the availability of oil supply, the availability of production capacity, adequate strategic petroleum reserves, protecting the environment, protecting and expanding the interests of U.S. businesses and oil companies, and having close and coordinated relationships with oil-producing and oil-consuming countries such as the Arab Gulf states, especially on professional and business levels. Privately, especially at the middle management level, most U.S. officials are logical and understand the oil market very well, and their decisions go beyond politics.

Therefore, the question is: Do American decision makers want or have in mind a price target for oil? The answer is simultaneously yes and no. During election years the price of heating oil or gasoline becomes a public issue, and the oil price becomes very important. After an election, oil prices become less important. At times, American officials may express concern about the impact of high oil prices on global economic growth, including growth of the U.S. economy. If prices are very low, officials may speak of the need to protect the U.S. domestic industry and "stabilize the oil market." In both cases, their comments are very general.

U.S. officials do not normally speak publicly about a specific oil price. Even in closed meetings, they may speak about a range but not a specific number. However, these ranges, or "about" as some American officials phrase it, are a moving target. To a great degree, they reflect different and even conflicting U.S. interests. When the oil price collapsed in 1998, the Clinton administration was pleased that Mexico was working with Saudi Arabia and Venezuela, among others, to push prices higher. And the United States did not complained to Norway, a member of the OECD, NATO, and the IEA, about reducing oil production and working with Saudi Arabia to manage the oil market.[13]

Whenever prices fell significantly, through private communication the United States would "understand" (but not directly and not through public statements) any effort to push them up. When oil prices rose, except in an election year, they would express their concern about the possible negative impact on economic growth. Most of the time the U.S. position and policy about the oil market has been in line with many oil-producing countries, such as the Arab Gulf countries and Mexico, and with oil-consuming countries.

During the last forty years or so, when U.S. decision makers have been concerned about market stability, they have communicated with Saudi Arabia directly or through their petroleum attachés at U.S. embassies. On these occasions, U.S. officials speak privately and without referring to a specific number. Here are some examples.

1. When the oil price collapsed in 1998 and began to recover in 2000, U.S. officials were comfortable with a price of "around" $20 per barrel. This was also the feeling of Saudis and the majority of OPEC countries.
2. When OPEC created a range and target oil price in 2002 (the range was $22 to $28 and the target was $25), U.S. officials did not have any problem with it either.
3. When oil prices were above $40 per barrel in 2004, the United States expressed displeasure for fear it might go higher, and they asked why OPEC was not defending its price target.
4. When the price reached $100 in 2007, the United States wanted to see it go lower and began speaking with their close allies, asking them to do something about it because of the concern that these high prices might harm economic growth and contribute to higher inflation.
5. In 2012, when the oil price was again above $100, the United States lobbied Saudi Arabia and others to help bring it down. Washington's acceptable price was "around $100 per barrel." This new preferred price continued until the collapse of 2014–2016. During this time, the United States did not express any preference for a certain price, even though the engineered price collapse targeted U.S. shale oil producers, among others.
6. When oil prices rose to around $75 in June 2018, President Trump began to tweet, attacking OPEC and Russia and asking for a lower price.
7. When the price collapsed below zero in April 2020, President Trump directly and strongly intervened to bring it higher (chapter 11).

OIL AND U.S. DECISION MAKERS

For U.S. decision makers, oil is not just a commodity that operates along economic rules and logic and by common international trade practices. It is an extension of power and influence with a clear geopolitical dimension.

Oil has been used to advance U.S. power and influence as well as to punish its enemies. It is part of "vital national security" and "national interest" issues. Only in the United States does the White House National Security Council, the State Department, the CIA, and even the Defense Department share involvement in international energy policy and relations.

For decades, American oil companies have worked hand in hand with Washington, taking advantage of and serving U.S. power in many parts of the world, including in the Middle East and South America. Since World War II, the only time oil has been used against the United States by oil producers to attain political goals was during the Arab-Israeli war of 1973. The so-called Arab Embargo was imposed to change the U.S. government's strong support for Israel. However, the United States has used oil for political ends a number of times against Iran, Libya, Iraq, Venezuela, and Russia. Measures have included reducing or even cutting off oil imports into the United States, and preventing U.S. and non-U.S. oil companies from investing in a particular country or prohibiting the transfer of U.S. petroleum-related technologies to a country, U.S. sanctions have been applied to third parties, countries, and companies.[14]

The United States has become the world's largest oil producer and a net oil exporter.[15] This leads us to look at the relationship between the United States and Saudi Arabia, the second largest producer, the largest oil exporter, and the only country with meaningful spare production capacity. Saudi Arabia plays an important role in international oil management within OPEC and OPEC+ and has significant influence in international energy-related organizations.

THE U.S.-SAUDI PETROLEUM RELATIONSHIP

In the past seventy years, the United States has had a strong and close relationship with the majority of OPEC countries through trade, investments, and information exchanges, but U.S. relations with Iran, Iraq, Libya, and Venezuela have had ups and downs. Saudi Arabia is the most important petroleum-producing country for the United States, and indeed for the world, for a number of reasons. First, the general relationship between Saudi Arabia and the United States has been very close for more than ninety years. Second, the United States recognizes the importance of Saudi Arabia not only because of its vast oil reserves, production, and exports but also for the role it plays in ensuring market stability. The United States recognizes that the Saudi oil industry is well-managed. And finally, Saudi Arabia has been the only oil producer with meaningful spare production capacity, and this is essential for oil market stability.

The personalities of decision makers are also important and continue to influence the direction and closeness of the relationship between the two countries. This close cooperation was initiated by a visionary man named Ibn Saud, who saw an opportunity to work with the United States. At the end of World War I, the United States was emerging as a world power on all fronts, and Ibn Saud welcomed U.S. financial help and investments. The Americans were looking for new opportunities and relationships in the Middle East, and oil pioneers were looking for new adventures abroad. With the support of the U.S. government, these Americans were willing to take the risk of oil exploration in Saudi Arabia and other countries. In May 1933, the first Saudi oil concession was signed, and production began five years later. In the decades following the end of World War II in 1945, the Middle East witnessed wars, conflicts, and ideological revolutions, but the relationship between the United States and Saudi Arabia grew stronger and went far beyond their interests in the petroleum sector. Today no other country in the region is a better U.S. ally than Saudi Arabia, and it is the same for Saudi Arabia, but to a much lesser extent.

When Saudi Arabia decided to invest in overseas refining and distribution in the second half of the 1980s, the United States was its first choice. U.S. companies have large petroleum and petrochemical investments in Saudi Arabia and supply petroleum equipment and training to the Saudis. In 1988, Saudi Arabia and the United States established an energy working group and a technical team that met annually to share information and methods of cooperation on bilateral and international issues. Prince Abdulaziz bin Salman, the energy minister and an adviser to the minister of petroleum at that time, suggested creating the bilateral Technical Committee, and he continues to head the Saudi side of the committee today. This was the first working group Saudi Arabia had participated in with another country. By exchanging information and establishing personal relationships, this working group proved to be very useful, especially during major oil crises. For example, after the Iraqi invasion of Kuwait in August 1990, the international oil market lost more than 4 MBD of oil in one day. Thanks to this personal relationship and daily technical and expert exchanges, the international oil market suffered no supply shortage. Oil prices initially moved higher, rising above $35 per barrel at one point, but this spike was short-lived. Officials from both governments coordinated their communications to the media and to the market.[16] Supply shortages during the following years were dealt with by the energy officials of both countries and the technical working groups.

There has been clear coordination between the two countries on international issues such as climate change and at international forums including the G20 and the International Energy Forum (IEF). The petroleum relationship between Saudi Arabia and the United States has been stable and steady for many decades, and individual personalities have had an impact on this stability. Throughout the last four decades, six types of personalities—kings, presidents, foreign officials, and oil/energy ministers supported by technical experts—have helped to nurture U.S.–Saudi Arabia petroleum ties. King Fahd, President Ronald Reagan, and President George W. Bush were close allies and friends and agreed on almost all issues, especially on the political side. King Abdullah and three U.S. presidents had their differences, but they also enjoyed a good relationship on oil-related issues. Saudi Arabia valued the relationship with the United States and came to Obama's aid when the U.S. president sought Saudi help to bring down oil prices in 2012. President Trump and King Salman and Crown Prince Mohammed bin Salman also were close and held similar opinions on many issues, including oil. President Joe Biden and some officials within his administration have expressed how important U.S.–Saudi Arabia relations are, and Crown Prince Mohammed bin Salman said that the U.S.–Saudi Arabia relationship is strong despite their differences.

Ali Al-Naimi was minister of petroleum from 1995 to 2016 and dealt with six U.S. secretaries of energy. He had excellent personal relationships with three of them (Bill Richardson, 1998–2001; Sam Bodman, 2005–2009; and Ernest Moniz, 2013– 2017). These close relationships enabled cooperation on issues related to the oil market, information exchange, collaboration in science and research, climate change, and energy conservation.

Khalid al-Falih, Saudi minister of energy (2016–2019), was a friend of U.S. secretary of energy Rick Perry; they both had studied at Texas A&M University. Prince Abdulaziz bin Salman (Saudi energy minister since 2019) had a close relationship with U.S secretary of energy Dan Brouillette, and now works with the U.S. Department of Energy secretary Jennifer

Granholm. Soon after her confirmation, Prince Abdulaziz bin Salman had a lengthy discussion with Secretary Granholm. They focused on their close energy relationship when it came to renewables, conservation, and climate change but did not talk about the international oil market.

In addition to relationships between heads of state and ministers, the personal relationships of professional and technical people who are concerned parties are very important. In the end, they are the people who conduct the needed studies, make recommendations, and deliver and implement policy objectives. Professionals from the Department of Energy and the State Department in the United States, and sometimes the White House, and from the Ministry of Energy in Saudi Arabia are fundamental to this work.

Majid al-Moneef, the secretary-general of the Supreme Committee of Hydrocarbon Affairs of Saudi Arabia and the kingdom's governor to OPEC from 2003 to 2012, stated that "the U.S. administrations and the Saudi leaderships since the end of WWII realized and appreciated the central role of oil market stability and supply security and based their mutual relations on such. Despite the testing of such relations during the Arab oil embargo of 1973 and the generally negative U.S attitude towards OPEC, the two countries have maintained close cooperation and consultations in oil matters for the past 75 years."[17] Yet, at the public level, mirror images about each other and oil policies largely reflect negative opinions that are being fed to the public by some politicians, interest groups, and some in the media.

The American public expresses little concern about the U.S. petroleum relationship with Saudi Arabia until the price of gasoline rises. However, many of the elite, or the political establishment, generally tend to have a negative view of Saudi Arabia and its oil policy. They accuse Saudi Arabia, together with the rest of OPEC, of market manipulation, greed, and causing harm to U.S. and Western economic interests. OPEC is described as a "cartel" even though this description is not correct, or is at least debatable. The No Oil Producing and Exporting Cartels Act (NOPEC) has been introduced (without success) in the U.S. Congress eight times between 2000 and 2021, with the purpose of punishing OPEC and its member countries for deciding the production level of its members. I do not understand what they want. Are they after a free market? The majority of U.S. oil-producing states and companies could not stand the heat, as we saw in 2020. Have they studied the long-term impact of an unmanaged oil market on almost all aspects? I doubt it. I think this legislation is driven by personal and political interests.

Some U.S. politicians and writers claim, from time to time, that the United States depends on Gulf oil and therefore must defend the region militarily, with additional costs to the U.S. taxpayer. After the collapse of the Soviet Union in the 1990s, many individuals and institutions began to question the importance and high cost of defending the Arab Gulf countries and protecting the region's oil export routes. It was hoped that Russia and other oil-producing former Soviet countries would supply any needed oil to the United States. They argue that importing oil from the Arab world costs U.S. taxpayers $40–50 billion per year. For example, in a 1996 report, Citizen Action, a consumer activist group, said that the real cost of each barrel of oil imported from the Gulf was about $90. At the time, the price of oil was about $20.

On the Saudi side, in normal times the public is not concerned about the petroleum relationship with the United States. However, the leftists, the Arab nationalists, and members of religious/political movements express a negative view regarding the motivation behind U.S. oil policy. They believe the U.S. policy is based purely on self-interest and is harmful to Arab and Muslim interests. Some economists and public figures also believe that oil reserves should be preserved for future generations and that the kingdom should limit its production and aim for higher oil prices. They argue that Saudi Arabia should not heed the calls of the Americans and other consumers for moderate oil prices and increasing oil production.[18]

Most decision makers and professionals at all levels understand and value the special petroleum relationship between the two countries, but some groups in both countries have more extreme views. They believe that oil is the cornerstone, or even the only reason, for the U.S. interest in the region and for maintaining a strong alliance on the political and military front with Saudi Arabia. In Saudi Arabia, at certain points in time, some decision makers were in favor of opening Saudi oil and gas investments to American companies. They also wanted to see more Saudi oil going to the U.S. market in the belief that this would strengthen the U.S.–Saudi Arabia relationship. Still others believe that the U.S. interest in Saudi Arabia, the Arab Gulf states, and the Middle East region is not limited to oil but extends into other policy areas.

Let's look at some of these other factors. The United States is Israel's strongest supporter—financially, economically, politically, and militarily—and has a significant interest in Israel's security and military superiority over other countries in the region. This, by extension, means that the United States has a regional interest in the Middle East. And that interest is reinforced by another area of interest—the wealth of historical and religious sites, especially biblical ones. Some Evangelical Christians, who are very powerful politically, believe that the Second Coming of the Messiah will happen in the Middle East, and therefore the United States has to maintain a presence there to support this "coming."

The Middle East is also a region in a state of transition, and regional powers such as Iran and Turkey aspire to become dominant forces that might threaten and weaken U.S. interests in the region. Equally important is the concern that any power vacuum in the region would likely be filled by Russia or China, as was recently the case in Syria. These worries were made clear in the U.S. military buildup in the Gulf in 2019 and 2020, even though the United States is a net oil exporter.[19]

U.S. policy (political, economic, and military) has a strong impact on the international oil market, including oil prices. For example, in 2018 when President Trump decided to put in place full sanctions on Iranian oil exports (down to zero, as he said), oil prices began to rise. Later, however, the U.S. administration granted waivers to eight countries and prices started to go down. During the CERAWeek conference in April 2019, a high-ranking Trump official said Washington would look at Iranian oil sanctions and falling Venezuelan production within the status of the international oil market, which meant oil prices. According to an oil expert who was at the conference, the United States is utilizing supply management to indirectly balance the market and influence oil prices and to control how much oil Iran and Venezuela may export.

During the OPEC+ Ministerial Monitoring Committee meeting in Baku, Azerbaijan, on March 18, 2019, then Russian energy minister Alexander Novak (now deputy prime minister) accused the United States of a lack of transparency and having a damaging sanctions policy on Iran and Venezuela. He said that it was "having negative effects on the global energy market, hindering long-term planning, and confusing reality in investment decisions . . . planning even a few months ahead is tough due to possible sanction-related volatility. . . . The country imposing sanctions was doing so in order to promote its own goods."[20] He was referring to the United States without mentioning it by name.

THE UNITED STATES AND THE FUTURE OF THE INTERNATIONAL OIL MARKET

Leaving rhetoric and short-term politics aside, U.S. oil policy and the future of the international oil market, including oil prices, will be one of the most interesting stories in the history of oil. Currently, the United States is the largest oil producer, a position that it lost in 1973, and it is exporting more and more oil and more liquefied natural gas (LNG). It is competing with other producers in the open international oil market. The United States under democratic leadership is also making climate change a top priority at home and abroad.

U.S. oil products and LNG exports began slowing down in 2020 and 2021, but they are likely to continue on an upward trajectory until 2025, if not beyond (especially if oil prices stay above $60 per barrel, which is the most likely case). The United States is a major oil exporter and importer, and its oil exports in 2020 were almost 4 MBD, making it the second or third largest oil exporter. This is a big change for the United States and for the global market. The United States is exporting oil to more than thirty countries all over the world and importing oil from more than twenty countries. Oil is becoming an important part of American trade and the import/export balance. U.S. crude production is largely light oil, but U.S. refiners need heavy crude grades, which is likely to lead to higher U.S. exports. U.S. decision makers should understand now the meaning of a truly open, free, competitive, transparent, and well-managed international oil market.

Another important development in 2019 was the beginning of U.S. oil flows into Rotterdam, the European oil hub. This is likely to lead to U.S. oil becoming one of the grades to be added to the Brent Blend, the global benchmark. As the United States becomes more dominant in the international oil market, it will need stable oil prices for U.S. oil consumers and oil producers. A stable oil market cannot be achieved without constructive involvement.

The United States has done a fair amount of management in the oil market in the past century through the Texas Railroad Commission and the Seven Sisters, but also through national regulations such as price fixing, export and import controls, and levies on imported oil and the uses of the

Strategic Petroleum Reserves. In the last forty years, U.S. administrations did not object to oil producers working together to manage the market as long as prices did not rise to a high level that might hurt the economy or make American consumers unhappy. The U.S. economy is very sensitive to high and low oil prices and sharp volatility.

In 2012, when oil prices were rising, the issue of spare production capacity was very important. Some U.S. officials suggested the idea that spare production capacity should and could be a shared responsibility, and not limited to Saudi Arabia. No detailed plans were discussed, but the idea was considered. Now that the U.S. status in the petroleum market has changed, the idea of shared spare production capacity should be reconsidered by all the major players, including the United States. With the growth of U.S. production, a clear economic and financial gain was achieved. For example, different estimates were put forward about the impact of shale oil on U.S. economic growth and its contribution to GDP, but it could be as high as 1 percent in some years.

The emergence of the United States as the world's largest oil producer provides leverage both in its bilateral relations with trading partners and in the international arena. Oil price movements will have an impact on U.S. oil producers, oil consumers, and the economy at large, and the United States will have to become more integrated and more sensitive to developments in the oil market. If there is a shortage or an oversupply of oil, or if prices move too high, the U.S. economy and consumers will be affected unless the government decides to halt oil exports or fix domestic oil prices (as it did in the 1970s). This outcome is unlikely, although some members of Congress have been talking about it since early 2020. Managing this important shift in the status of the United States as a global petroleum power and adapting its policy accordingly calls for enlightened leadership. Empty rhetoric and political posturing are counterproductive when assuming a leading role in the international oil market.

Top U.S. decision makers, especially the president and the secretary of state, have usually not been involved in international petroleum issues unless there was a major energy crisis or it was an election year. When they did get involved, they did so at the bilateral level rather than through international collective efforts. Occasionally, when pressured by friends and allies, they sometimes became involved in collective work through the IEF, the IEA, and at the G20. Each president's involvement reflected his personality and beliefs, and the political, economic, and petroleum circumstances of the time. Now the United States must change its stance because it is one of the most important players in the oil market.

This period is different from any time in the past in almost every dimension, and Americans need to shed their old method and engage in international collective actions, including the possibility of continuous direct management and participation to stabilize the market. This became clear when the industry faced its biggest crisis in many decades in 2020.

Some signs of a change of approach have been noted, but they are only visible to those who follow these matters closely. In the second half of 2019, for the first time the U.S. government proposed a candidate for the position of secretary-general of the IEF. Joseph McMonigle worked with the U.S. Department of Energy when Spencer Abraham was the secretary of energy (2001–2005), and he has worked in the private sector as well. Joseph McMonigle began his term in 2020, and he has been active, participating in a clear and positive way in the debates on energy issues.[21]

Another sign of changing attitudes by U.S. officials toward the international oil market was clear in the answer of Secretary Dan Brouillette in 2020 to a question regarding OPEC and its desire to have a meeting to cut production. He said, "we're not concerned about the decision that OPEC may make, and whatever decision they make will be good for them and we appreciate what they are doing."[22] However, Washington expressed major concerns a few weeks later. When oil prices started to collapse during the second week of March, President Trump thought it was good for American consumers, but members of Congress from oil-producing states pressured the administration to doing something. Later on Trump concluded that these low prices would harm the U.S. economy and hurt his bid for reelection. During election years, many things become extra sensitive and important. The "I can do it alone" thinking and policies of Trump, including an aversion to international cooperation, began to shift for the first time, and Washington discovered the importance of collective global action.

President Trump called King Salman and Crown Prince Mohammed bin Salman as well as Russian president Putin, asking them to work together, alongside others including the United States, to bring stability back to the oil market (i.e., increase prices). More important, President Trump told them that the United States was willing to contribute to any production cuts and asked other non-OPEC+ countries to contribute more (chapter 11).

Jason Bordoff, the founding director of the Center on Global Energy Policy at Columbia University, had told me that the new status of the United States as the largest oil producer and a major exporter would undoubtedly bringing some economic and geopolitical benefits, but it also exposes the United States to new risks and vulnerabilities. The March/April oil crisis proved that he was right, and the United States played an important role in global management by working directly with other producers. Although the method of participation may change over time, President Trump established a new direction for the United States in international oil management. No future U.S president will be able to easily reverse this trend toward increasing integration of the United States in the international energy market. When oil prices were rising in March 2021, the Indian government attacked OPEC openly and decided to increase its oil imports from the United States and reduce them from the Arab Gulf states.

The new administration of President Joe Biden is focused on national and international environmental issues that include restricting exploration and transportation of oil and gas on federal land. The Biden administration has also rejoining the Paris Agreement to address climate change. Climate change issues are global and need collective international cooperation. These policies are likely get support from the public, but the economic side of this could be more difficult.

Oil prices might increase to $100 per barrel, or likely more, in the near future because of increasing demand and lower energy investments. Petroleum companies, oil-producing states, and other organizations may lead a political or legal campaign against the Biden administration (some have already begun doing this). Added to all of this is the fact that many countries, although appearing to act in support of measures that tackle climate change, will simply act based on their national economic interests.

The challenges are global and the solutions are not easy. In mid-February 2021, when a cold wave hit some southern states, leading to partial collapse of clean energy and the electricity supply and high gasoline prices, the new administration faced its first challenge. It is clear that energy is a highly important and highly complex issue.

Chapter Nine

ALI AL-NAIMI

The Road to Doha

The first half of 2014 was normal. Oil prices were similar to what they had been since early 2011 (around $100 per barrel), a level that was considered reasonable and acceptable to producers and rich consumers, including the United States and Europe. Prices fluctuated from one day to the next due to the usual mixture of geopolitics and market forces, included oil sanctions against Iran, the possibility of Israel attacking Iran, and Iranian threats to close the Strait of Hormuz. The major talk was about the rise in U.S. shale oil production, the availability of production capacity to make up for the loss of Iranian barrels, and the status of Libyan production. However, the market was about to change direction. A snowball had been forming, which led to a dramatic fall in oil prices. This was not due to fundamental forces alone but was mixed with negative sentiment, which played the larger role.

The main player in these events was one important decision maker. Ali Al-Naimi, the Saudi minister of energy (1995–2016), was beginning to change his stance regarding the oil market, OPEC, and Saudi oil policy. This shift in thinking began in 2012–2013, and there were four reasons for it.

First, some people within Saudi Arabia, including at the Ministry of Energy, thought Saudi Arabia's policy was protecting the interest of some high-cost oil producers, such as U.S. shale oil, and Russia, Canada, and Brazil. These oil producers were increasing their production because of high oil prices. Personally, I did not see anything wrong with that increase, as long as it didn't directly hurt Saudi Arabia, especially in terms of its income, and stable oil production.

Second, some reports were claiming that Saudi Arabia had lost its market leadership. For example, in February 2012, Ergo, an oil and gas consultancy, issued a report titled "The Waning Era of Saudi Oil Dominance: Current Challenges and Future Threats to Saudi Arabia's Influence over the Oil Market."[1] I gave it to Al-Naimi, who read it with great interest.

Third, Saudi oil consumption (products and crude) was growing at an alarming annual rate of about 6 percent, more than double the world average. This was a concern for Saudi officials as well as many international oil experts. In December 2011, the Royal Institute of International Affairs (Chatham House), a London-based think tank, published a study on this subject. It concluded that Saudi Arabia's oil exports would decline significantly within a few years because of increasing domestic consumption. Saudi Arabia needed either to increase production to keep its exports steady or slow unsustainable growth in domestic consumption, which was difficult at that time.[2]

Fourth (and very important), Al-Naimi believed that expensive oil, such as shale oil, could not survive at low oil prices. If the oil prices went to $80 per barrel, not only would investments stop but the production of expensive oil would decline, and the fall in production would be deeper if prices fell to $60 or $50 per barrel. An important oil expert said that shale oil producers could operate even if oil prices fell to $45 per barrel; Al-Naimi was unhappy, but he dismissed that opinion. Al-Naimi was not the only oilman who believed in the negative impact of low oil prices on shale oil and other high-cost oil production. The International Energy Agency (IEA) reported in October 2014 that oil prices below $80/BBL would threaten about 2.6 MBD of global production (table 9.1).

Al-Naimi was about eighty years old and had been in the ministry for around twenty years, and he was unwilling to lead an international campaign to manage the market. King Abdullah was also getting old and not in good health (he was over ninety at the time); he had complete trust in Al-Naimi and left oil policy to his minister. In addition, Prince Saud al-Faisal, the Saudi minister of foreign affairs who used to have a strong say in Saudi oil policy, was not in good health and had lost interest in oil issues. For the first time in his career as minister of energy, Al-Naimi had a high

TABLE 9.1
Low oil prices and estimated production decline

Sector Output (threat at sub-$80/BBL)	Output (thousands of B/D)
Deepwater crude (125m+)	650
Canadian synthetics	250
U.S. light tight oil (incl. condensate)	150
Nigeria onshore-shallow water	200
Russia conventional onshore	160
Indonesia onshore-shallow water	150
China onshore	135
Malaysia shallow water	85
U.S. conventional onshore	80
UK shallow water	75
Other conventional	665
Total	2,600

Source: International Energy Agency, "IEA Monthly Oil Market Report," October 2014.

level of freedom and was able to make decisions as he saw fit. He had more freedom than any other Saudi energy minister had enjoyed.

Some time, during the second quarter of 2014, Al-Naimi asked Saudi Aramco's Department of Planning to prepare a study listing different options for Saudi Arabia's oil production and its future status in the oil market. They presented four options for the kingdom's future production and exports:

1. Saudi Arabia could play the role of swing producer to keep oil prices at a certain level by reducing production when needed. But Saudi Arabia might lose market share and even lose control of oil prices.
2. Saudi Arabia could retain market share by increasing production in line with the rise in global demand.
3. Saudi Arabia could fix oil production at the existing level of production at the time, which was 9 MBD.
4. Saudi Arabian oil exports could be fixed at a certain level and not go below it. The number discussed was 7 MBD as an export floor.

After a long discussion, Al-Naimi decided to adopt the fourth option (fixing the floor for oil exports) and mix it with the second option (increasing production and exports gradually).

This meeting was not attended by the ministry's regular OPEC and international market team. OPEC was not given any role during the discussion. Neither were the Saudi Ministry of Finance and the Ministry of Economics and Planning consulted nor informed. The minister of finance, a Saudi Aramco board member, learned of the decision one year later during Aramco's board meeting in Seoul, Korea, on April 20, 2015. The minister of finance was not happy with falling government income, but he trusted Al-Naimi's judgment.[3]

THE SNOWBALL

That decision was made when the price was over $100/BBL. Nobody knew about it, so it had no impact on the market. However, by September 2014 the oil price fell to $90/BBL. Some analysts thought it was the new OPEC floor and that Saudi Arabia would not allow the price to go lower. But that was not the case.

On October 9, 2014, PIRA Energy Group had its annual meeting in New York and hosted a private dinner attended by Nasser al-Dossary, an adviser at the Ministry of Energy and the Saudi representative to the OPEC Economic Commission board. If oil prices continued to fall, he was asked whether Saudi Arabia could handle a price of $80/BBL, to which he answered yes. The Saudis did not prefer this level, but al-Dossary said that they could deal with this price. This response was quickly circulated among oil consultants in the United States. The following week at a meeting in London, the same question was put privately to a high-ranking Aramco official. He gave the same answer as al-Dossary had, that Saudi Arabia could handle a price of $80/BBL. They both did not say or even indicate that these prices were preferred by the Saudi.

Some oil analysts interpreted this response by two important Saudi oil officials to mean that Saudi Arabia could not only handle $80/BBL oil but that it might even prefer to see a lower oil price. Word spread quickly to other analysts and hedge fund managers, and it became public when the specialized petroleum media reported it. Prices began a rapid slide the following month, and the market's sentiment turned negative.

Al-Naimi was vacationing in Romania's mountains in October 2014. I telephoned him when prices started to fall with the suggestion that he issue a denial that Saudi Arabia wanted to see lower prices. Al-Naimi replied, "No, we should not say anything." The minister and other Saudi officials remained silent for more than two months. This created a sea of rumors that were reinforced by questions left unanswered by the Saudis, such as why the Saudis wanted the price to go down and what price level would be unacceptable. Those rumors slowly came to be seen as fact and even as part of a hidden agenda. Some reports were written by non-oil-experts or people with no deep understanding or connection to the oil market and Saudi oil policy, but the people were well-known.

In October 2014, Saudi Aramco issued its monthly pricing formula, adjusting the price and lowering the price differential. The *New York Times* reported that Saudi Arabia was getting into a price war in Asia to drive other producers, especially other Gulf producers, out of the market.[4] This explanation showed a lack of understanding of the Saudi Aramco pricing system and the marketing procedures of other Gulf countries. Refinery margins are the main parameters used by Saudi Aramco to set monthly prices for their five crude grades. The company has three marketing regions (Asia, Europe, and the Americas), and its sophisticated computer model analyses each of the three regions independently. Aramco also takes into consideration comments and feedback from its regular customers about the differential of the previous month.

After Saudi Aramco issues its prices, other Gulf countries—Kuwait, Iraq, and Iran—use the same pricing formula with some adjustments. This has been the procedure since the end of the fixed oil price and netback pricing system and the establishment of Saudi Aramco in 1988. Saudi Aramco's senior management—as well as Saudi Ministry of Energy officials, including the minister—does not interfere with the formula or with the monthly pricing system. Most of the time they don't even know the price differential until it is issued. Nevertheless, the *New York Times* story about Saudi prices was widely quoted and pushed oil prices into further decline.

New York Times columnist Thomas Friedman wrote that the oil price collapse was engineered by Saudi Arabia and the United States to hurt Russia because of its actions in Ukraine and Syria. That month Russia had taken over Crimea and Eastern Ukraine, a move condemned by the United States and the European Union (EU). The Russians were also helping Syrian president Bashar al-Assad against U.S.- and Saudi-backed rebels. Friedman repeated reports that the collapse of the oil market in 1986 was engineered by President Reagan and King Fahd to bring the Soviet Union down, but these reports were not true (chapter 8). Friedman wrote,

> Is it my imagination or is there a global oil war underway pitting the United States and Saudi Arabia on one side against Russia and Iran on the other? One cannot say for sure whether the American-Saudi oil alliance is deliberate or a coincidence of interests, but, if it is explicit, then clearly we're trying to do President Vladimir Putin of Russia and Iran's Supreme Leader, Ayatollah Ali Khamenei, exactly what the Americans and Saudis did to the last leaders of the Soviet Union: pump them to death—bankrupt them by bringing down the price of oil to levels below what both Moscow and Tehran need to finance their budgets.[5]

Friedman's knowledge about the oil market was limited. He might have discussed it with some U.S. officials who wanted to gain political credit even though they were not directly involved.

On December 6, 2014, the cover of the *Economist*, a respected London weekly, featured an expressive cartoon of an Arab sheikh and an American shale oil cowboy back to back, getting ready to duel using gasoline pump handles instead of guns. Its report speculated on the reasons for the collapse in oil prices. Unlike Friedman's article, there was some truth in this article, but it was exaggerated.

In May 2015, the Bloomberg monthly magazine had Minister Al-Naimi on the cover. It showed him wearing eyeglasses covered with the words "Crude, Gambit." Peter Waldman reported, "Last fall, as oil prices crashed, Ali Al-Naimi . . . went mum. He still popped up, as is his habit, at industry conferences on three continents. Yet, from mid-September to the middle of November, while benchmark crude prices plunged 21 percent to a four-year low, Al-Naimi didn't utter any word in public." Why? Waldman's answer was "Buying time: The Saudis plan to extend the age of oil: The biggest exporter has let prices plummet—delaying the day when climate concerns, efficiency, and fuel switching break the world's dependence on crude."[6]

This conflicting and inaccurate reporting spawned more rumors and conspiracy theories about why the Saudis would allow the price to go down. One theory was that the Saudis were trying to hurt Iran, which was believed to be working to develop a nuclear weapons capability. Another was an attempt to hurt the Syrian government or the Islamic State in Iraq and Syria (ISIS/ DAESH), which controlled some oil fields in Syria and produced oil and sold it at a discounted rate.[7]

These false or exaggerated stories swirled around while prices continued to fall, but Al-Naimi kept a low profile and made no attempt to clarify Saudi policy or take action to halt the slide in oil prices. He did not take an international leadership role, as he had done in 1998–1999 and 2008, nor did he allow his associates to speak with the media and the market. Al-Naimi was silent. This brings to mind the words of the great Arab poet, al-Mutanabbi, who said more than one thousand years ago:

> I slumber oblivious of the hidden meaning of my thinking, while people are awake arguing and contending over what I might mean.
>
> (أنامُ مِلءَ جفوني عن شواردها . . . . . . ويسهرُ الخلقُ جرّاها ويختصمُ)

Al-Naimi knew what he was doing and why, but others were just guessing. Oil market fundamentals are very important, but market psychology is equally important. Perceptions can influence the oil price on a daily or weekly basis and might even create a trend or snowball. Negative interpretations, rumors about Saudi intentions, and silence from the Saudi Ministry of Energy pushed oil prices down rapidly in the second half of 2014 and into 2015. Other members of the Gulf Cooperation Council (GCC) could have stepped in and assumed a leadership role, but they normally do not do so unless they have Saudi Arabia's full support.

Algeria and Venezuela had taken leadership roles in the past, and they worked hard to coordinate action in 2014, 2015, and 2016. Venezuela called for an emergency OPEC meeting in October 2014 after the oil price had declined by about 30 percent from its peak in June. Al-Naimi was on Margareta Island in Venezuela at the time to attend the United Nations Conference of the Parties (COP20); the Saudi minister of energy had led the Saudi team to all international climate change negotiations since the late 1980s. Al-Naimi had a long meeting with Rafael Ramirez, Venezuela's foreign minister and former oil minister. Ramirez was very close at that time to the new president Nicolás Maduro, and Ramirez was hoping that the two countries could work with OPEC to stop the oil price slide. Venezuela, like other oil producers, was suffering from the oil price decline, and it was a strong believer in OPEC and its ability to manage the oil market.

It was a long meeting. Al-Naimi had an excellent command of English and an ability to argue in a logical manner based on sound information and market data. He explained to Ramirez, whose English was poor and who did not use a translator, that the recent oil price decline was due to slow global demand and increasing non-OPEC supply from the United States, Russia, and Brazil, among others. He went on to say that OPEC alone could not rebalance the market and that it needed at least Russian and Mexican participation. If this was achieved, Al-Naimi said that Saudi Arabia would be willing to support any decision. Ramirez promised to take on the mission to bring non-OPEC producers, especially Mexico and Russia, to work with OPEC for a production cut. Ramirez had high hopes for this mission.[8]

Al-Naimi thought there was zero chance that Ramirez would succeed in bringing non-OPEC countries in for joint actions, but Ramirez was more than willing to take on this task. Ramirez visited many OPEC countries as well as non-OPEC producers, including Russia, and coordinated his mission closely with Saudi Arabia.

Two days later Al-Naimi left Venezuela for Acapulco, Mexico, to attend the International Energy Forum on natural gas. There he met Pedro Joaquin Coldwell, the Mexican energy minister. Coldwell expressed his government's willingness to cooperate with other producers but said it would be difficult to cut production at that time because of a planned opening of Mexican oil acreage to foreign upstream oil investments. Nevertheless, he kept the door open for all options and possibilities. It was clear that the Mexican delegation did not have good rapport as they used to with Venezuela.

In the end, Saudi Arabia, Russia, Mexico, and Venezuela agreed to a ministerial meeting one day before OPEC's regular conference on November 27, 2014; international media were not present. Igor Sechin, the Russian deputy prime minister and head of the state-owned oil company Rosneft, and Russia's energy minister Alexander Novak were both in attendance. Ramirez had organized the meeting and began by expressing his hopes that the meeting would lead to a good outcome. He asked Al-Naimi if he wanted to comment, but Al-Naimi said that the Russian delegation should go first.

Sechin explained at length that Russia wanted to see a stable oil market but that it could not cut its production for two reasons. First, there were many oil-producing companies in Russia, and it was difficult to organize a joint production cut among them. Second, some Russian oil fields were not flexible enough to bring their production down and then up again. Therefore, he said that Russia could not be part of any international production cut. Novak spoke next, making a general statement about the stability of the international oil market and Moscow's desire to work with other producers. He repeated what Sechin had said but in a softer tone and simpler language, which suggested that Moscow might be open to some form of coordination. Both Sechin and Novak talked about shale oil producers in the United States as the source of the problem.

The Mexican oil minister spoke of Mexico's falling production and its plan to open the upstream to international oil investors, which meant it could not cut production. Al-Naimi was pleased that he had predicted the failure of Ramirez's initiative to get non-OPEC countries to agree to cut production, and details of the meeting and its failure were later leaked. That day I received a call from a high-ranking Mexican who was familiar with the international oil market and with the Mexican-Saudi petroleum relationship, and she suggested the possibility of a compromise. But it seemed that it was too late, especially with Russia's unwillingness to cut production.

The following day OPEC held a regular ministerial meeting in Vienna. Algeria and Venezuela wanted OPEC to lower production by 1–2 MBD, but Al-Naimi and the ministers of other GCC OPEC members (Kuwait, Qatar, and the United Arab Emirates) opposed the proposal. The final decision was to roll over the 30 MBD ceiling of December 2011.

What happened in the closed-door ministerial meeting was more interesting. Al-Naimi lectured the other ministers about how OPEC risked losing market share as they did in the 1980's to U.S. shale oil producers and to Russia, Canada, and Brazil, among others, if it cut production. He added that high-cost producers were benefiting from OPEC's oil policy. He reminded them of the first half of the 1980s when OPEC cut and cut production to defend targeted oil prices while other producers continued to increase production, which resulted in OPEC losing both the price and the volume. Therefore, OPEC should not cut production, especially because high-cost oil producers would not be able to continue at the same production level in a weak oil price environment. His argument was convincing and supported by sound data. He also had in his favor the outcome of the meeting the previous day when Russia and Mexico indicated that they were not willing to reduce their production.

Somehow Al-Naimi's remarks to the ministers in the closed-door meeting were leaked to the international media, and the story that emerged was spicy. The media reported that Saudi Arabia and the Gulf countries were against U.S. shale oil, and these stories made headlines and the cover of some magazines.[9]

In the following month, the market was more or less stable, and prices held at around $60/BBL. If oil prices reached $60, it was expected that shale oil production would begin to decline, but this did not happen. In a sign of confidence in and support for U.S. producers, the U.S. government lifted a ban that had been in place for some forty years and allowed oil exports, but Al-Naimi still resisted proposals for a production cut by OPEC alone. Saudi Arabia could not reverse the oil price decline with an actual production cut, but Al-Naimi thought Saudi Arabia could stop it from falling further by sending out positive messages.

The opportunity to express this positive message came during a conference of the Organization of Arab Petroleum Exporting Countries (OAPEC) in Abu Dhabi on December 21–23, 2014. The conference drew a large number of participants from all over the world, and the media was there in force. Al-Naimi's speech was carefully written to send a positive message to the international oil market. It had four important points. First, Saudi Arabia was optimistic about the oil market and its future. Second, there is a need for cooperation among all oil producers for a meaningful and effective oil cut. Third, and contrary to what was being reported, Saudi Arabia did not use oil for political goals against this or that country. Fourth, the Saudi economy was so strong that it could cope with the existing oil prices without any problems.

But in his interactions with the media, the script changed. When Al-Naimi walked out of the building after his speech, CNN correspondent John Defterios asked him if Saudi Arabia planned to cut production, and Al-Naimi replied that he would never cut production. Defterios then asked Al-Naimi about working with the Russians, and he said it was too late.[10]

Subsequently, Al-Naimi spoke with his three favorite journalists in special interviews: Randa Takieddine from *Pan Arab Al Hayat*, Samira Kawar from *Petroleum Argus*, and Kate Dourian from the *Middle East Economic Survey* (MEES). What he told them was a bombshell. Al-Naimi said that Saudi Arabia would not reduce its production even if oil prices were as low as $40 or even $20 and that expensive oils from other countries would not be able to continue production. Al-Naimi's reasoning to everybody, especially the international media, was that he did not want Saudi Arabia to repeat the mistake of the 1980s—playing the role of swing producer and reducing oil production when others were unlikely to do so as well.

Oil prices did not move right away, and Bassam Fattouh, the head of the Oxford Institute for Energy Studies, explained that it was the end of the year and the markets had not priced this in and financial analysts and hedge funds had not yet fully absorbed what was happening. Fattouh also mentioned that this might not happen until the first quarter of the next year and predicted that the price might go down to $40.[11] Fattouh is a distinguished energy academic, not a regular market analyst, and his prediction proved to be right.

The policy of Al-Naimi in 2014–2015 was not questioned by the Saudi leadership; King Abdullah had full confidence in him. But there was growing disapproval by some important figures within Saudi Arabia, and many oil-producing countries, such as Oman, began to feel the pain of low oil prices. The Saudi leadership is very sensitive to the feelings and interests of their Arab allies when oil prices, and therefore income, are falling.

The assumption by Al-Naimi and some in Saudi Arabia that production of high-cost oil, such as shale, would fall and prices would rise turned out not to be the case. It is not that simple. This became clear before the end of 2015 as commercial stock increased and market sentiment changed. The economies of the oil-producing countries were facing difficulties. Stock markets in Saudi Arabia and the other Gulf states fell, and the real estate and construction market in Saudi Arabia entered a period of steady decline. The Saudi government's financial system was also under strain in 2015. In Saudi Arabia, the sharpest criticism came from three important figures: Prince Al-Waleed bin Talal, Abdulaziz al-Dakheel, and to a lesser extent and indirectly, Ahmed al-Malik.

Prince Al-Waleed bin Talal, the nephew of King Abdullah and one of the world's richest men, was direct in his criticism of Al-Naimi. Al-Waleed harshly criticized Al-Naimi's oil policy and his statement that the declining oil price was "no cause for alarm." Al-Waleed's attacks pointed out that low oil prices hurt Saudi Arabia and its citizens. He wrote a three-page letter to the head of King Abdullah's office, with copies to the ministers of finance, economy, and planning, and to a few other members of the Saudi cabinet. The letter was widely circulated inside and outside Saudi Arabia.[12]

Abdulaziz al-Dakheel is a Saudi economist and a consultant, and he was the assistant deputy in the Ministry of Finance for Economics and Financial Policy during the 1970s. His writings were normally critical and widely read in Saudi Arabia, and in December 2014 he wrote about the negative impact of low oil prices on the Saudi economy.[13] At the same time, Ahmed al-Malik, former vice president of the Saudi Central Bank (SAMA), provided a comprehensive analysis in the widely circulated Saudi newspaper, *al Riyadh*. He did not criticize Ali Al-Naimi nor Saudi oil policy directly, but he analyzed the negative impact of low oil prices on the economy of Saudi Arabia.[14]

There were important developments politically and in negotiations among oil producers during the first few months of 2015, but there were no signs of improvement in the oil market in terms of oil prices and the supply and demand balance. Equally important, shale and other expensive oil production did not decline, even when prices fell below $40/BBL. The oil price crisis forced shale oil producers to restructure, cut spending, and refinance some of their operations, but there was no substantial decline in production.

OPEC and non-OPEC oil producers continued to suggest doing something—anything. Algeria and Venezuela proposed new initiatives, and Oman, a non-OPEC producer, expressed readiness to cut its production.

Venezuelan president Nicolas Maduro visited Saudi Arabia on January 11, 2015, to meet Crown Prince Salman (King Abdullah was in the hospital). Maduro and his minister of foreign affairs attended a meeting with Saudi oil ministers to discuss the oil market and ways they could work together and with other oil producers to stabilize the market. Al-Naimi told them what he had said many times since oil prices started declining in 2014: OPEC should not do it alone. Al-Naimi said that Saudi Arabia was willing to cooperate if the Venezuelans could bring along non-OPEC producers. The Venezuelans had an interesting suggestion. They had been told that shale oil production in the United States was causing earthquakes and suggested starting an environmental campaign inside the United States to slow its growth. At the same time, there was talk of a possibility thatt Norway could join OPEC in a production cut. Gro Anundskaas, the assistant director general of the Ministry of Petroleum of Norway, contacted me to ask whether any initiatives were coordinated with Saudi Arabia or OPEC. The answer was that it was not the case. She also asked what Saudi Arabia's position was regarding a production cut. I told her that Saudi Arabia would support such a cut provided major producers and exporters took part in it. She later told me that Norwegian participation in any production cut was not possible at that time because oil prices at that level would not clearly harm the country's economy, which goes against the legal prerequisite for any production adjustments.

Norway had cooperated with other producers in reducing oil production in 1998–1999. However, they preferred not to do it within a collective decision-making process because they were members of both the Organization of Economic Cooperation and Development (OECD) and the IEA as an observer. They also preferred to coordinate their decisions with Saudi Arabia because of its weight in the oil market and its credibility.

The petroleum relationship between Norway and Saudi Arabia began with Saudi petroleum minister Hisham Nazer's visits to Norway in 1987 and 1995, but the relationship was consolidated with Al-Naimi. The oil ministers of both countries scheduled annual visits and shared some social activities such as desert camping, hiking, and fishing. This strong personal relationship between ministers and professionals strengthened their petroleum ties on both the bilateral and international level.[15] This relationship cooled after Al-Naimi was out of office.

Khalid al-Falih, with his wide-ranging responsibilities and busy schedule, had little time to directly coordinate with Norway, let alone to undertake social activities with the Norwegians or with ministers from other countries. Equally important, the Norwegian energy ministers were changing too frequently to allow for personal relationships to develop. While these new oil-related changes were developing, a major event took place that had a significant influence on Saudi oil policy.

KING ABDULLAH PASSES AWAY

In the early hours of Friday, January 23, 2015, the royal court announced the death of King Abdullah. Even though the king had been seriously ill for months and his death was expected, it was a big shock nationally and internationally. The transition to the new king, Salman bin Abdulaziz Al Saud, was immediate, smooth, and easy. In the evening, Ali Al-Naimi and I went to the royal palace in Riyadh to pay allegiance to the new king, and King Salman received the minister with high respect (without waiting long). The palace was packed, and the line to meet the new king was very long.

For three days, foreign dignitaries, kings, presidents, and prime ministers from all over the world came to Riyadh to offer their condolences. One of them was the prime minister of Russia, Dmitry Medvedev, who arrived in the afternoon of January 24, 2015. With him was the Russian minister of energy, Alexander Novak, who expressed his desire to meet the Saudi minister of petroleum. Al-Naimi asked Prince Abdulaziz bin Salman to go to the airport to greet the Russian delegation and meet Novak because he had to go to the royal palace with other ministers. Prince Abdulaziz bin Salman and the Russian minister met for more than two hours while the Russian prime minister went to see King Salman to offer condolences.

I was with Prince Abdulaziz bin Salman, and the discussion about the international oil market and the energy relationship between the two countries was very frank. The prince explained to Novak that media reports about the Saudi oil policy were wrong, especially the ones about a Saudi-engineered oil collapse for political reasons against Russia. "They were absolutely baseless," Prince Abdulaziz bin Salman said more than once. In the end, it was agreed that the two countries should work together to help stabilize the international oil market. I asked Novak if Russia was willing to cut oil production and if there was a collective decision. He replied yes, with a confident voice, but nothing tangible happened during the next couple of months.

However, the will to do something continued, with Algeria and Venezuela leading the process. On February 11, 2015, the Algerian minister of justice, Tayeb Louh, visited Saudi Arabia as the special envoy of Algerian president Abdelaziz Bouteflika. The Algerian minister spoke about the negative economic, political, and social impact of low prices on the Arab world and suggested that in the interest of Arabs and Muslims we should all have a meeting. Algeria was willing to do whatever was needed to pressure other producers to join them.

During the meeting, Al-Naimi was calm. He spoke of his bad experience with the Russians and their lack of commitment to production cut agreements in the past, adding that high-cost marginal producers would soon reduce their production and that the price would stabilize between $50 and $70 per barrel. During the summer of 2015, oil prices fell below $50/BBL. In August, Al-Naimi took his annual vacation, and on his return he still would not change his mind.

International pressure by some oil producers, and even some oil consumers, was growing. In September 2015, the Qatari minister suggested an extraordinary OPEC meeting. That same month the president of Venezuela visited Russia and Qatar along with other countries. His intention was to arrange a meeting of OPEC heads of state, plus Russia, in Venezuela. Perhaps he thought to do what Chavez had done in 2000, but he did not realize that the people and the circumstances were completely different in 2015.

In 2015, Al-Naimi had to adapt to a changed political environment in Saudi Arabia that was new to him. There were big changes. In April 2015, Al-Naimi was removed as chairman of Saudi Aramco's board. After twenty one-years in this position of prestige and importance, Al-Naimi found this hard to swallow. Furthermore, the new administration, especially the Council of Economic and Development Affairs, which was headed by Crown Prince Mohammed bin Salman, was filled with young dynamic people with open working hours. Al-Naimi could not easily adapt to this new system and lifestyle. For example, he normally went to bed at 9 p.m. or 10 p.m., whereas the council might start working at that time.

Al-Naimi was no longer active in international oil management and OPEC, and the Algerians began to give up as well. It was left to Venezuela and, to a lesser extent, the Qatari oil minister, who was the president of the OPEC conference, to assume leadership. They suggested calling a summit of heads of state of OPEC producing countries along with Russia and other non-OPEC producers. Venezuela and Qatar both expressed willingness to host such a summit, but Al-Naimi was against it, and so were other countries, including Russia. Al-Naimi had already made up his mind, and he could not easily change it. He wanted the marginal producers out (at least partially) and for oil prices to find a new floor without interference from Saudi Arabia or OPEC.

On October 5, 2015, I delivered a lecture at a special seminar organized by OAPEC in Kuwait. The topic was recent developments in the international oil market and expectations for the future. One of the points I emphasized was the importance of having leadership or management in the oil market throughout its history. I went on to say that "there is a lot of uncertainty in the market because there is no anchor. This created a lack of capability for price discovery. Therefore, there is a high level of volatility which has a negative impact on the oil producers, consumers, and the oil industry. This current vacuum in the oil market leadership is not natural and it is impossible to imagine its continuity."[16] Al-Naimi was not happy about this part of the speech, especially after it was leaked to the media.

Al-Naimi did not blink. He was not willing to change his view, but he was gradually losing his importance inside Saudi Arabia. After many years in office, he was not in full synergy with the new Saudi administration and the emerging style of work, but he kept working as hard as he could.

NEW PROCEDURES

King Salman created two new institutions: the Council of Political and Security Affairs and the Council of Economic and Development Affairs. The latter was headed by Crown Prince Mohammed bin Salman (deputy prime minister and minister of defense). He was very dynamic and hard-working and had ambitious goals for reforming the Saudi economy, including the energy sector. The government of King Salman, with Crown Prince Mohammed bin Salman's clear and strong emphasis on economic issues, began to develop a new energy strategy. The basic goal was to diversify and enlarge the Saudi economy and reduce its dependence on oil. Ideas included raising the price of energy domestically, introducing some form of taxation, and partial privatization of some businesses (such as Aramco). They also considered the possibility of increasing Saudi oil production capacity beyond 12.5 MBD.

Al-Naimi could not easily deal with these changes. In Saudi Arabia, older people are respected and rarely questioned by their younger superiors, and Al-Naimi often left meetings that started late at night. There were other major changes as well. During the administration of King Abdullah, ministers wrote reports and policy options and sent them directly to the king, who might take the necessary actions, including making the decision himself, or send it to the Council of Ministers or one of its committees, or any other concerned parties. If the king or the minister wanted to discuss a special issue, they were likely to meet either on Friday afternoons at the king's palace or in the king's office on Monday, before the weekly cabinet meeting. When Al-Naimi sought King Abdullah's guidance, he would either call the king or report the results of a meeting. King Abdullah used to call Al-Naimi as well.

King Salman's new system was very different. Any suggestion, policy, development, or guideline had to be debated and approved by the economic council. After that, it might go to the king or to the cabinet for final approval. Al-Naimi and some of the people around him had not fully adjusted to this new working process, and it was a major reason for the failure of the Doha meeting on April 17. 2016.

The lead-up to the Doha meeting was building week after week. Failure of a proposal to have an emergency meeting, or an OPEC/non-OPEC summit, and the idea of freezing oil production came up some time in early 2016. The new initiative was suggested by Russia, and it signaled a big change in Russian oil policy (chapter 10). Russia was willing to take a leadership role, and the Russian production-freeze initiative soon gained support from almost all countries within OPEC and outside it. Al-Naimi backed the proposal because it did not require a production cut, and the Saudi production freeze would be at a higher level than the Saudi official OPEC quota, which had been ignored by the Saudis and others for at least two years.

The Saudi ministry accepted the idea provided all countries would freeze their production, and they informed the leadership about it. Russia called for a meeting in St. Petersburg on March 20, 2016. Al-Naimi wanted to delay the meeting until April, believing that the price might improve because of expectations of higher demand and declining production in the United States and in other high-cost producers.

OPEC had two problems. First, Libya and Nigeria had domestic conflicts that affected their production and wanted to be exempted until they could restore output to normal levels. Second, Iran had just begun raising its production after UN economic sanctions were lifted. Iran also claimed that its production before sanctions had been 4 MBD, but independent sources estimated it at no more than 3.75 MBD. Iran demanded an exemption from any freeze, meaning that Iran would be able to continue to increase its production. After much discussion, the decision was made to have a general freeze of oil production except for Libya and Nigeria.

The OPEC meeting was to be held in Doha, Qatar, because it had the presidency of the OPEC conference. Also, the Qatari oil minister, Mohammed al-Sada, was very active in the negotiations and was a close friend of Al-Naimi's and looked to him for guidance. A small committee was formed, and Saudi Arabia and Russia took part in drafting a communiqué.

The problem with Iran was solved by not inviting them; Iran would not be part of the agreement. Saudi leadership was quickly informed about the meeting and the deal.

WHAT WENT WRONG?

Al-Naimi believed that it was sufficient to inform the royal court, but in the new system it was necessary to get approval from the economic council, which was headed by Crown Prince Mohammed bin Salman. Al-Naimi and some of his assistants (including me) argued that there was no need for official approval because the royal court was informed and did not have any objection—and time was very short. But Prince Abdulaziz bin Salman suggested having clear approval before going to Doha, so Al-Naimi went to Doha without the full approval of the Saudi government. Work on the agreement and the communiqué was finalized, and we were ready to go to Doha the following day, April 17, 2016.

When the Saudi delegation arrived in Doha, Crown Prince Mohammed bin Salman's interview with Bloomberg was published in which he stated that he was not currently worried about the oil market and prices.[17] The Bloomberg interview was not intended for the Doha meeting, as some speculated at the time. It was one of several interviews with Western media, including the *Financial Times* and the *Economist*, as well as some off-the-record interviews. However, the big shock for Al-Naimi came at 9 p.m. when he received a call from the royal court saying that any agreement should involve all producing countries with no exceptions.[18]

Al-Naimi called for a meeting of the Saudi delegation. Prince Abdulaziz bin Salman said he would first talk with the Qatari oil minister, Mohammed al-Sada, and later with the Russians. Prince Abdulaziz bin Salman and the Saudi team worked all night drafting a new agreement and hoped it would be acceptable. Early in the morning, the prince and Qatari Oil Minister Al-Sada had a meeting, with the new draft to be discussed during the general ministerial meeting. Al-Sada was flexible and supported the Saudi position.

The official opening of the ministerial conference was delayed to allow for more discussion of the new agreement with the other delegates. The Russians were not happy with the changes, but they were willing to go along with them if others accepted them as well. The new agreement did not explicitly require a production freeze. Instead, the production freeze was linked to a freeze by other producers, some of whom were not present in Doha.[19]

With the failure of the meeting, as well as other signs, it was clear that Al-Naimi's career as minister of petroleum was coming to an end. On May 17, 2016, just twenty days after the Doha meeting, Al-Naimi called me and with a happy voice said, "Now you can retire." I immediately understood that he was no longer the minister of energy, and it seemed appropriate to reply, "Congratulations Abo Rami" (his nickname). Al-Naimi had talked about his desire to retire for about ten years. He told me that the royal court had just called and told him that the official announcement would come that afternoon, and he would be named "Minister without Portfolio."

After the phone call ended, I took a moment to reflect on our relationship and his career. Al-Naimi had become a friend more than a boss. His career was interesting and included both achievements and failures and to great extent reflected his personality. Al-Naimi is quiet, gentle, and easygoing, but at the same time he is hard-headed. When he made up his mind, he could be inflexible. He felt that being a minister was a duty to his country more than a career, and he was highly dedicated to his boss (the king) and to his responsibilities. He led the team that established the King Abdullah University of Science and Technology, which is one of the most distinguished research institutes in the region and beyond. During his tenure, the production and capacity of the Saudi gas system has almost doubled; the Saudi mining company (Ma'aden) was established; and the minerals railroad between northern Saudi Arabia and its eastern coast was built. Two industrialized mineral cities, one in the Gulf coast and the other in the far north, were built. Moreover, Saudi Aramco signed joint petroleum and petrochemical ventures in both Japan and China.

But above all, Ali Al-Naimi was lucky. Most of the time during his career the oil market was favorable to Saudi Arabia. After twenty-one years as a minister, in only five years were oil prices and Saudi income below the needs of the government's budget. Al-Naimi will be remembered inside Saudi Arabia as well as outside mostly as a simple boy growing up in the desert who gradually advanced his education and career, becoming the minister of energy of the most powerful and influential oil-producing country in the world.

Chapter Ten

VLADIMIR PUTIN

Placing Russia on the Global Oil Map

Khalid al-Falih, the Saudi energy minister, met with a small group of people early in February 2019 to discuss a new petroleum management system based on the petroleum relationship with Russia. Al-Falih remarked that he spoke with Energy Minister Alexander Novak (now deputy prime minister) more often than he spoke with his own colleagues in Saudi Arabia. He even jokingly said that he spoke with Novak more than with his own wife. Al-Falih was the Saudi energy minister from 2016 to 2019, and these meetings with Novak were an important part of a long-term effort that contributed to Saudi Arabia and Russia becoming close energy allies and sharing leadership roles in the oil market. It should be noted that Prince Mohammed bin Salman was the driving force behind improving Saudi-Russian relations in the oil sector, as well as in other areas.

Saudi Arabia has been one of the most important members of the oil-producers club since the creation of OPEC in 1960, and OPEC became more influential when it began setting oil prices in the early 1970s and setting production levels in the early 1980s. Russia was not part of OPEC or any international oil management group, even though it has been a major oil producer and oil exporter. Moreover, oil is an important component of the Russian economy and was often used in pursuit of its geopolitical interests. Moscow controls much of the country's oil industry, but it took the

Russians about five decades to become part of the oil management structure and to develop an international energy strategy.

When Prince Saud al-Faisal, the Saudi foreign minister, visited Moscow
in 1982 as part of an Arab delegation to discuss an Arab initiative regarding the Arab-Israeli conflict, he spoke with Soviet officials about reestab-
lishing the political relationship between the two countries. The Russians
did not respond to the Saudi proposal, but trade between the two countries continued.[1] In 1983, OPEC contacted the Soviet embassy in London,
where Andrei Glebovich was stationed, asking for Moscow's cooperation
with OPEC members and with Saudi Arabia to discuss possible production
coordination to prevent a price collapse. The embassy conveyed the message to the government, but Moscow did not respond.[2]

In the 1980s, the Soviet bureaucracy and the administrative system
functioned poorly, and effective communication with OPEC, or even with
the Russian embassy in London, was difficult. At that time, the Soviet
leadership faced larger issues, including Russia's war in Afghanistan and
the arms race with the United States under the Reagan administration.
Another possible reason for their lack of response might have been that the
Soviet oil industry was starting to fall apart due to bad management and
underinvestment and could not have handled a production cut. Finally,
Moscow's relationship with Saudi Arabia and some other OPEC members
was strained because of Saudi Arabia's involvement in the war against the
Moscow-controlled regime in Afghanistan.

The first direct contact between Saudi Arabia and the Soviet Union on
petroleum issues came in 1987, when Prince Bandar bin Sultan, the Saudi
ambassador to Washington, spoke with his Soviet counterpart about the
subject. This time the answer was positive. Oil prices were very low, and
the Soviet economy needed help. One man in Moscow was responsible
for the change of heart—Mikhail Gorbachev. He was the general secretary
of the Communist Party and was involved in important decisions on internal affairs and external relations.

In January 1987, the new Saudi oil minister, Hisham Nazer, visited Moscow and was well received, but the visit did not lead to an agreement on oil
production cooperation. It was a good start, however, and it led to meetings and formation of a new group made up of OPEC and the "independent oil producers." The new group included Russia, China (at that time
an oil-exporting country), Oman, Malaysia, Norway, and Mexico. It also

included the Texas Railroad Commission, the U.S. state of Alaska, and the Canadian province of Alberta. The group met in 1988 and planned to hold further meetings to work toward market stability. However, two events complicated matters in the ensuing years. The first was the Iraqi invasion of Kuwait in August 1990, which led to a tightening of the oil market and higher oil prices. When the war ended seven months later and oil prices collapsed, OPEC alone was able to balance the market, mainly by increasing production levels for individual OPEC members because of the absence of Iraqi production for a number of years and the gradual return of Kuwait's production, along with a strong growth in demand for oil.

The second event, which was more important, was the collapse of Russian oil production as a result of the breakup of the Soviet Union in 1991. Russia went from producing almost 11 MBD in 1989 to about 6 MBD in 1995, and stayed at that level until 2000. This decline in Russia's production was much more than could have been achieved through any production cut agreement with other producers. Russian production eventually recovered and reached more than 10 MBD by 2013.

Although Russia's high and low production levels spanned twenty years, the international oil market was able to absorb these remarkable changes with little impact on market balance and oil prices. OPEC and Saudi Arabia, in particular, did not complain about Russian oil production even when the oil price collapsed in 1998. Their real complaint at that time was with Venezuela, which was an OPEC member.

OPEC AND RUSSIAN OIL POLICY

Russia is rich in oil and natural gas and is one of the three most important oil producers and oil exporters in the world. It has the world's largest natural gas reserves and is the leading producer and exporter of natural gas, especially to Europe, where gas prices are closely linked to oil prices. Historically, oil and natural gas have played an important role in Russia's economic and political power and influence, especially within Europe, and recently in Asia and beyond. However, the way oil wealth is managed has changed over time.

During the Soviet era (1917–1991), the entire energy sector was under strict state control. Before the collapse of the Soviet Union, oil production totaled 12 MBD, and Russian production alone was 11 MBD in 1989. But the energy sector was badly managed and suffered from massive amounts of waste and low productivity. In addition, oil was provided at a discounted rate to Moscow's allies (mainly the Eastern Bloc). In the 1980s the Soviet Union began to face internal difficulties (economic, administrative, social, military, and political), and political developments and changes in leadership have affected Moscow's relations with the West and the rest of the world since that time.

In 1985, Mikhail Gorbachev became secretary-general of the Communist Party and gradually gained national and international political influence. (It is interesting to note that he came into his position before the collapse of oil prices and fabrication of the false conspiracy theory of Saudi Arabia–U.S. cooperation to harm the Soviet Union through low oil prices.) Gorbachev adopted some Western concepts, such as freedom of the press, and opened some sectors of the economy to national and international private investment. He called his new policy Perestroika and Glasnost, and he worked closely with Washington on a number of major international issues, including the liberation of Kuwait from Iraqi occupation and the Palestinian-Israeli peace process. He also supported President George Bush's effort to create a new international order. He tried to revive the oil industry and was open to the idea of Russian cooperation with OPEC. Internal opposition hindered his ability to follow through on these commitments, and Russian oil production began its decline during his administration.

The Soviet Union disintegrated in 1991, and Boris Yeltsin became the first president of the newly formed Russian Federation. He instituted major dramatic changes for the economic and petroleum sectors and spoke of establishing a free market without a clear vision of how to achieve it. He sold off parts of the Russian oil industry at low prices, including the reserves, and corruption was the norm. Some people made billions of dollars owning businesses without doing very much. It was one of the major sell-offs in the history of the petroleum industry. Yeltsin's government created a system called "loans for shares" in which wealthy individuals would lend money to the government in exchange for shares in some state oil companies. If the government did not repay the loans on time, shares of these companies would be transferred to those wealthy individuals. This became known as the "sale of the century." It was from this chaotic situation that the Russian oil "oligarchs" emerged—rich individuals with no experience in the oil industry but who now owned it.[3] Moreover, the industry was failing and no longer served the interests of the country. Russia's production was in a steady decline, reaching its lowest point of less than 6 MBD in 1996.[4]

Yeltsin also threw Moscow into the arms of Washington, politically and economically. The United States rewarded him in 1997 by inviting Russia to join the Group of Seven (G7), the club of rich nations. Russia joined what became the G8, alongside the United States, Canada, the United Kingdom, France, Italy, Germany, and Japan. This was clearly a political decision by the United States because at that time Russia was a waning economic power.

OPEC needed the cooperation of the Russians and other non-OPEC producers when the oil price collapsed in 1998, and visits by Minister Ali Al-Naimi and other OPEC ministers to Moscow secured a Russian promise of a small cut of about 100 KBD. However, many people believed that cut did not take place.[5] Indeed, the Russians themselves said they would not adhere to the promised cut after a meeting of the energy ministers of the G8 countries in Germany in 1999 (Russia was part of the group at that time and was very cozy with the West).

When Vladimir Putin came to power in 1999, oil and natural gas were among his priorities, and the country adopted a new strategy. Putin reorganized the oil industry under strict state authority, and some of the largest companies became state-owned or ended up with mixed ownership. At the time, more than one hundred international and small local private companies were operating in the Russian upstream oil sector. From 1999 to 2004, Putin's power grew, eventually extending to almost total control over all aspects of Russian policy. Unlike Gorbachev and Yeltsin, he was a strong believer in the power of the state and wanted to restore the superpower status enjoyed by Moscow under the Soviet Union and the Czars.

The petroleum industry is an important contributor to the Russian economy, and it is more exposed to low oil prices than some other producers, such as the United States, Norway, Canada, and the United Kingdom. Oil production and oil prices affect the Russian government's income, the value of the national currency (the rouble), economic growth, government spending for military needs and for social projects, and the balance of payments. The cost of oil production is higher in Russia than it is in most OPEC countries, but Russia's oil exports provide income and facilitate relationships that help Russia achieve one of its important goals—to be a major international power.

It serves Russia's interests to be part of a collective effort to stabilize the oil market and to have an oil price that is good for the oil industry, the economy, and the government. But there are conflicting opinions and interests inside Russia, especially among oil producers and nonpetroleum economic decision makers. One group, including the ministers of energy and finance and the head of the government's investment fund, prefer relatively higher oil prices that generate more income for the government. They also strongly supported Russian participation in international oil management. The other group, headed by Igor Sechin, chairman of Rosneft Oil Company, is against production restrictions. Sechin is a close ally of President Putin but is also a hardline national conservative who does not trust the West, especially the United States and its allies. His opinions about the oil market are clearly colored by his political beliefs. For example, he might even have an anti-Saudi tone,[6] but he follows what the president wants. Other Russian companies, including some international oil companies operating in Russia, backed Moscow's participation in oil supply management, but they did so privately.

It is important to examine the strategic role of oil in the relations between Moscow and Washington. When the United States was on good terms with Russia during the Yeltsin era and the early years of the Putin presidency, the United States encouraged American and European energy investment in Russia and the construction of oil and gas pipelines to export Russian oil and gas to Europe. At the same time, a number of U.S. decision makers and oil experts were unhappy with what they called the dependency on imported oil from the Arab world, the Middle East, or OPEC. They saw an opportunity to replace Middle Eastern oil with more "secure" supplies from Russia and the former Soviet republics in Central Asia. Later when Russia and some Central Asian countries were looking for new oil and gas export outlets through Iran, Washington opposed the proposals and endorsed new pipelines through Turkey, a project that received Western financial support. However, "the winds do not always blow as the sailor wishes," as the Arabic saying goes.

Putin's growing power coincided with the election in the United States of President George W. Bush, whose administration included several influential people who saw the U.S.-Russian relationship in Cold War terms. They were part of the neoconservative school and included Vice President Dick Cheney, the secretary of defense Donald Rumsfeld, and Condoleezza Rice, the secretary of state and former national security adviser. They wanted to curb Russia's power and international influence in Eastern Europe and Central Asia.

Nevertheless, Putin was hoping to establish a good relationship with the West on the political, economic, and petroleum fronts. Putin wanted to retain Moscow's influence over what was called the "near abroad," that is, neighboring countries that had previously been part of the Soviet Union. He wanted Russia to be a major international player, but the United States, and the West in general, viewed Russia as a regional rather than a global power. American author and politician Angela Stent wrote that Putin "believes Russia has a right to sit at the table on all major international decisions and will insist on inclusion. The West should recognize that Russia belongs to the global board of directors."[7] But the United States Has not been willing to acknowledge this status under the Bush, Obama, and Biden administrations, and it set the stage for a sour relationship between Russia and the United States, which was often suspicious of Russian motives.

These tensions were certain to bubble to the surface with any major international changes, including leadership changes in neighboring countries. In 2004, a change of leadership in Georgia, a small country that lies at the crossroads between Europe and Asia and that had been under Moscow's sphere of influence for centuries, led to the beginning of a major conflict. Mikheil Saakashvili was elected president of Georgia, and he had close ties to the neoconservatives who wielded power in Washington at the time. Saakashvili wanted Georgia to join the U.S.-dominated North Atlantic Treaty Organization (NATO). Some U.S. officials declared that it was only a matter of time before Georgia would join NATO, which caused alarm in Moscow. Putin saw this as a breach of an agreement with the United States not to expand the West's military presence into Russia's spheres of influence (near abroad). Matters came to a head in August 2008 when Russia invaded Georgia. The war lasted only five days. Georgia was defeated, and Russia occupied the regions of Abkhazia and South Ossetia, claiming that the two regions wanted to be independent.

The relationship between Russia and the West worsened in 2014 when the pro-Moscow president of the Ukraine, Viktor Yanukovych, was removed from power. Russia considered this another Western attempt to curb the influence of Russia and to contain its access to power within what Russia considers its spheres of influence. Russia intervened militarily,

annexing Crimea and seizing control of some parts of the pro-Russian eastern Ukraine region. Relations with the United States deteriorated further,
and the G8 members cancelled a planned summit that was to be held in
the Russian city of Sochi in June 2014 and suspended Russia's membership
in the group.

The U.S subsequently imposed selected economic sanctions, including
on oil-related investments and technologies, and the Obama administration even considered imposing sanctions on Russian oil exports. On May
15–16, 2014, Russia hosted a ministerial meeting of the International Energy
Forum (IEF), the largest gathering of energy ministers of producing and
consuming countries. The United States and some European countries boy-
cotted the meeting because of the Ukraine crisis.

In 2018, the Trump administration continued Obama's policy against
building a pipeline project known as Nord Stream II to carry gas from
Russia to Germany without going through Ukraine. The Biden administration is expected to maintain, if not strengthen, these anti-Russia policies
on many issues.

CHANGING OIL POLICY

Russia changed its oil policy in 2016 and began to take a leading role
together with Saudi Arabia in the OPEC+ arrangement. The big question is
why—why did Russia change its energy policy? Were these decisions based
on the energy sector, or were there political and economic considerations?
What part did personalities and personal beliefs and relationships play?
Russia's realization of the strategic role of petroleum in its international
relations was growing year by year, and it began to ship more oil and gas to
Asia, especially to China, and away from the West. These and other policy
decisions involving oil and gas were important factors in the development
of Russia's international strategies, including their relationship with other
oil producers, such as Saudi Arabia and OPEC.

When Gorbachev came to power in 1985, many people in Russia and
some in the West had hoped for a strong alliance in many areas of mutual
interest, including oil and gas investment opportunities. But in the 1980s
and the 1990s, the political, economic, and administrative systems in Russia were fragile. This made it difficult for Russia to design a coherent and
clear international petroleum policy, let alone a comprehensive strategy

outside the simple issues of production and exports. This was one of the main reasons OPEC was unable to establish meaningful cooperation with Russia despite attempts on all levels for more than thirty years, starting in 1983.

In December 1991, after the fall of the Soviet Union and the end of the second Gulf War, Western European countries established the European Energy Charter to open up and integrate Russian oil with the Western European energy market. This included opening investments in oil exploration and production in Russia. The charter did not achieve its goals because of opposition from several countries. Norway refused to join, arguing that it might lead to a loss of its sovereignty over its natural resources. Russia was against it for the same reason. Saudi Arabia was against it because it felt that it might create a new petroleum alliance against OPEC. The United States was also opposed, objecting to the charter's regional focus, but the most likely reason was that European energy companies would have more access to Russian oil than the Americans had.

Some U.S. experts provided insights into the new U.S. thinking about Russian oil and gas. For example, Edward L. Morse and James Richard had close ties in Washington in the oil industry and in the financial establishment, and they wrote a widely circulated article about rising Russian oil exports and the implications of this increase in a global context:

> The American campaign against terrorism may be grabbing the headlines, but another battle is being waged with perhaps equally significant long-term implications: the contest for energy dominance between the world's two largest oil exporters, Saudi Arabia and Russia. This battle will have fundamental consequences for the world's economy, U.S. energy security, the Russian global role, the future relevance of Saudi Arabia, and the influence of the Organization of the Petroleum Exporting Countries (OPEC).

They concluded by saying that Russia would become more relevant to the United States and the West than Saudi Arabia is, which would have important political implications for the alliance between the United States and Russia.[8]

In 2003, Putin visited the United States, and oil was at the top of his agenda. Putin suggested "that Russia could deliver stability and reliability at a time when the Americans needed it, or at least craved it."[9] During a visit to New York, Senator Chuck Schumer gave Putin special attention and was looking forward to close petroleum cooperation not only between the two countries but also between the state of New York and Russia. Schumer said during one meeting, "I hope OPEC is hurt by this so that they don't have a stranglehold on the oil market anymore."[10] But the honeymoon period between Moscow and Washington quickly ended, especially after the conflict over Georgia and the return of a policy of containment of Russia's power.

Putin began looking for new alliances, and his first choice was China. The two countries had some conflicting interests concerning Central Asia, but this did not prevent Russia from signing a friendship treaty with China in 2001. Russia is also a member of the Conference on Interaction and Confidence-Building Measures in Asia (CICA), which was established in September 1999 with twenty-seven countries. In 2003, the Shanghai Cooperation Organization (Shanghai Pact) was established to ensure security and maintain stability in the region. Its full members included Russia, China, India, Kazakhstan, Tajikistan, Uzbekistan, Pakistan, and Iran. Russia and China wanted to create a new economic system that was not dominated by the West. Together with India, Brazil, and South Africa, in 2009 they established a new informal arrangement known as BRICS (the first letter of the name of each of the five countries). The goal was to establish an economic bloc for the major emerging economies, similar to, but not necessarily competing with, the major economic powers known as the G7.

Russia and China also established a petroleum alliance in which Russia would export more oil and gas to China and away from the West. China wanted to diversify its imports to be less dependent on the Arabian Gulf region, so this alliance served the interests of both countries very well. But Putin was looking for a larger international petroleum role and alliance.

CROWN PRINCE MOHAMMED BIN SALMAN AND PRESIDENT PUTIN

With consolidation of President Putin's power and low oil prices, the possibility of creating a petroleum alliance with Saudi Arabia and OPEC became a strategically winning idea. It fit perfectly with the new direction and strategy that was evolving in Putin's mind. At the same time Saudi Arabia was also facing major economic challenges and looking for a new direction.

Crown Prince Mohammed bin Salman took charge of Saudi Arabia's economic policy in 2015, introducing Vision 2030, a plan to diversify and expand the Saudi economy and reduce its dependence on oil income. The prince is young, dynamic, ambitious, and has clear futuristic goals. He wants to make Saudi Arabia a major international power in many aspects, above all in energy and oil. In addition to good relations with the United States and Europe, he wants to expand and strengthen Saudi relations with other major powers such as Russia, China, and India. With Russia, oil policy, industry, and investment can be the cornerstones of a strong relationship.

The personalities of the players are important for successful collaboration. When important decision makers "click" with each other and work on common goals, they can change policy and influence the world. That is what happened between Crown Prince Mohammed and President Putin. The crown prince visited Russia with a large delegation in June 2015 to lead the meeting of the Saudi-Russian Business Council and to participate in the nineteenth St. Petersburg International Economic Forum. This meeting was only five months after a change in the Saudi government and was a clear sign that Crown Prince Mohammed wanted to have a close relationship with Russia. During the visit, the Saudi Ministry of Energy and the Russian Ministry of Energy signed an agreement on implementation of a joint program of action. The signatories were Alexander Novak and Ali Al-Naimi. The prince then went to Moscow for an official visit and had a long meeting with Putin. This visit was the beginning of a close relationship between the two men, and it was to have a big impact on the international oil market.

The second development with clear implications beyond the bilateral relationship that affected the oil market took place on September 4, 2016. Crown Prince Mohammed met Putin on the sidelines of the G20 summit in Hangzhou, China. One of the main purposes of their meeting was to see how the two countries could work together to bring stability to the oil market. For political, economic, and energy-related considerations, Putin was willing to work with Saudi Arabia and take on a role in managing the international oil market. Like Crown Prince Mohammed, Putin wanted to create a wide-ranging relationship between the two countries that was not limited to oil matters, but oil could be used to cement it.

The importance of oil for Saudi Arabia goes beyond generating income for the state budget; it also gives Saudi Arabia more international power both economically and politically. The two men directed their energy ministers, Khalid al-Falih and Novak, to discuss the issue and draft a future joint action plan and issue a joint statement to be announced at a press conference, which they did the following day. "The Ministers agreed to act jointly or with other producers. In addition, the Ministers agreed to continue consultations on market conditions by establishing a joint monitoring task force to continuously review the oil market fundamentals and recommend measures and joint actions aimed at securing oil market stability and predictability."[11] During the press conference, al-Falih and Novak explained how they would work together and with other oil producers. Novak stated that "we are opening a new era of cooperation today. Our energy cooperation is moving towards a deeper and closer interaction, a strategic partnership . . . I am confident that this is a new stage of relations between the two countries, OPEC and non-OPEC. This is a historic moment, in my opinion."[12] The plan was put into motion, and the market began to improve.

Crown Prince Mohammed took the initiative, and President Putin later credited the prince for the improvement in oil prices. However, there is no doubt that Putin wanted Russia to have strong relations with Saudi Arabia and to play a leading role in the international oil market for economic and political reasons. To deliver on the leadership's desires, their energy ministers must be capable and be in sync with each other as well.

ALEXANDER NOVAK AND KHALID AL-FALIH

Alexander Novak, the Russian minister of energy, and Khalid al-Falih, the Saudi minister of energy, both played important roles in the evolution of energy cooperation between the two countries. The two men are close to the same age and had assumed a variety of responsibilities during their career before becoming energy ministers. They had climbed the ladder gradually and were both enthusiastic, hardworking, and well-informed.

Novak (born in 1971 in Ukraine) was appointed energy minister in May 2012 and has remained in this job after the big changes in the Russian cabinet in January 2020. He is soft-spoken and uses clear language and logic in his arguments. His English is not good, and he prefers to use a good English interpreter who understands petroleum issues. Some oil ministers insist on speaking English, even if they are not proficient, which hinders their ability to present their ideas and to convince others to accept them.

Novak has also earned the favor of his bosses, President Putin, Prime Minister Dimitri Medvedev, and in 2020 Prime Minister Mikhail Mishustin. He is the first Russian energy minister to have a close relationship with the Russian president and to enjoy his trust. His personality, knowledge, experience, and background, particularly in finance and financial management, were a distinct advantage in getting his view accepted by the president and the Russian government at large. Putin respects and values Novak and his opinions, and Novak has been loyal to the president. Putin calls Novak by his nickname "Sasha," a sign of affection and familiarity.

In November 2020, Novak was appointed deputy prime minister of Russia, but he kept his role as the head of the Russian delegation to OPEC+ meetings. This is a clear sign of the heavy weight that the Russian president gives OPEC+. Novak has helped to advance cooperation between Russia, Saudi Arabia, OPEC, and other producers through a gradual process. Novak had to persuade his boss and win his case against others, including Igor Sechin, the powerful CEO of Rosneft and a Putin ally known as Russia's "energy czar."

In November 2014, at a meeting in Vienna attended by representatives from Mexico, Venezuela, Russia, and Saudi Arabia, it was Sechin and not Novak who led the Russian delegation. But it was obvious that Sechin was in step with Novak. When Novak came to Riyadh with Russian prime minister Dmitry Medvedev to offer Russia's condolences on the death of King Abdullah in 2015, Novak made it clear that Russia was willing to participate in any production cut, which suggested that he had the blessing of the Russian leadership. In early 2016, Russia took the initiative by proposing an oil-production freeze. This proposal likely came from Novak with Putin's blessing.

Khalid al-Falih was appointed the Saudi Arabia minister of energy on May 7, 2016, and was given a wider mandate than that of any previous energy minister; he became the minister of energy, industry, and mineral resources. His varied portfolio included responsibility for electricity and petrochemicals, and he was also the head/chairman of about fifteen important government organizations, including two universities.

Three months after his appointment, al-Falih started thinking about how to restore stability to the oil market and eliminate "meaningless fluctuations of oil prices." After discussing the issue with Prince Abdulaziz bin Salman, on August 11, 2016, al-Falih issued a carefully written statement that contained two messages: first, Saudi Arabia was not satisfied with the prevailing market situation and price fluctuations and was willing to take a leading role in restoring a stable oil market; and second, Riyadh was willing to work with both OPEC and non-OPEC oil producers toward market stability. When giving a presentation in Kuwait a few months later, I explained that "the statement sent shock waves through the market. Prices rose by about three dollars in one day and continued to rise in the following week. The market was hungry for the leadership of a powerful country such as Saudi Arabia."[13] The timing of the statement was good; the message was clear to oil producers, and concrete actions started to evolve.

Three weeks after the September Hangzhou G20 meeting, the IEF held its ministerial meeting in Algeria. Before the conference, Novak and al-Falih had a bilateral meeting in which the Russians agreed to cut production, and Novak was confident that Moscow would deliver. However, he asked that OPEC first agree to cut production. The following day, OPEC held an Extraordinary Ministerial Meeting. After five hours of hard discussion, which lasted until midnight, the ministers recommended cutting OPEC's production by 1.2 MBD, which would be decided during the upcoming ordinary OPEC ministerial meeting. The final statement also referred to a contribution from non-OPEC producers.

As Saudi-Russian oil cooperation moved forward, al-Falih invited Novak to take part in the annual meeting of the energy ministers of the Gulf Cooperation Council (GCC) in Riyadh on October 22, 2016, a rare invitation for a non-GCC minister. Novak's trip to Riyadh was preceded by a full-day visit to Saudi Aramco, where he was given a red-carpet welcome. Al-Falih, Novak, and the Qatari minister of energy, Mohammed al-Sada, who was then president of the OPEC conference, gave a joint press conference after the Riyadh meeting. The three ministers had clear, strong, and positive messages about the future of the oil market and the cooperation between OPEC and non-OPEC countries, especially with Russia. Novak emphasized that Russia and Saudi Arabia were determined to cooperate closely on oil at all levels, which had never been the case before, and he reinforced the initial understanding by Russia and other non-OPEC producers to slash output by 0.6 MBD from January 1, 2017.

A NEW OIL MANAGEMENT AGREEMENT

On December 10, 2016, more than twenty countries, led by Saudi Arabia and Russia, agreed to implement production cuts totaling 1.8 MBD, and a Joint Declaration of Cooperation between OPEC and the participating non-OPEC countries was issued. A framework was also established for oversight and monitoring the agreement to ensure compliance by all participants.

Two important proposals were adopted at the conference. The first was creation of an OPEC/non-OPEC Joint Ministerial Monitoring Committee (JMMC) that would meet regularly to evaluate market fundamentals and monitor compliance of member countries with the agreed cuts. The committee also would follow up if there were problems of compliance from any member country. OPEC used to have a ministerial monitoring committee, but it was weak and had little importance in the decision-making process. This was not the case with the JMMC.

The second important decision was creation of a Joint Technical Committee (JTC), and oil experts from participating countries were required to meet every month to discuss technical and fundamental issues, such as current and future supplies, demand, commercial stocks, and price behavior. The JTC would also study monthly production estimates published by secondary sources as well as those communicated directly to the OPEC secretariat by the twenty-three members of OPEC+. Although similar to the OPEC Economic Commission Board (ECB) that had existed for more than forty years (chapter 4), the JTC experts from OPEC+ are more professional and more effective. They have a businesslike mentality, which has proved helpful to ministers and their decision-making.

Another important development was adoption of a new yardstick (conformity level) to measure the performance of the whole group and of individual countries. The yardstick measures how closely members are complying with their agreed production levels, and it has proven to be more effective than the old OPEC ceiling and quota system even though some OPEC members are not fully committed to it.

The agreement came into force in 2017, and its impact was felt in the first quarter of 2018 when the market was stable and prices were at a level that most OPEC+ members deemed suitable. It was even good for oil producers who were not part of the new agreement, including the United States, Canada, the North Sea, and Brazil. But he new group and its leadership faced a major challenge in the summer of 2018.

THE UNEXPECTED CHALLENGE

The price of oil climbed higher than expected during 2018 and was above $86 a barrel by October, and some experts thought prices might go even higher. Russia was constrained by the agreement and neither expected nor welcomed these high oil prices, fearing that they might lead to higher production from other countries, especially U.S. shale oil. And oil consumers were unhappy about high oil prices.

In the summer of 2018, a new player unexpectedly appeared to take part in international oil market management—Donald Trump, the U.S. president. High oil prices were bad news for President Trump and the Republican Party. During the midterm elections in 2018, the Democratic Party and their candidates were using high gasoline prices to influence voters. President Trump tweeted negative and harsh statements directly attacking OPEC, and this proved to be a major factor in the movement of oil prices. The situation became more complicated when the Trump administration decided to persuade consuming countries to stop importing oil from Iran. U.S. officials said at that time that the goal was to reduce Iranian oil exports to zero.

It was not only Trump who was unhappy about higher oil prices. The Indian government faced a dual challenge: higher oil prices and a weakening national currency (the rupee). The government imposed new taxes on some oil products, but this was difficult for the general public in India. Some Indian officials attacked OPEC privately and in closed meetings, and in August 2018, one high official described OPEC as a "greedy organization." This was unusually harsh coming from India, which had always defended the interests of fellow developing countries.[14] There was also concern that commercial stocks were lower than normal because of high demand and tighter oil supply.

Saudi Arabia normally thinks first about its immediate and long-term interests, but it seriously considers requests and the interests of its major allies, partners, and consumers (the United States, China, Japan, Korea, India, and Europe). Developing countries are usually the first to complain about high oil prices, but their voices are not loud enough to be heard and reported by the international media.

The decision to raise output was first discussed between al-Falih and Novak at the St. Petersburg International Economic Forum in May 2018. In this atmosphere, OPEC+ decided during their June meeting to increase oil production. Iran and Venezuela were against any increase and argued that if there was to be one it should be small. They and some other OPEC members were not happy that the decision had been made by Saudi Arabia and Russia. Saudi Arabia, Russia, the United Arab Emirates, and Kuwait, among others, wanted to reverse the previous production cut, which would translate into raising oil production by 1.8 MBD.

Many bilateral ministerial meetings were held in Vienna in June, as well as two important ministerial meetings. The first was an OPEC conference, and the second was a joint OPEC+ ministerial meeting. A decision by OPEC alone was almost impossible because OPEC needed a consensus from all members to increase oil production. In addition, the decision in December 2017 to cut production by 1.8 MBD was a combined agreement between OPEC and OPEC+. Because of the complexity of the situation, it was decided to increase production through OPEC+ using the newly created yardstick, the conformity level. They decided to bring it down from 147 percent to 100 percent, which meant logically and legally adhering to the agreement but in reality increasing production by 1.2 MBD. The decision was made by all twenty-four ministers of OPEC+, and it was done without providing the volume of the total increase or individual output allocation to avoid objections by some participants, especially the Iranians. In the beginning, the Iranian minister gave his blessing to the idea, but he did not understand the full details. Al-Falih and Novak explained the agreement during their meeting with the press.

Market circumstances did not work out as the Russians and the Saudis had expected. Washington did not enforce the zero Iranian oil exports it had announced before the OPEC+ meeting. Trump gave eight countries exemptions to continue importing Iranian oil, which included major Iranian oil consumers: China, India, Japan, South Korea, and Turkey. As a result, Iranian oil exports continued to flow for another year at lower levels than before the sanctions but still much higher than expected. At the same time, non-OPEC supply, especially U.S. shale oil, was rising higher than expected, and some OPEC+ members increased production above their agreed levels. For example, in November 2018, the reported Saudi oil production was 11.016 MBD, higher than the Saudi conformity level by about 0.7 MBD.

Nobody expected the increase to harm the market because it was reflecting the demand from customers, but that was not the case. Inventories began rising week after week, depressing the price of oil to below $51 in December 2018, almost the same level as before the Saudi-Russian deal. The only way out was an agreement to reduce production, first with Russia and later with OPEC and the other members of the new group. The agreement reached in December 2018 was to slash oil production by at least 1.2 MBD. Novak returned to Moscow for consultation with his government, and after further discussions between the two ministers, the Russians went along with the idea of cutting production.

The experience of Russian-Saudi cooperation beginning in 2016 shows that the market needs good management and leadership by individuals willing to take the initiative in forging good alliances, communicating clearly, and taking action when necessary. Support and intervention when needed from heads of state are crucial to ensure success and to build trust, but alliances and coordination should not be limited to ministers only. They should include professionals and experts who lay the groundwork for any action. A good alliance does not mean agreement on all issues, but understanding and appreciating the position of each side is critical.

THE CHARTER OF COOPERATION

In 2016, the year the Russian and Saudi petroleum alliance began, OPEC chose Mohammed Barkindo of Nigeria as secretary-general. Barkindo created a positive image of OPEC and established friendly and constructive relations with producer and consumer countries. He is an excellent public speaker and has extensive experience in the oil market and the energy industry, and he has strong ties with non-OPEC oil producers such as Russia. He also has highly professional relationships with energy officials and experts in Europe, Asia, the United States, and China. Nevertheless, the oil ministers of Saudi Arabia and Russia occasionally have had to work beyond OPEC. The secretary-general is accused by some inside and outside the secretariat of weak management, including not controlling the leakage of confidential information. In January 2022, OPEC ministers by acclamation, approved the nomination of Haitham Al Ghais of Kuwait as the new secretary-general. He is highly competent with extensive experience in petroleum and OPEC affairs.

An important development in the management of the international oil market and the relationship between Russia and Saudi Arabia took place in Vienna on July 2, 2019, when the countries of OPEC+ adopted the Charter of Cooperation, essentially formalizing the alliance. *Petroleum Argus* described it as "a landmark charter that provides a permanent framework for long-term cooperation on oil production policies." I also told the international media that it "transforms the ad hoc coalition of producers into a formal organization to provide long-term stability to the oil market."[15]

Speaking at a news conference after the charter was signed, Novak said, "We have been speaking about this document for quite some time now, and I can say that we have come today to a consensus around this document, and we have signed it. It is not only a historic document which solidifies our cooperation in the long run, but it also gives us a solid foundation for future joint analysis of the market, and a platform for making decisions to stabilize the market." For his part, al-Falih said the gathering "is also historic because the commitment of this now formalized partnership is being guaranteed by the top leadership. . . . Saudi Crown Prince Mohammed bin Salman and the President of Russia, Vladimir Putin."[16]

However, the charter did not come into existence easily. Prince Abdulaziz bin Salman strongly supported the alliance and contributed to its success, but the Iranian minister stood against the new charter. After more than two hours of discussion, Prince Abdulaziz talked to him on the side and found that his objections were not in principle, so Iran was brought on board after some linguistic changes were made in the charter. Apparently the Iranians were looking for recognition and attention rather than objecting to the issue based on its merit.

For Saudi Arabia and Russia to work together effectively and successfully on oil market management, they created a new system for the major oil producers. OPEC had become rigid and riddled with problems between members over the years, and political disputes often stood in the way of reaching a consensus. OPEC was slow in dealing with major developments in the international oil market, and OPEC would roll over its ceiling for many months, perhaps years, even if actual production was much higher, to avoid conflicts and long negotiations. At one point, the difference between the official ceiling and actual production was more than 2 MBD. Most of the time, Iran and two or three other countries were in the hard-liner camp, whereas Saudi Arabia, Kuwait, the United Arab Emirates, and Nigeria were in the moderate grouping. Other countries shifted alliances based on the issue.

Russia played an important part in moderating the policy of some countries, especially Iran. Iran and Saudi Arabia have major disagreements and levels of mistrust on many issues, including oil, but this is not the case between Moscow and Tehran. The Iranians cannot accuse the Russians of being influenced by Washington as they accuse the Saudis. At a time of rising tensions with the United States, Iran needs Russia more than ever before.

The big question for the future is whether the Russians will continue to act as copilots with the Saudis. The answer is most likely yes. The appointment of Prince Abdulaziz contributed to stronger relations between the ministers of the two countries, and it is clear that Novak has a lot of respect for and trust in the prince. Recent developments on the energy, political, and economic fronts have made it clear that a collaborative approach is needed to overcome challenges faced by oil producers. Above all, the emergence of Novak (replacing Sechin) as a decision maker on international energy matters for Russia has clearly improved cooperation.

The Saudi-Russian relationship is also evolving in other areas, including cross-country investment. The Russian Direct Investment Fund (RDIF) and the Saudi Public Investment Fund (PIF) are working together to identify investment opportunities in all sectors, and trade between the two countries has been on the rise. The relationship between the Saudi and Russian leaders reached a higher level during the Russian president's visit to Riyadh on October 14, 2019. In addition to the special welcome and attention Russia's president received, the two countries signed twenty agreements covering a range of topics, especially focusing on economic and energy-related cooperation. Saudi Aramco signed nine petroleum Memorandums of Understanding with Russia, and other energy-related investment agreements were made between the Sovereign Wealth Funds of both countries.

After visiting Saudi Arabia, Putin went to the United Arab Emirates where energy investments and cooperation were also high on the agenda. He then returned to Moscow and met with Turkey's president, Recep Tayyip Erdoğan, signing a major agreement regarding Syria. The following day, Putin met the Egyptian president and other African leaders to discuss cooperation between African nations and Russia, including potential Russian energy investments.

Putin has attacked the West for their treatment of Africa, and in recent years Putin has been increasingly playing a significant role in international affairs. Putin has involved Russia in some regional conflicts and problems directly or indirectly: indirectly in the case of the civil war in Libya and directly in the case of Syria. Putin has also tried to find a solution to the conflict between Egypt and Sudan with Ethiopia over the Renaissance Dam, which Ethiopia is building. In 2020, Russia played an important role in ending the Nagorno-Karabakh war between Azerbaijan and Armenia.

Abdel Monem Said Aly, a member of the Egyptian Parliament and a distinguished Arab and Egyptian thinker and author, told me "there is no doubt that President Putin's goal is to end the conflict between the three countries [Egypt, Sudan, and Ethiopia], and therefore be seen as an important global leader. However, President Trump took on this responsibility and deployed the heavier weight of the U.S. It is sad to see that the U.S failed."[17] The Biden administration is now trying to end the conflict.

Daniel Byman and Kenneth M. Pollack discussed the important roles of individual decision makers in modern history. They mentioned Crown Prince Mohammed bin Salman as "the most obvious example of a leader defying the pressure on both domestic politics and international circumstances and, in so doing, redefining both." They note that "he defied the risk averse logic of Saudi politics and is betting everything on his far-reaching reforms." With regard to the Russian leader, they wrote that "fortune favors the bold, and some leaders are skilled at seizing opportunities as they arise. . . . Putin has proved a master of Russian and international politics, and cutting and thrusting whenever his does present an opening . . . Putin . . . has evinced a combination of pride, cynicism, nationalism, and comfort with risk."[18]

President Putin's overconfidence may create new problems at home and abroad. This was clear, for example, in the oil market crisis of March–April 2020, which is discussed in the following chapter.[19]

Chapter Eleven

CROWN PRINCE MOHAMMED BIN SALMAN AND PRINCE ABDULAZIZ BIN SALMAN

The Forty-Five Day Oil Shock

On September 8, 2019, more than fifty Saudi energy officials and experts gathered in Abu Dhabi, United Arab Emirates, to take part in the World Energy Council's (WEC) triennial World Energy Congress. Saudi Arabia is an important member of the WEC and would host many activities during the congress. It organized the largest exhibition and sponsored a major workshop on Saudi domestic energy policies and new initiatives. Many Saudis were due to participate in sessions during the congress.

The Saudi energy minister, Khalid al-Falih, was not sure that he would attend the congress, and he decided not to take part in the ministerial panels. Prince Abdulaziz bin Salman, minister of state for energy and head of the Saudi National Committee in WEC, would take part in two main events: officially open the Saudi Energy Workshop and host a live interview with Helima Croft, the managing director and global head of commodity strategy at RBC Capital Markets. Prince Abdulaziz wanted the Croft interview to focus on domestic energy issues, leaving the international issues to Minister al-Falih when he met with the media.

On the sidelines of the congress, two major events were taking place: the Asian Energy Ministerial Round Table, which is organized by the International Energy Forum (IEF), and the Joint Ministerial Monitoring Committee (JMMC) of OPEC+, chaired jointly by al-Falih and the Russian energy minister Alexander Novak.

In the past, the Asian Energy Ministerial Round Table had been a large energy gathering of major Asian producers and consumers, but this event had become less influential and al-Falih was not planning to attend. The most important meeting for Minister al-Falih was the Joint Ministerial Monitoring Committee (JMMC) of OPEC+ on September 12. In addition to al-Falih and Novak, the energy ministers from Iraq, the United Arab Emirates, Venezuela, Nigeria, Algeria, Oman, and Kazakhstan planned to attend the meeting. Al-Falih was going to strongly emphasize the issue of noncompliance by some countries.

On Sunday evening, September 8, the Saudi delegation went to their beds after another long day of meetings and conference sessions, but a few hours after midnight unexpected news came out. I woke up and by chance looked at my mobile phone around 2:30 A.M. on September 9 and noticed many missed calls from Prince Abdulaziz, his assistants, journalists, oil analysts, and friends from all around the world. The news was astounding: Al-Falih was ousted as minister of energy, and Prince Abdulaziz had been appointed as his replacement.

Some people in Saudi Arabia were expecting the replacement of al-Falih and had seen signs pointing in that direction for several weeks. But there had been no information or rumors about when it might happen or who might replace him. The news was momentous, both at home and internationally, and came as a big surprise to many people and generated these questions: Why had this change happened? and What would the consequences be for Saudi oil policy? A rumor circulated widely that al-Falih had been opposed to the IPO of Saudi Aramco, a major objective for Crown Prince Mohammed bin Salman, but to say that al-Falih was ousted because he was against Aramco's IPO makes no sense and shows a misunderstanding of the Saudi government system. In fact, al-Falih fully supported the IPO and worked hard to deliver it.[1]

After talking with Prince Abdulaziz, we worked until sunrise to disseminate a clear message: The fundamentals of Saudi oil policy will not change. After all, Prince Abdulaziz had played a central role in forming and implementing this policy for more than thirty years. The idea that Prince Abdulaziz would one day become minister of energy had been raised from time to time. However, in recent times, most people, including those who thought he was best suited for the job, had stopped making such a prediction.

Many international observers and journalists had an unusual reason for ruling the prince out. It was perceived wisdom that a member of the royal family cannot become the minister of energy and that the position had to be filled by a technocrat. It was not clear why this perception was so widespread even though Prince Abdulaziz is an energy technocrat par excellence; his education, training, experience, responsibilities, and achievements since the early 1980s underline this. Clearly, being a member of the royal family should not prohibit anyone from taking any position in government if that person is qualified. In fact, there was and is no policy, formal or informal, in this regard. Since formation of the first Saudi cabinet in the early 1950s, many members of the royal family have been ministers in so-called Technocrat Ministries, including the ministries of finance, education, agriculture, housing, municipalities, and trade. Ministers from the royal family, just like other ministers, come and go.

International media coverage also misunderstood the recent evolution of al-Falih's responsibilities from being minister of health and chairman of Aramco in 2015 to becoming the minister of energy, industry, and mineral resources in 2016. Three years later, in the late summer of 2019, the Ministry of Mining and Industries Policy was removed from al-Falih's portfolio, and on September 2, the chairmanship of Aramco was transferred to the chairman of the Public Investment Fund, Yasir al-Rumayyan.

The international media generally seemed to like al-Falih. He was forthcoming and talked to the media more than what was considered normal for a Saudi energy minister. Some international observers who followed OPEC closely for many years said that al-Falih was very articulate but that talking to the media so much might create misunderstandings. Inside Saudi Arabia, especially within energy circles, the picture was different. The common belief was that al-Falih gradually lost his high stature because some were uneasy with his working style. Saudi Arabia is a traditional society, and what ministers and decision makers say privately can easily spread. Abdallah Jum'ah (president of Saudi Aramco 1995–2008) said that "Khalid is a smart engineer and hard-working manager with excellent knowledge, but his working style does not please some people who work with him."[2]

The second difficulty al-Falih faced was related to being overburdened with responsibilities. He was unable to deliver on some promises made at the beginning of his ministerial tenure, including promises related to industrial policy, the development of the minerals sector, and expectations regarding oil prices in 2018 (chapter 10). Some undelivered promises were partially the result of an overreliance on international consultants who have a tendency to say what their clients want to hear and create a rosy picture about the future.

When al-Falih was relieved of his duties, many people thought that was the end of his career. To their surprise, less than six months after his removal as minister of energy, in February of 2020 al-Falih was appointed the minister of investment. This signaled confidence in al-Falih by Saudi Arabia's leadership.

THE NEW MINISTER

As the new Saudi minister of energy, Prince Abdulaziz will balance his experience and knowledge with his working style. He was well-known and highly respected even before he became the energy minister. He is realistic and unlikely to make big promises that are not easily delivered. This is largely due to his nature and his long firsthand experience within the government. Prince Abdulaziz relies more on national experts than on international consultants, and when he uses consultants, he rigorously questions their opinions and suggestions. His management style is different from that of the four previous Saudi energy ministers discussed in this book.

Prince Abdulaziz knows the working system of government very well and has a wide range of relationships inside Saudi Arabia with links beyond the energy sector. He has taken a leading role in intellectual and economic gatherings and debates and enjoys reading and watching documentary movies on history and geopolitics. He is also the head of various charity programs. Prince Abdulaziz is a modest man who walks to the mosque in his local neighborhood. He became chairman of the Board of Trustees of the King Fahd University of Petroleum and Minerals, and in early 2021 he announced policy changes that paved the way for women to enroll in the university for the first time since its establishment sixty years ago.

Prince Abdulaziz is well-known internationally, especially for his connections and extensive understanding of economic and political policy and energy issues. He had been the second ranking official in the Saudi delegation to the OPEC ministerial meetings for more than thirty years and led the international team within the ministry on policy decisions related to the international oil market and OPEC. He was instrumental in the formation of the IEA-OPEC dialogue, which led to creation of the International Energy Forum (IEF). Prince Abdulaziz had supported creating a petroleum and energy research center in Saudi Arabia since the late 1980s, and after more than twenty-five years of debate and discussion and a lot of bureaucratic problems, the King Abdullah Petroleum Studies and Research Center was established in 2007 in Riyadh. Prince Abdulaziz also oversaw many international energy conferences in Saudi Arabia, including the producer-consumer meeting in 2000, the OPEC summit in 2007, and the Jeddah energy summit in 2008.

These activities, in addition to being a chairman or a member on boards of many Saudi and international economic and energy organizations, reveal a man who is well-connected in the energy world on both the technical and policy sides. Because of his strong love and dedication to the petroleum and energy sector, he once told me that he was unwilling to take on a more prestigious position outside the energy field. Prince Abdulaziz is in regular and direct communication with the media, oil consultants, and energy research centers, and above all with his own Saudi advisers in the ministry.

POLICIES OF THE SIXTH SAUDI ENERGY MINISTER

The Saudi Ministry of Energy was established in 1960, and five ministers have preceded Prince Abdulaziz. Will Saudi oil policy change under Prince Abdulaziz? In terms of style and his approach to challenges, the answer is yes, but the fundamentals of Saudi oil policy have remained the same for thirty-five years and are based on the kingdom's oil, economic, and political interests. This position was consolidated in the Saudi Petroleum Strategy, which was written in 2000 and revised in 2006. During that time, Prince Abdulaziz was leading the team that was developing this strategy.[3]

One of the major goals of the strategy was to generate a reasonable income for the country and the government within a stable international oil market. Contrary to the thinking of some outsiders, this is a highly complex objective. A Saudi energy minister has to match the desired government income with Saudi exports, as well as other factors such as OPEC and OPEC+ agreements. In addition, Saudi Arabia is the leading country within OPEC and OPEC+ and has to set a good example of adhering to its production quota. If the Saudis do not adhere to these agreements, then nobody else will. Also, Saudi Arabia prefers stable prices, taking into account that it's the market that determines prices in the end.

The Saudi minister of energy has to take into account several important factors. First, balancing short- and long-term interests of its oil operations is a key priority. This has technical elements, such as the depletion rate of the oil fields, the rate of replacement of the produced oil, and economic elements for future production. At the current production rate and replacement level, Saudi Arabia will be able to produce oil for more than eighty years.

Second, any decision should not undermine the interest of oil consumers and Saudi energy partners. More than eighty companies in fifty countries buy oil from Saudi Aramco, which include some major producing and exporting countries such as the United States, the United Kingdom, Canada, Indonesia, and Malaysia. Ahmed al-Subaey, Aramco's vice president for marketing, sales, and supply planning, stated that "Saudi Aramco enjoys a special and unique relationship with its world-wide customers that has stood the test of time . . . these institutionalized relationships span from 20 to 80 years."[4]

Third, the Saudi energy minister must consider the health of global energy industries and the health of the global economy, especially their effects on developing and emerging economies.

Fourth, one of the major responsibilities of the Ministry of Energy is to promote a clean environment and address climate change concerns. The ministry's team has taken the lead in global negotiations on this issue and is promoting projects, such as carbon capturing and storage, that can reduce the amount of carbon dioxide in the atmosphere. Through the Ministry of Energy, Saudi Arabia has employed highly qualified people who have international respect in this area. Currently, Prince Abdulaziz is strongly promoting the Circular Carbon Economy (CCE) approach, which was endorsed by the leader of the G20 in 2020.

A fifth important role is to explain energy policy and its direction and gain the approval of the king, the crown prince, the Economic Ministerial Committee, the Council of Ministers, and the Hydrocarbon Committee (depending on the relevant issue). The minister also has to take public opinion into consideration, which is increasingly vocal on social media.

Prince Abdulaziz suggested the creation of technical bilateral committees with many oil-consuming and oil-producing countries in the late 1980s, and the number of participants continues to grow. Although the United Kingdom, France, Russia, China, Japan, India, and Korea are committee members, international attention focuses on the relationship between Saudi Arabia and the United States. Another significant relationship that receives little international media attention is the Saudi petroleum relationship with less developed economies. They truly are the ones most affected by higher oil prices and supply shortages. During periods of energy crises, these countries talk with Saudi Arabia and express their concerns.[5]

A new and important objective for the energy minister is to integrate the various components of the Saudi energy sector. Saudi Arabia has many sources of energy and many types of users spread out in a country as large as Western Europe. The current sources of energy are oil and natural gas, but more renewables will be added in the future, especially solar, wind, and possibly thermals and nuclear. The kingdom's goal by 2030 is for 50 percent of power generation to come from renewable energy sources. Prince Abdulaziz's goal is to create synergy matches between users and sources, taking into account the relative advantage of each source in terms of type, cost, needs, and location. For example, in the northwest region of Saudi Arabia, a future NEOM megacity with resorts and international tourist attractions will largely use solar energy. The energy needs and costs of each region are different, and integrating them is not an easy task. Yet, the work with natural gas to connect many regions started in 2021.

Part of this task is to increase the integration of the energy sector with the economy at large. Energy should be a major driver for economic growth, increasing demand for local products and services and finding more opportunities for small businesses, enterprises, innovators, and local content providers, and Prince Abdulaziz plans to devote much more attention to them.[6]

In 2000, Prince Abdulaziz took on the mission of improving energy efficiency in the kingdom following years of uncontrolled increasing energy consumption. He collaborated with international organizations and governmental and private stakeholders to establish the Saudi Energy Efficiency Center. This led to creation of the Saudi Energy Efficiency Program (SEEP), whose mandate is to improve energy efficiency in the kingdom as an intergovernmental effort. SEEP was instrumental in rationalizing the kingdom's domestic energy demand through more than eighty initiatives (regulatory, funding mechanisms, target setting, etc.) to improve efficiency, which led to improvements in energy savings.

Internationally, Prince Abdulaziz's major goal is for the kingdom to be the most trusted and reliable oil supplier in the world. During a speech in Moscow on October 2, 2019, less than one month after his appointment, Prince Abdulaziz emphasized this goal, pointing out that having spare production capacity is important to maintain and enhance the kingdom's role as the most reliable supplier.

When Iran (or one of its clients) attacked major Saudi oil facilities at Abqaiq and Khurais, the world lost about 5.7 MBD of production capacity. The major concern of the Saudi Government was to maintain Saudi Arabia's reputation as the most reliable international oil supplier. Prince Abdulaziz explained that Saudi Arabia will use local and international storage and reduce the supply to local refiners, and petroleum products of the strategic reserve will be used to meet national needs. The prince was judged by many inside and outside Saudi Arabia to have risen to the occasion and was praised by the public and the national and international press. It was a major challenge nationally and internationally, and he passed it with flying colors. This was the sixth time the kingdom took on this role (1979–1980, 1990, 2003–2004, 2008, and 2020).

Prince Abdulaziz is unlikely to make significant international changes to overall Saudi oil policy unless the market and other producers force him to do so. But changes related to emphasis, personality, and style are important in the decision-making process. For example, the minister is being very robust with other members of OPEC+ when it comes to adhering to their quotas. He introduced a new concept—compensation—requiring a country that produces above its quota in one month to further reduce its production by more than its allocation in the following months to fully adhere to its overall production level.

Prince Abdulaziz is likely to strengthen the bilateral Saudi oil relationship with other countries. He believes it is important to respect the opinion and participation of all countries, both large and small. It sounds like an idealistic concept that would be difficult to achieve. Nevertheless, he is respected by OPEC officials, including the Iranians, who are often difficult to deal with, and the Iranian former energy minister, Bijan Zanganeh, has called him a "longtime friend."[7]

Being energy minister is different from being the second in command in the ministry. The buck stops with Prince Abdulaziz now. Saudi oil ministers may become unhappy with domestic developments such as the economic and financial situation or their relationships with others, and they may be frustrated by the market, OPEC, and their fellow ministers. Prince Abdulaziz is capable of maneuvering around any of these problems.

THE SAUDI ARAMCO IPO

One of the goals of Crown Prince Mohammed bin Salman since 2016 has been privatization of many government-owned companies, including Saudi Aramco. It is part of the Vision 2030 initiative to improve, expand, and diversify the Saudi economy. In my opinion as well as that of many others, privatizing Aramco was the right thing to do. It accomplished many goals at the same time:

1. Provided more transparency nationally and internationally
2. Created a business-like mentality (not cost plus as used to be the case)
3. Expanded Aramco's activities nationally and internationally, upstream and downstream (the company had not been allowed to look for international upstream opportunities)
4. Provided more accountability to shareholders
5. Competed on the same level with other major international oil companies (which should increase efficiency and productivity)
6. Generated money for the Public Investment Fund of Saudi Arabia
7. Enlarged the Saudi stock market

Prince Abdulaziz was engaged in this process from the beginning and led the legal team for the privatization. "He was working day and night with the lawyers, financial, technical, political, and media advisors. Sometimes, we would spend many hours on how to settle the meaning of this or that word or phrase. National interest was the driver and the framework of all of his works," said Turki Althunayyan, consultant to the minister and supervisor of legal affairs.[8]

When the final decision was taken to implement the IPO, Prince Abdulaziz was the energy minister and a member of the Supreme Committee of Hydrocarbon Affairs. He was a leading advocate for floating the shares on the national stock market (Tadawul), betting that Saudi individuals and institutions would cover the entire subscription and that there was no need for an international listing. That is what happened, and the prince was proved to be right.[9]

To prepare Saudi Aramco for the IPO launch in November 2019, the government had to enact a hydrocarbon law and renegotiate its concession agreement with Aramco. The company also had to redraft its bylaws and revisit its governance structure. With the energy minister no longer de facto or de jure chairman of the board and the government's shareholding changing with an initial offering of 1.5 percent to the public, financial supervision and regulation of the company has increased in importance.[10] With the floating of Aramco's shares, the energy ministry needs a strong technical department and a qualified workforce to carry out this responsibility.

There has long been speculation in international circles about the relationship between the Saudi government and Aramco. Since Aramco became a Saudi registered international oil company in 1988, the government has kept its intervention in the affairs of Aramco to a minimum.[11] Unlike other national oil companies, Aramco has been relatively independent and will be even more so now that some of its shares are owned by the public. The Saudi government is very sensitive to the Saudi public's reaction to its behavior in the stock market. Close to five million Saudis, about 25 percent of the total population, own shares in the stock market, and more than a dozen major Saudi companies listed on the market are partly owned by the government through the Public Investment Fund.[12]

RESTRUCTURING THE MINISTRY

Prince Abdulaziz has dedicated a lot of time and effort to improving the functions and structure of the ministry. In addition to OPEC, OPEC+, and other international activities, it is essential that the ministry supervise and regulate the oil and gas industry in all phases of exploration and production, refining, distribution, and marketing. The ministry also supervises the power industry, including the development of renewables and nuclear energy, and implements energy efficiency rules and regulations. To successfully create a well-functioning ministry, Prince Abdulaziz needs to achieve two things: build human capability and restructure activities within the ministry with a clear business line.

Over the past forty years, the ministry's responsibilities have evolved. No clear structure or processes were established inside the ministry. Instead, the ministry relied on Saudi Aramco and Petromin for human resources, information and data, studies, and some financial resources. During Ali

Al-Naimi's tenure as energy minister, more than sixty people from Aramco worked for the ministry, and that number reached 150 as the duties of the ministry increased during Khalid al-Falih's tenure. Prince Abdulaziz ended this practice, and Aramco personnel were either transferred to the ministry or went back to work at Aramco. Two areas have been neglected since the mid-1990s and require special attention and are expected to be strengthened, especially with the new structure and responsibility of the ministry and the partial floating of Aramco's stock nationally and perhaps internationally.

Before the Saudi government's acquisition of Aramco in 1980, the ministry regulated the American oil company under the terms of the 1933 concession and its amendments. This included supervising its technical and safety operations as well as managing its financial records for collection of taxes and royalties. Two dedicated ministry directorates operating from the Eastern Province fulfilled those roles. The first supervised the technical activities of Aramco and other companies working in Saudi Arabia (including in the neutral zone) in areas such as drilling, the production level of each oil well and field, the depletion rate, and other technical and petroleum engineering issues. The second role was fulfilled by the government controller, ensuring compliance with the tax code and verifying the financial practices of the companies. After the government created Saudi Aramco in 1988, these two regulatory functions were marginal because it was thought that the national oil company would be as keen to implement the government's dictates as was the ministry itself.

As a young leader from a new and enlightened generation, Crown Prince Mohammed bin Salman has given the climate issue special attention based on his personal beliefs. In 2017, he began to focus on renewable energy and the creation of highly sophisticated clean energy projects in such areas as the Red Sea and NEOM. In 2019, Crown Prince Mohammed initiated a project to make Riyadh a green city, and this idea was expanded in 2021 to include not only the kingdom but also the whole Middle East region. Instead of focusing on military, political, or economic issues, regional cooperation is now focused on environmental issues.

Prince Abdulaziz believes in these ideas and projects and is working hard to implement them. He is likely to lead a transformation in the Saudi energy sector, not just because of his background and knowledge but also because of changing circumstances and his personality. Prince Abdulaziz has already made major structural changes in the electricity sector, and he wants to leave his mark on the industry and deliver long-term achievements. Many people believe that he will do so. With regard to the new Saudi policy on climate change and global warming, Prince Abdulaziz used his diplomatic and negotiation skills to promote acceptance of the Circular Carbon Economy, which was endorsed by the leadership of the G20 in 2020 during Saudi Arabia's presidency. It is an important tool to capture carbon from fossil fuels and protect the environment.

I follow Twitter because I believe it reflects what Saudi citizens think about their energy ministers and energy issues. For example, Ali Al-Naimi is greatly admired for his modest attitude and his achievements from a humble upbringing. Khalid al-Falih received mixed opinions based on interpretations of what he said, and Prince Abdulaziz is greatly admired by the Saudi public. Somebody tweeted, "Why did we not have him as a minister before?"Another asked, "Where was this man, hidden from us all this time!" Prince Abdulaziz's time as energy minister will be judged in the fullness of time, but I worked with him for thirty years and am confident that Prince Abdulaziz will continue to be an outstanding minister of energy.

THE SIXTH OIL MINISTER AND THE SIXTH OIL CRISIS

One important measure of an energy minister's tenure is how the ministry deals with the international oil market during a price collapse or a steep price rise. Each Saudi energy minister has dealt with these challenges in his own way and achieved different results, and Prince Abdulaziz will not be an exception.

In January 2020, the oil market began to face major challenges regarding demand and prices as a result of the coronavirus pandemic. It was a challenge to the new global leadership and to the ministers of OPEC+, especially Saudi Arabia and Russia. On Monday, March 8, 2020, the oil price dropped by 25 percent—the second largest one-day drop on record. A number of factors were driving this slide, including the impact of the pandemic on the global economy, a drop in oil consumption, high uncertainty about almost everything, negative sentiment arising from the failure of the OPEC+ meeting, and reduced oil prices by Aramco and others.

As the crisis intensified, no clear solution was in sight. This crisis was not the result of human misjudgment or economic circumstances, as was the case with previous crises. This time an invisible virus resulted in major disruptions in the international oil market and wreaked more damage than ever before. But the solution to this sixth crisis still depended on human judgment and actions.

The first crisis was in late 1985 when Ahmed Zaki Yamani decided to restore market share using the netback pricing mechanism (chapter 1). This led to the collapse of the market. It took a couple of years and a new OPEC policy for the market to recover, supported by strong demand growth.

The second crisis occurred during the Iraqi invasion of Kuwait in August 1990. The oil supply was cut by more than four million barrels per day, and the price doubled. This crisis lasted about six months and led to major changes in the structure of the international oil supply (chapters 2 and 3).

The third crisis began with the Jakarta agreement of 1997 and its aftermath. Oil prices collapsed for more than fourteen months, and OPEC and other oil producers had to implement deep cuts (more than four million barrels daily) to bring the market into balance and stabilize oil prices. This was the first such case and perhaps the last of its kind. A change of government in Venezuela and production cuts by Saudi Arabia, Kuwait, and the United Arab Emirates on behalf of Iran facilitated the end of this crisis.

The fourth crisis created perhaps the most interesting effects on the international oil market. The global economic crisis of 2008 unhinged the oil market. Within a year, oil prices went up from just under $100/BBL at the beginning of the year to around $145/BBL at midyear and then down to below $35/BBL by year's end. OPEC alone had to cut production three times in the second half of 2008 by a total of 4.2 MBD (chapters 7 and 10).

The fifth crisis was a price crisis. From 2014 to 2016, oil prices dropped from over $100/BBL to almost $26/BBL in less than twenty-four months. The price drop began with a new policy initiated by Saudi oil minister Al-Naimi that spun out of control and failed to meet expectations (chapter 9).

With the exception of 2008, these five crises resulted from the judgments or misjudgments of the decision makers. The sixth crisis had a completely different driver—it started with a virus in one city, Wuhan, China, and spread all over the world within three months. It first hit the Chinese economy and then the global economy, and transportation, tourism, trade, and the industrial and service sectors—the backbone of oil consumption—were destroyed. Predictions about the future of the international market changed almost weekly, from bad to worse.

Prince Abdulaziz was charged with a heavy burden and had two major responsibilities: he is the minister of energy of the most important oil country, and he is the head of the Joint Ministerial Monitoring Committee (JMMC) of OPEC+, where decisions regarding the international oil market begin and end. For OPEC+ to succeed, Prince Abdulaziz believed they needed to act big and get ahead of the curve. He knew this from having lived through the experiences of the previous five crises.[13] Prince Abdulaziz emerged as the undisputed OPEC leader following the OPEC meeting in December 2019.

When the Joint Technical Committee met in late February, they recommended an additional production cut of 0.6 MBD on top of an existing production cut of 1.7 MBD agreed on in December of 2019. (Saudi Arabia had pledged to make an additional voluntary cut of 400,000 B/D.) It was felt that this would be enough to halt the slide in oil prices. But at the OPEC meeting in early March, this sentiment was changing as new information about the virus, the global economy, and the prospects for a strong decline of oil consumption became known. After a careful assessment by the ministers and their experts, an additional reduction of 1.5 MBD on top of the 1.7 MBD already in place was needed. This would take the total to 3.6 MBD until the end of 2020. This new proposal was to be taken to the OPEC+ meeting the next day.

Early in the morning of March 6, everyone was waiting for Minister Novak to return from his consultations in Moscow with President Putin. The expectation was that he would agree to the new cuts because it was felt to be the minimum that could be done to balance the market in 2020. Within the proposed 1.5 MBD cut, the share allotted to non-OPEC countries was one-third, or 500,000 B/D. OPEC would decide how to divide its share of the one million (pro rata, as usual), and Russia would coordinate the shares of non-OPEC producers.

Novak had a meeting with Prince Abdulaziz in which they discussed the developments of the previous day. Then Novak had another meeting with non-OPEC producers (Kazakhstan, Azerbaijan, Oman, Mexico, Malaysia, and Brunei) and asked each country how much it could contribute to the 500,000 B/D total cut. Novak was able to collect 160,000 or more barrels daily from the other countries. One minister asked how much Russia was willing to contribute, but Novak did not answer. Without Russian participation in the cut, as one of the participating delegates told me later, a deal would be almost impossible to achieve.

After the failed meeting of non-OPEC ministers, Prince Abdulaziz and Novak had a special meeting. They realized the impossibility of reaching an agreement acceptable to all, mostly because of domestic or political issues. However, both ministers emphasized the importance of maintaining the continuity of their personal dialogue, the Saudi-Russian close energy relationship, OPEC+, and the Charter of Cooperation. They also discussed the upcoming meeting of the Saudi-Russian Joint Cooperation Committee, which is headed by Prince Abdulaziz and Novak and covers economic issues between the two countries.

The joint meeting among all OPEC+ ministers went as planned: the opening statements, the presentation, and the discussion. But it was decided not to have joint press conference or a press release, which was normally done, and decisions about the dates of future meetings were not made. After the failed OPEC+ meeting, all knew that oil prices would collapse in light of negative global demand, high inventory levels, and no possibility in sight of a big cut if needed. In the absence of an agreement, it was clear that every country would work independently to defend its interest using the tools it had to gain market share by selling more oil if it had the capability to do so.

It was clear that we were in the midst of a free for all oil market. What triggered it is the subject of much debate. Daniel Yergin said it was the coronavirus. Javier Blas, the chief energy correspondent for Bloomberg, laid the blame elsewhere in his tweet on March 8: "If there is a smoking gun for the price war, that was Russian Oil Minister Novak leaving the OPEC building and saying everyone was free to pump-at-will from April. That was the start of the price war. Everyone else is just reacting."

Saudi Arabia, Russia, Kuwait, the United Arab Emirates, Kazakhstan, Azerbaijan, and Nigeria believed that they had spare production capacity and could increase their production in April. Some of them thought raising production would compensate for part of their lost income due to lower oil prices. Saudi Arabia has the highest capacity, with more than 12 MBD. Russia, for example, said it could produce 200,000 to 300,000 more barrels per day, rising to 500,000 B/D within months.

After the failure of the meeting, Saudi Arabian officials felt that oil prices would drop, perhaps into freefall. They also believed that there would be additional competition among oil producers. After careful study, assessments, and close coordination within the government, Saudi Arabia had no choice but to act, and to act first, big, and fast. It had to capture market share before other countries did so. It needed to replace some lost income as a result of expected lower oil prices. Crown Prince Mohammed was the decision maker in this regard, and it later proved to be a good move.

To set this plan in motion, Saudi Aramco had to get involved. Prince Abdulaziz flew directly from Vienna to Dhahran on March 7 to meet with Aramco's management and discuss how to increase Saudi production and find customers for the newly produced oil at a time of decreasing demand. The company decided to cut the differential between Saudi crude and benchmarks for Asia, Europe, and the United States, leading to the lowest differential ever. Aramco would also increase production and exports to the maximum. "The goal was to capture market share for Saudi Arabia which reflects its production capacity and oil reserves, just as other countries would in the absence of a cooperative framework," said Adeeb al-Aama, the Saudi OPEC governor.[14] This was not an oil price war, as some international media and oil experts claimed; it was not an action against Russia or any other party.

THE RUSSIAN FACTOR

Why did Russia refuse to be part of the non-OPEC 0.5 MBD production cut or even negotiate a smaller one? By talking to some officials and oil experts, reading interviews and statements from Russian officials, and looking at media and other reports, a number of factors may have been considered.

First, President Putin believed that he had become a very successful, big, and important leader internationally, and he was popular at home and was consolidating his power domestically. In early March, Putin backed a constitutional amendment in Parliament that would allow him to remain president until 2036. At that time, President Trump's importance on the world stage was weak. Boris Johnson of the United Kingdom was new and busy with many domestic problems and with Brexit. Angela Merkel of Germany had never tried to take on a global leadership role, and she was stepping down in 2021. The Chinese president, Xi Jinping, was intent on becoming a distinguished international leader, but China's trade war with the United States and the coronavirus slowed down this ambition. The president of France, Emmanuel Macron, had little charisma abroad and had made few attempts to take on an international leadership role. The Indian prime minister, Narendra Modi, had many domestic problems and had developed little leadership importance beyond India and Hindu nationalism.

President Vladimir Putin of Russia had become involved in many international issues, and he had created a positive image for himself in some parts of the world.[15] There was some talk, which is unconfirmed, that Putin was feeling so important that he had refused to answer telephone calls from presidents of less important oil-producing states when the oil crisis began in early March.[16]

In the early morning of March 6, before Novak returned to Vienna, Putin met with Novak, the heads of some Russian oil companies, and other important officials at a Russian airport to decide on the Russian stance regarding the new OPEC+ production cut. The decision not to participate was made there, most likely because the anti-OPEC+ and anti-production-cut voices had the upper hand.

Within this context we must consider the Russia-U.S. relationship (chapter 10). Beginning in 2008, the United States had introduced a number of measures targeting Russia's energy sector, investments, and technology transfers. The latest U.S. sanctions targeted Russia's Nord Stream II gas pipeline from Russia to Germany and the marketing of Venezuelan petroleum products by the Russian oil trading company Rosneft. Some decision makers in Russia believed that they had to fight back. They believe that the growth in U.S. shale oil and gas production would enable the United States to become an oil and gas exporter again, competing with Russia in some energy markets, especially in Europe. They also did not want to promote the visibility or certainty of U.S. shale oil investors and producers. Others thought that the OPEC+ decision to limit production and keep oil above $50 helped U.S. shale oil grow. Therefore, if oil prices dropped below $45, U.S. shale oil production would fall. This would weaken U.S competition and expand room for Russia to increase its production.[17]

Decision makers in Russia, like those in other countries, base their beliefs and decisions on the information they have, their interpretation of it, and their expectations and forecasts. Sometimes they look at this information and interpret it to fit their own beliefs or wishful thinking. They also base it on the behavior and statements coming from other countries, especially if they are adversaries. Apparently, Russian energy officials did not believe that there was a clear picture about the international oil market and the impact of the coronavirus on the global economy and the oil market. Therefore, they preferred not to take big steps, instead dealing with the situation quarter by quarter, or perhaps remaining less involved. They did not share the opinion that OPEC+ needed to get ahead of the curve and commit to a big response.

Oil officials and oil companies in Russia did not think the price would go below $40, and a price of $41–$42 would meet the Russian government's needs. Even if the price went lower, Russia has the financial resources to handle it with little negative impact on Russia's overall economic, financial, and oil interests.[18] Equally important, the pro-OPEC+ side of Novak, Kirill Dmitriev, head of the Russian investment authority, and some Russian private companies were losing their argument against the anti-OPEC+ campaign led by the powerful boss of Rosneft, Igor Sechin.

In Vienna, the picture was different. Prince Abdulaziz worked hard to secure a sound agreement and a good working petroleum relationship with Russia, but it seemed that the decision was not up to Novak and there was no room for compromise. The Saudis were frustrated with Russia but also with other countries that were not willing to fully adhere to their agreed cuts. Saudi Arabia had no choice but to act rapidly and decisively, increasing production and lowering price differentials to find buyers for the new crude.

The failure of the OPEC+ meeting and the Saudi oil price differentials precipitated the oil price decline, but the underlining reasons were more complex. The coronavirus pushed the global economy into recession, and the demand for and consumption of oil took a big hit. Oil demand lost more than twenty years' of growth, returning to levels similar to those at the beginning of the century. Even worse was the news that some oil companies in Texas could not find buyers or places to store their oil, pushing prices into the negative level, something that had never been seen before.

The first five oil crises led to big changes in the structure of the international oil market and relationships, and sometimes these relationships went beyond oil. The fifth crisis brought Saudi Arabia and Russia close to each other, but the sixth crisis drove them apart. However, unforeseen and unexpected circumstances emerged a short time later.

DEMAND DESTRUCTION, A PRICE COLLAPSE, AND RECOVERY

Unprecedented dramatic events shook the international oil market in the spring of 2020. The U.S. oil benchmark (West Texas Intermediate oil) fell from $50 in early March to −$30 on April 20, the first time it had moved into negative territory. Week after week global oil consumption estimates plunged, from about 1.5 MBD in early March to more than 20 MBD by April. Equally important were changes in the decision-making process. After the failed OPEC+ meeting of March 6, media and experts talked about a price war, the end of the Russian-Saudi oil alliance, a free international oil market, and the end of oil management.

Talk of an end to the Russian-Saudi oil alliance proved to be premature. Although bilateral discussions about the oil market had stopped, they resumed a week later.

The free-for-all oil market, actual or perceived, lasted for only thirty days. On previous occasions, this type of free oil market had survived for a couple of months or even as long as two years. Some oil experts I talked to said that a true free oil market, which some American officials promoted, would be damaging to all.

For more than one hundred years, the oil market had followed one type of supply management or another, and individual decision makers made significant contributions to this process. In the spring of 2020, a new oil market manager came to town—the U.S. president, Donald Trump. This was a clear sign of the depth of the crisis and signaled a change in the role of the United States in the oil markets (chapter 10). Trump took the initiative, suggesting a reduction in the oil supply by all major oil producers and urging President Putin, King Salman, and Crown Prince Mohammed to work together to restore stability to the market. The result of this process was a major production cut (up to 19 MBD, the largest ever) and introduction of a new type of supply management.

Other government officials also influenced the decision-making process. One of them was Kirill Dmitriev, a powerful, smart, and articulate young decision maker within the Russian establishment who had a special relationship with President Putin, including at a personal level.[19] Dmitriev was a frequent visitor to Saudi Arabia and had well-established relationships with Crown Prince Mohammed and many Saudi ministers and top government officials. Dmitriev met with Prince Mohammed on March 20, and he had been encouraging cooperation between the leadership of the two countries since 2016.

The second man in this group was the U.S. secretary of energy Danny Ray Brouillette, who formulated President Trump's international oil policy and shaped the opinions of influential U.S. decision makers.[20] Soft spoken, with a logical and easygoing personality, Brouillette was loyal to his boss. His knowledge and experience in energy and related industries enabled him to make good judgments based on sound reasoning. In addition, he understood the political and working relationships inside Washington and was in contact with the White House. Brouillette and Prince Abdulaziz also liked and respected each other, which is a critical component for decision makers struggling to resolve a crisis.

The third person in this group was the executive director of the International Energy Agency (IEA), Fatih Birol. He had worked with OPEC before joining the IEA in 1995 as their chief economist. After the failure of the OPEC+ meeting and the fall in oil prices, Birol framed the situation as an international problem that was not limited to oil producers. After consultation with the United States and other members, he felt that the IEA should get involved, and Birol began working with Saudi Arabia in March 2020.[21] Prince Abdulaziz and Birol had known each other for many years, and they agreed that oil producers, including some IEA members, should join OPEC+ in cutting production, but this would have to be done through a new format.

The United States and some other Western countries were unwilling to sit down with OPEC+ to discuss the international oil market, especially if Iran and Venezuela were at the table. So a new venue had to be found. Saudi Arabia held the presidency of the G20 in 2020 and called for an emergency meeting of G20 energy ministers. Norway was not a member of OPEC+ or the G20, but Saudi Arabia was able to invite Norway to join the discussions at the G20 as a special guest and to join the discussion among OPEC+ countries as an observer. In the end, Norway made a very positive contribution by reducing their production.

In Riyadh, Prince Abdulaziz set up a crisis room and worked around the clock with his team of Saudi oil experts to assess the international oil market and its future. This effort reminded me of the oil crisis room Prince Abdulaziz had set up during the military campaign to liberate Kuwait in 1991. The prince and his team were in daily contact with the oil-producing and major oil-consuming countries as the level of demand destruction continued to change not only weekly but even daily.

Saudi Arabia, Russia, and the United States agreed to do whatever was possible to bring stability back to the market. The responsibility of delivering the desired goals rested on the shoulders of Prince Abdulaziz because he was the minister of the most important oil-producing and oil-exporting country, was chairman of the OPEC+ Ministerial Monitoring Committee, and was the head of the G20 energy ministers. Decisions had to be made as quickly as possible through virtual meetings due to health precautions required during the pandemic.

Prince Abdulaziz was active on many fronts both domestically and internationally. He had to consult and coordinate closely with Crown Prince Mohammed and get approval from related institutions within Saudi Arabia as well. Using the best possible information from different sources, his team made proposal after proposal for the amount and duration of oil production cuts. The prince also had to discuss these issues with many participants, including the United States, Russia, the Arab Gulf states, and Algeria (which held the presidency of the OPEC conference).

Saudi Arabia and Russia succeeded in getting OPEC+ to collectively agree on the amount, duration, and method of the cuts, and it was decided to conduct the OPEC+ meeting first, where a production cut of 10 MBD would be approved. Subsequently, there would be a meeting with the G20 oil ministers. Before the two meetings with all forty-three member countries (OPEC+ and G20), they agreed that the proposed amount of the total reduction would be 19 MBD; they also suggested contributions for each country and the method of reduction. The agreement would last for two years (the first of such duration).

The first meeting for OPEC+ was on April 9, and the meeting dragged on for more than six hours because of a disagreement between the Saudis and Mexicans over the proposed reduction. The agreement required Mexico to cut their production by 0.4 MBD, but Mexico did not accept this and insisted on only cutting 0.1 MBD. Prince Abdulaziz was worried that if this was accepted other countries would also look for exceptions and special treatment. In addition, the prince knew that such an exception would make the agreement weak, and it would be difficult to achieve the desired results. President Trump intervened and proposed that the United States would make up the difference on behalf of Mexico. This was not legally possible, nevertheless it helped ease the problem.

After four days and three very long separate meetings, it was agreed to cut the production of all participating countries. OPEC+ incurred a 10.0 MBD straight production cut, and contributions from other countries would come via two methods: (1) an expected natural decline as a result of lower oil prices, and (2) reducing the oil glut by allocating it to U.S. strategic oil storage. Other G20 countries promised to increase their strategic reserves as well.

There is no doubt that the forty-five days that shocked the market proved that the international oil market needs good cooperation, strong management, and enlightened individuals to steer it. Although people will debate issues such as the oil price war, who blinked first, and who won and who lost, one thing is certain—this shock brought about major structural changes in the thinking and workings of the international oil market. The United States, Western countries, and OPEC+ are no longer adversaries; they have become partners who need to work together for mutual benefit, especially in times of major crises.

After the second OPEC+ meeting, I called Prince Abdulaziz to congratulate him on the terrific job he and his team was doing, to which he responded, "Tonight, I hopefully will sleep eight hours, after forty-five sleepless nights," but then added, "tomorrow will be another day. It might be as difficult as yesterday." He was right. A couple of weeks later, Prince Abdulaziz faced a new challenge that would test his ability to keep the OPEC+ countries together to achieve the desired results.

When the designated secondary source production estimates for the month of May came out, at least five countries failed to adhere to their pledged cuts (Iraq, Nigeria, Kazakhstan, Angola, and Gabon). Their total overproduction was more than one million barrels a day, which was a lot of oil during a major crisis like this. Over the years, OPEC and OPEC+ have experienced this problem from various countries. Nonadherence is like a virus that can, and does, spread from country to country and increase month after month, and it has to be contained. Sometimes the market or political circumstances take care of it, but on other occasions that is not the case.

This time was different, and Prince Abdulaziz realized this. Saudi Arabia and its major allies (Kuwait and the United Arab Emirates) were making additional cuts over and above the agreement, totaling approximately 1.2 MBD, and the kingdom needed to push others to at least adhere to their official cuts. Prince Abdulaziz demanded full adherence from those who were failing to comply in May, and he required a transparent program to compensate for any overproduced barrels with deeper cut in the coming months. This was done for the first time and by talking to individual countries, one by one.

The Ministerial Monitoring Committee of OPEC+ met in early June 2020, and Prince Abdulaziz played a vital role at this meeting. The next day an analysis by Julian Lee was titled "Saudi Arabia Lays Down the Law to the Oil Market."[22] Another article stated that "the deal is a victory for Saudi Arabia and Russia, who spent a week cajoling fellow members to fulfill their obligations. It's a particular vindication for the Kingdom's Energy Minister Prince Abdulaziz bin Salman, who has consistently pushed fellow members to stop cheating on their quota since his appointment last year."[23] After reading these two pieces by Bloomberg, I reflected on the ten months that had passed since Prince Abdulaziz had been appointed Saudi Arabia's energy minister.

Ten months is a brief moment in time in the history of oil, but what a roller coaster the past ten months had been. Major challenges came one on top of another, shocking the energy markets and the global economy. The world looked to Saudi Arabia for leadership, and the kingdom provided it, thanks in no small part to Crown Prince Mohammed and Prince Abdulaziz. No other energy minister has faced such difficult multilayered challenges in such a short space of time. It would have been a daunting task for any minister, let alone one newly appointed. The combination of Prince Abdulaziz's experience, knowledge, personality, diplomatic capabilities, and wide range of contacts meant that he was able to navigate these issues with aplomb. There can be no doubt that Prince Abdulaziz rose to the occasion in his first year in office.

In February 2021, the international oil market and energy consultants gave their judgment on Prince Abdulaziz's performance. Not only has the oil price returned to precrises levels, but it has gone even higher. The majority of analysts credit Prince Abdulaziz with this achievement. After the prince delivered his opening speech to the Joint Ministerial Monitoring Committee (JMMC) on April 1, 2021, Javier Blas, chief energy correspondent at Bloomberg, tweeted the whole transcript, and Roger Diwan, vice president of IHS Markit, commented, "We will call this 'The Great Helmsman' speech." Commenting on the successful OPEC+ meeting, Blas said that "the fact that after the JMMC, the OPEC+ ministerial meeting 'took' place on Tuesday—even if that was virtually, interchanging phone and diplomatic messages—is another sign that Prince Abdulaziz bin Salman can continue pulling rabbits out of a hat at each meeting."

From time to time, the international energy market faces major and unexpected challenges. The autumn of 2021 saw a major fragmentation among different energy sources and disintegration among major parts of the world. High energy prices in the United States, shortages of gasoline in the UK, and skyrocketing natural gas prices in Europe. China and India, among others, went back to using more and more coal. The price of natural gas was up by 500 percent, coal by 200 percent, and NGL by 200 percent. Yet the price of oil went up only 29 percent. Prince Abdulaziz, during the Russian Energy Week in October 2021, correctly attributed the small increase in oil prices and the lack of supply shortages to oil management through OPEC+.

CONCLUSION

Thoughts About the Future

Yan Xuetong, a professor of international relations at Tsinghua University, wrote, "When all states are in the same leaky boat without an automatic operating system, one of them should wield the biggest dipper for the security of the boat as a whole. If the leading power does not lead, the other states cannot follow, and the world boat will lose direction."[1] I believe this is true not only for the international system as a whole but also for many of its parts, including the international oil market.

The personality of decision makers affects outcomes from the household level to the policy level of the most powerful country on earth (the United States) in peace and war. The three most recent U.S. presidents—Barack Obama, Donald Trump, and Joe Biden—all have different personalities, and their policies and relationships with the leaders of other countries have been different as well. Saudi Arabia's energy ministers— Abdullah al-Tariki, Ahmed Zaki Yamani, Hisham Nazer, Ali Al-Naimi, Khalid al-Falih, and Prince Abdulaziz—as well as ministers from other major oil-producing countries also have different personalities that affect their relationships with others and influence their policy decisions. All of these decision makers have had an impact on the international oil market and on the global economy, and it is important to understand how personality influences these decision makers.

Personality does not operate in vacuum; it is influenced and shaped by internal and external factors. Internal attributes include knowledge, background, ambition, desires, beliefs, relationships, information, age, and the length of time the individual has held the office. This includes having the right and qualified people. External factors include political, legal, economic, and social systems and the global environment within which individuals work.

Petroleum is a highly important part of the global economy, and the personality of these decision makers is as important as the commodity itself. Oil has been a great gift to humankind, but it brings challenges such as maintaining oil market stability and dealing with climate change. So far oil is our most important energy source, and it has had a huge impact on economic development and human prosperity. As economies grow, their need for energy resources increases. In 1990, global GDP was $23 trillion, whereas in 2020 it was almost $84 trillion. Oil consumption was little over 65 MBD in 1990, and today it is about 100 MBD. The world needs to manage this important commodity and address the uneven productions and consumptions of this resource.

Some countries have a lot of oil, and other countries have little or none. Seven countries (the United States, Russia, Saudi Arabia, Canada, Iraq, the United Arab Emirates, and Kuwait) have about 60 percent of total global production. Consumption is uneven as well. Four entities (the United States, the European Union, China, and Japan) consume more than 60 percent of total global oil. Consumption is dependent on the level of wealth and prosperity. Reserves depend on geological circumstances, but production levels depend on good management of this resource. Equally important, production and consumption changes year after year. The United States was once the major oil-producing and oil-exporting country, then it became the major importer, and now it is a major exporter. China was an exporter, and now it is the major importer of oil.

Oil is a capital-intensive industry that requires long-term planning from the day of exploration to retail consumption in our cars and airplanes. The cost of production also varies from one area to another (from as low as $3 per barrel to as high as $50). Networks for processing crude, refining the oil, and distribution are large and global. The players involved in the value chain and related businesses number in the millions, and the beneficiaries are almost the entire global population. No country is independent, or stands alone, in the oil market, even if it is not importing oil. The U.S. experience provides a clear example of changes in this resource—from net importing as much as 7 MBD in 2015 to gross exporting 4 MBD in 2020.

Yet its sensitivity to oil shortages and to price fluctuations has increased, as was shown by falling prices in early 2020.

Taking all of these factors together, oil needs to be under good and responsible management. This has been the case since oil became an important commercial commodity more than one hundred years ago. The importance of good management has grown with the increasing diversification of production and consumption, as well as concerns about climate change and the need to institute energy transitions.

Supply management needs strong, innovative managers. Attempts to manage the demand side in the late 1970s and early 1980s, in the name of reducing dependency on OPEC oil, had only limited success. Today new attempts are being made to manage the consumption side to protect the environment. Personality plays a critical role in management on both sides of the equation. Equally important is cooperating with other decision makers to achieve desired goals. Climate change has forced us to contemplate some kind of energy transition, and there is an increasing need for close cooperation, good management and great managers.

Personalities are as important as market fundamentals in shortening or lengthening a crisis on the supply side and stabilizing prices. Equally important, decision makers influence market sentiment, which is an important factor in stabilizing the oil market and protecting long- and short-term investments. Fundamentals and market sentiment sometimes work together and on other occasions work against each other. The media, information, and interpretation are part of these processes.

Market fundamentals (supply, demand, and commercial inventory) keep changing, not only monthly but sometimes weekly or daily. There is a lot of uncertainty in interpreting market fundamentals, and more than fifty different monthly outlooks provide information. The margin of error in the majority of market forecasts is between 2 and 3 percent, which is equal to two to three million barrels per day from global production and consumption. During a market crisis, this margin might rise to 10 percent or more. Research is done by individual analysts or by a small group of experts, then it is up to the leaders to make appropriate decisions based on the information they have and their short- or long-term goals. What serves the interests of one decision maker may not be appropriate for another or for the market as a whole. Decisions are based on the best understanding of the perceived interests of the decision maker's own country. The role of decision makers is likely to be more important and more dynamic in the future.

The global petroleum map keeps growing and changing, and other energy sources, such as solar, will also continue to grow. But contrary to what some believe, the growth or decline of these alternative energy sources will be connected to changing oil prices unless the world has a major technology breakthrough. If oil prices become very low, for example, $10 or lower, many oil producers will be priced out of the market. Moreover, the majority of alternative energy sources cannot compete with oil without strong government support (which is very costly in a competitive and globalized economy). The personalities of our energy decision makers will help shape the world as we work to solve this global dilemma.

Some people doubt the continuity of a high demand for oil in the next ten, twenty, or thirty years. They are referring to "peak oil demand" and the transition away from fossil fuels. This viewpoint is a personal judgment based on selective information. The transition process will not be easy, and some of the people who promote this view are likely to have political agenda or personal interests. We have seen all of this many times within the context of peak oil supply, among other issues.

The moment demand stops growing, oil prices could collapse. Strong competition among energy producers and energy sources would increase, leading to a free fall for energy and oil prices and the collapse of some energy sources. This would lead to disorder in the energy market similar to what we experienced in March and April of 2020, if not much worse. Any transition has to be gradual and carefully managed globally. Yet, political, military, and economic conflicts between nations would make it very difficult to achieve this easily.

If oil prices collapse, there might be no bottom. Then high-cost oil would gradually decline and demand would grow. Some renewables and other expensive energy sources could not survive the competition. Again, in this scenario you need good management by capable individuals to get the world of energy and the global economy out of such a mess. It is a mess we have seen before, and the negative consequences would increase if prices remained low for many months.

The international oil market has seen major price collapses during the last forty years. The role of decision makers was critical in causing the collapses and in bringing the market back to stability. There seem to be big ups and downs in prices every decade. The possibility of a major price rise or decrease in this or the coming decade is highly likely. Again, there will be a need for leadership, as has been the case in the past.

The demand side of the energy map is interesting. Demand is likely to grow across the world, with the exception of countries with major economic problems or those that are politically unstable. Mature economies facing increasing demands by the populace to control climate issues, such as the United States, Western Europe, and Japan, will witness little or negative growth. Globally, we are likely to see uneven growth. Stronger growth will occur in emerging and developing economies such as India, Sub-Saharan Africa, and Central Asia. Some large economies, such as Indonesia and Brazil, are likely to become major economic powers with high oil and energy consumption. Yet price fluctuations are expected to continue on the oil market.

Contrary to what some believe, many leaders of oil consuming/importing countries worry about low oil prices as much as they worry about high oil prices, but when prices are low, they express their concerns privately. Perhaps they do not want to be seen by the public as wanting higher prices. They know that low oil prices would lead to a decline in oil and energy investments, which would lead to supply shortages and spikes in oil prices. Oil producers and consumers alike prefer stable and reasonable oil prices.

The crucial question is what are reasonable prices? Decision makers have different opinions about reasonableness that are not limited to oil producers but also can be found among oil consumers. The desired price for Saudi Arabia is different from that for Russia and is different again for producers such as Algeria, Venezuela, and Iraq and is likely to change from one year to the next. The same can be said about oil consumers. Apart from election years, U.S. politicians would like to see a $50 or $60 oil price whereas Europe prefers a lower price. Indian leaders would like to see low prices, especially if their currency is going south, as was the case in 2018 and 2020.

It should be noted that the desired oil price is a moving target that depends on many factors. It is not necessarily related to market fundamentals. In the early 1980s, different OPEC ministers targeted different oil prices (from $35–$45). After the market collapse of 1986, Saudi Arabia targeted a price of $18, which was soon adopted by other OPEC countries. During the 1990 Jeddah meeting of Iraq and Saudi Arabia and other Arab Gulf countries, the new target was $21. The Iranians wanted $35, which was most likely a political price.

After the collapse of the market in 1998 and its recovery in 2000, a new price system was adopted with a target of $23 and a range of $22 to $26. Decision makers in major consuming countries accepted this, but when the price went above $40, OPEC ministers felt unable to defend the target prices. When the price went over $100 in early 2008, the preferred price was between $80 and $100. The British prime minister suggested a range of $60 to $80. When prices increased to $127 again in 2012, both Saudi and U.S. officials preferred a price drop to $100. With the collapse of the oil market in 2014–2015, Ali Al-Naimi was hoping for a price of $60. With the price recovery in 2016, the Saudis preferred a range of $70–$75, but the Russians preferred a range of $60–$65 and later changed their preference in 2019 and early 2020 to $45. This moving target for prices among oil decision makers is likely to continue in the future.

OPEC is likely to continue to be an important international oil organization, and OPEC+ will become more important especially if Russia remains on board and acts with a strong interest and commitment. Saudi Arabia will maintain its commitment and leadership within OPEC and OPEC+. It benefits Saudi Arabia financially, economically, politically, and the global economy and energy industries at large. Other oil producers are likely to continue as a part of the oil management club, not only for economic reasons but also for their countries' prestige. Saudi Arabia leadership was challenged in the past, but this has not been the case since 2020.

Major changes in supply and demand often create the need for new arrangements, new management, and new leadership on the international oil scene. The oil crisis of March-April 2020 had international consequences, and the U.S president jumped into the international driver's seat with the goal of attaining market stability. President Trump was successful, but many U.S. taboos were broken related to price targets, price management, and working with Russia and OPEC+ to attain these goals.

The United States is now a major oil producer, consumer, exporter, and investor, and its status in the oil industry has changed. Most U.S. oil (shale and deep sea) is very expensive to produce. For about fifty years, the United States dominated the consuming end of the oil market, and decision makers blamed OPEC or the Arabs when the price went up. U.S leaders cannot attack OPEC so easily today when there is a crisis. When President Biden rejoined the Paris Agreement, U.S. leadership highlighted its return to participating on energy and climate issues, which require close international cooperation and good management. Domestic energy issues are also very complex and require cooperation by parties with different interests. With this complexity, U.S. leadership at the federal and state levels, as well as in business, is needed more than ever before. The United States must assess its responsibility in international oil and energy management in a realistic way far away from narrow and short term political goals.

Looking to the future through the experience of the past, international energy and oil market stability benefits oil producers, oil consumers, and the global economy at large. The emerging circular carbon economy, climate issues, and possible transitions within and between energy sources means that the energy business in general, not only oil, will benefit most from stability and predictability. Achieving stability and predictability requires good management, which is only possible with enlightened leadership and decision makers who are willing to work together collectively to deliver these goals. That is the essence of the lessons learned in the last forty years, and this will remain the case well into the future.

NOTES

FOREWORD

1. Norman E. Nordhauser, *The Quest for Stability: Domestic Oil Regulation, 1917–1935* (New York: Garland, 1978).

INTRODUCTION: DECISIONS, DECISION MAKERS, AND OIL

1. Nicholas Moore, a respected oil journalist and the chief energy reporter of Reuters, wrote: "The new Saudi Minister, Hisham Nazer, was too taciturn among reporters, but his spokesman Ibrahim al Muhanna was gold dust. He never lied. After Iraq invaded Kuwait, I trusted him on a story that Saudi had enough spare capacity to prevent any shortage of oil now that the West banned Iraqi-controlled exports. Some pundits said I'd gone mad, but it had." Nicholas Moore, "Mr. Shake Your Money," in *Frontlines: Snapshots of History*, ed. Nicholas Moore and Sidney Weiland (New York: Pearson Education, 2001), 210.
2. "As the voice behind the scenes for the biggest producers in the Organization of Petroleum Exporting Countries, a few words from a late-night briefing with al Muhanna flashed across news wire screens could move world oil prices in a second." Amena Bakr, "Saudi Arabia's OPEC 'Gulf Source' Bowing Out," *Reuters*, May 30, 2013.
3. Walid Khadduri, the former editor in chief of the *Middle East Economic Survey* (MEES) and a highly respected writer and journalist, told me on many occasions that if my name was mentioned in the media whenever they quoted me, I would be one of the most quoted energy sources in the world.
4. Daniel Yergin, *The Prize: The Epic Quest for Oil, Money and Power* (New York: Free Press, 1991), 14.

5. Some recent studies about the role of decision makers in shaping major events include Daniel Byman and Kenneth M. Pollack, "Beyond Great Forces: How Individuals Still Shape History," *Foreign Affairs* (November/December 2019): 148–61; Yan Xuetong, *Leadership and the Rise of Great Powers* (Princeton, NJ: Princeton University Press, 2019); Jocko Willink and Leif Babin, *The Dichotomy of Leadership* (New York: St. Martin's, 2018); Margaret MacMillan, *History's People: Personalities and the Past* (London: Profile, 2016); and Robert Jervis, *How Statesmen Think: The Psychology of International Politics* (Princeton, NJ: Princeton University Press, 2017).

1. AHMED ZAKI YAMANI: GOOD START, DIFFICULT ENDING

1. Hassan Youssef Yassin, a businessman and a Saudi government adviser, has told me this story many times in slightly different ways since I first met him in the late 1980s.
2. Yamani's main responsibility in the 1960s had to do with surveillance and Saudi Arabia's borders, and respected people who worked with Yamani during this time emphasized these achievements. They include Jawad al-Sakka, the legal adviser to the minister of energy from 1958 to the present day, and the late Ahmed M. al-Ghazzawi, who joined the ministry in 1961.
3. Some people, especially in the West, thought that Yamani was in the room during the assassination of King Faisal because he had a close relationship with the king. However, the reality is that Yamani came with Abdul Mutalib al-Kadhimi, the Kuwaiti minister of oil, who was there to greet King Faisal. When a minister or high-ranking official from another country visits Saudi Arabia, the official practice is for the Saudi counterpart to be with them during their official meetings, especially with the king and crown prince.
4. During the late 1970s and early 1980s, the theory of exhausted oil resources was common. See Majid al-Moneef, *Petroleum: Between Historical Inheritance and 21st Century Challenges* (Beirut: Arab Cultural Center, 2017); Yousif al-Yousif, *The Political Economy of Oil: An Arab Perspective on Its Development* (Beirut: Center for Arab Unity Studies, 2015).
5. According to some people familiar with Aramco board meetings, in which business and technical details are usually discussed, Yamani rarely engaged in these discussions.
6. Bhushan Bahree worked for the *Wall Street Journal* and covered the international oil markets, including OPEC, from 1975 to 2015, and he knew Yamani very well. Currently he is an oil and OPEC analyst for IHS Markit Inc., and I interviewed him many times between 2018 and 2020.
7. In 1990, Edmund Ghareeb, a professor at the American University (Washington, D.C.) and a media adviser, told me that Yamani would contact some of his friends and ask them to inform the media that he would be in the United States and might be available for interviews. Therefore, this notification did not seem to come directly from Yamani. I reconfirmed this with Ghareeb in early 2021.
8. Interview with Pierre Terzian, publisher and editor of *Petroleum Strategies*, in Paris in April 2018. Terzian covered OPEC meetings in the 1980s.
9. Ahmed al-Malik stated, "with declining oil prices; what are the best solutions: withdrawing reserves or mixing different options?" Quoted in Arabic in *al Riyadh*,

November 19, 2015. Al-Malik was the assistant president of the Saudi Central Bank, which published a study analyzing how the Saudi government had dealt with three major financial crises related to oil (1986, 1998, and 2014).

10. Yamani said many times in 1985 and in early 1986 that low oil prices would not continue for long. See, for example, Ian Seymour, "Current Soft Market Will Be Only Temporary, Says Yamani," *MEES* 28, no. 30 (May 6, 1985).

11. Interviews with Abdulsamad Al Awadi in London in the summer of 2018 and 2019. He was the head of Kuwait Petroleum Corporation in Europe and a member of the Kuwaiti delegation during OPEC ministerial meetings from 1981 through 2000.

12. See William M. Brown, "Can OPEC Survive the Glut," *FORTUNE Diary*, November 30, 1981. This article was released March 16, 2007, and is now available at the CIA Library. Also see U.S Ambassador, "Telegram 944 from Riyadh," sent to the U.S. State Department on June 11, 1979, describing a meeting with Yamani. This telegram was made public by the State Department on March 20, 2014, and is now available in the U.S National Archive. During the private meeting with the U.S. ambassador, Yamani expressed his concern about Kuwait's and the United Arab Emirates' oil policies and how OPEC members were at odds regarding whether the price should be $17.50 or $20.00 per barrel. I also interviewed some Saudi and Kuwaiti officials who are familiar with these issues but do not want to be mentioned by name.

13. Many news stories featured American oil companies and Aramco's pricing methods. See, for example, Mark Potts, "IRS Tangles with Big Oil Potential $8 Billion Tax Case," *Washington Post*, May 07, 1991; and "Exxon, Texaco Win Case, Needn't Pay Aramco Tax," *Associated Press*, December 26, 1993.

14. When Norway and the United Kingdom lowered their oil prices in 1984, Yamani dismissed the economic reasons behind it and suggested that "the decisions were politically motivated." See press conference with Yamani after October 31 OPEC meeting in Geneva: *MEES*, November 5, 1984. On December 26, 1984, Yamani told the Arabic daily newspaper *al Sharq al Awsat* that "the current crisis facing OPEC is part of a long-term plot to end its role in the oil market." *MEES* 28, no. 12 (December 31, 1984).

15. Ali Al-Naimi, *Out of the Desert: My Journey from Nomadic Bedouin to the Heart of Global Oil* (London: Penguin, 2016), 134.

16. I talked with some of Aramco's top managers during the 1980s and with officials from the Saudi Ministry of Petroleum, but they did not recall this.

17. The late Faruq al-Hussani, an economic adviser to Yamani for three decades, told me that Yamani expressed his appreciation of Ali al-Sabah's suggestion that Saudi Arabia play the role of swing producer.

18. Interviews with Walid Khadduri on July 20, 2020, former editor of *MEES* who covered OPEC at the time.

19. Ahmed Zaki Yamani, "Statement of Saudi Policy," in Robert Mabro, ed., *Organization of Petroleum Exporting Countries and the World Oil Market: The Genesis of the 1986 Price Crisis* (New York: Oxford University Press, 1986). The book has many good and informative chapters about what was happening in the oil market during the first half of the 1980s.

20. As a general practice in Saudi Arabia, if the king asks a minister to do something, the king's orders must be followed. However, if the minister has a convincing argument

regarding a different approach or policy, the minister can persuade the king to change the initial order. The minister's position is stronger when he has the support of other ministers.

21. For many years, articles and debates were ongoing in the United Kingdom about the Al Yamamah deal. Some were against it or the way that it was done; others were not. The split was along party lines, with the Conservatives supportive and Labour against it. However, the Labour Party changed its attitude when it became the ruling party.

22. Some people might have had a negative opinion of this deal. Nevertheless, it proved useful when Aramco facilities were attacked on September 14, 2019. To keep the crude oil flowing to Aramco's international customers, the company reduced intake to local refineries and supplied domestic needs from these strategic storage locations.

23. On October 31, 1984, Yamani said during a press conference that "the barter deal was not used to increase output levels. It was used for internal fiscal reasons." See *MEES* 28, no. 4 (November 5, 1984).

24. Jeffery Robinson, *Yamani: The Inside Story* (London: Simon & Schuster, 1988), 272.

25. The late Saudi petroleum minister Hisham Nazer told me this story. On many occasions, I also talked with Sulaiman al-Mandeel, the deputy minister of finance who had been involved in the issue. He confirmed that the Ministry of Finance and the Ministry of Petroleum disagreed on the issue.

26. Ali al-Juhani, "Petroleum and Apple," *Asharq al-Awsat*, March 11, 1984. Al-Juhani became an adviser to Crown Prince Sultan bin Abdulaziz, the minister of defense, and was the minister of communication from 1995 to 1999. I talked with al-Juhani by phone in 2018 about this issue, and he confirmed this story.

27. I talked with many Saudi officials and business people who were involved in the Saudi economy during that time, and they stated that there were some misgivings about Yamani's oil policy and its negative impact on the Saudi economy.

28. This information has been gathered from some Saudi and Kuwaiti officials and international insiders over the years. They do not like to be mentioned by name.

29. From an April 2018 Paris interview with Pierre Terzian, founder and publisher of *Energy Strategy*.

30. Ghazi al-Gosaibi held many ministerial portfolios. He was a diplomat, a technocrat, a poet, and a novelist, authoring many books. While al-Gosaibi was a minister of health in 1984, he wrote a poem about his relationship with King Fahd, expressing his feelings of love and unhappiness. When the poem was published in the well-known Saudi daily newspaper *Al Jazirah*, both al-Gosaibi and the editor-in-chief of the newspaper, Khalid al-Malik, were fired. Al-Gosaibi continued to work in the government as the ambassador to Bahrain and the United Kingdom and, later, as a minister from 1984 to 2010. Khalid al-Malik, the editor-in-chief of *Al Jazirah*, was back in his job in 1998 and has kept it until today.

31. April 2018 telephone interviews with Mike Ameen, who worked in Aramco and was closely associated with Yamani during the 1970s and early 1980s.

32. One of the journalists who did not have a good relationship with Yamani was *New York Times* correspondent Youssef Ibrahim. In 1985, Ibrahim wrote a negative article about Yamani and some OPEC ministers. OPEC tried to ban Ibrahim from attending their meetings even though other journalists strongly protested. After Yamani lost his position, Ibrahim visited Saudi Arabia in 1989 at the invitation of Minister

Hisham Nazer. They became good friends, and Ibrahim wrote many positive stories about Saudi Arabia's economy, society, and oil. My first assignment with the ministry was to organized Ibrahim's visit and to accompany him during his two-week trip to many parts of the kingdom. One of his front page stories about economic and social developments in Saudi Arabia began with my small village, al Dakhlah. My picture was next to our house in the village and was featured in the report. See Youssef M. Ibrahim, "Shaping a New Saudi Arabia: Oil, Peace and Steady Hand," *New York Times*, April 17 1989.

33. Associated Press (AP) News Agency interview with Yamani, November 22, 1973.

34. AP News Agency interview with Yamani, December 15, 1978.

35. When Yamani was dismissed, an atmosphere of sadness permeated the international media, especially among his friends. *MEES*, which was close to Yamani, described his dismissal as happening "abruptly." *Petroleum Intelligence Weekly*, a competing petroleum publication also close to Yamani, was quoted by *MEES* on December 1, 1986, commenting on the loss of Yamani. This is a rare situation in which competing publications quoted each other. The *New York Times* published an interesting story about the ousting of Yamani, citing ten reasons for his dismissal, some of which contradicted each other and others that made no sense. They included problems with his health, his use of "Sheikh" in his title, his views on Iran, his relationship with the king and the royal family, and suggesting that Yamani wanted to leave the ministry so he could practice law. See Lee A. Daniels, "Yamani Ousted as Oil Minister of Saudi Arabia," *New York Times*, October 30, 1986.

2. HISHAM NAZER: SHIFTING INTERESTS AND LOOKING NATIONALLY

1. Interviews in 2019 in Riyadh with Abdurrahman Abdulkareem, former deputy minister of energy, who was also the secretary of the Follow-Up Committee in the Ministry of Planning during the 1970s and early 1980s.

2. Ghazi al Gosaibi, *A Lifetime in Administration*, 17th ed. (Beirut, Lebanon: Arab Establishment for Studies and Publishing, 2017 [in Arabic]), 232.

3. During the late 1980s and early 1990s, far-right religious leaders such as Salman al-Ouda distributed free tapes with speeches that attacked the liberals, especially government officials Ghazi al-Gosaibi, Hisham Nazer, Mohammed Aba al-Khail (minister of finance), and Mohammed al-Taweel (head of the Institution of Public Administration).

4. In addition to the five people listed, Nazer hired others from Saudi universities and from the Ministry of Planning. They included me (a teaching professor at King Saud University in Riyadh before I moved to the ministry in 1989); Ahmad al-Ghamidi (a teacher of economics at the Military College who joined the ministry as economic adviser in 1993 and was a member of the Shura Council from 2013–2020); Mohammed al-Saban (from King Abdulaziz University, Jeddah, who joined the ministry in 1989 and led the Saudi delegation in international climate change negotiations until 2014); Abdullah Basodan (from King Saud University, who was with the economic and international team from 1989 to 1993, then became president of Nimir Petroleum, the first private Saudi upstream oil company); Turki al-Wosemer (who joined

the ministry in 1988 and worked for four ministers and is now chief of staff for the minister of energy); and Mansour al-Ayyaf (from the Ministry of Planning, who joined the Ministry of Energy in 1987 and worked with four ministers, assuming responsibility mainly for the file of the Aramco board).

5. There was a lot of debate about renaming the company once it was Saudi-registered. The original brand enjoyed widespread international and national recognition, importance, and value, so it was decided to call the new company Saudi Aramco. The original company, the Arab American Oil Company (ARAMCO), became the Saudi Arabian Oil Company.

6. I was a member of the board of Petronal, the overseas service company for Petromin, representing the Ministry of Petroleum. I made some proposals to improve the company's work and activities and had the approval of the minister, but SAMAREC management did not follow the minister's orders.

7. For a more complete history of Petromin, see Steffen Hertog, "Petromin: The Slow Death of a Statist Oil Development in Saudi Arabia," *Business History* 50, no. 5 (September 2008): 649–67.

8. I heard this from Hisham Nazer many times and on different occasions during my work with him from 1989 to 1995.

9. Turki al-Dakhil, *Hisham Nazer: Untold Biography* (Dubai: Madarek, 2016 [in Arabic]), 211–18. Al-Dakhil is a well-known and respected Saudi journalist, intellectual, and publisher. He is currently the Saudi ambassador to the United Arab Emirates. He spent hours and hours talking with Hisham Nazer and recording their conversations, including Nazer's thoughts and discussions about the details of his life and career. This is an excellent and comprehensive book about Nazer.

10. Al-Dakhil, *Hisham Nazer*.

11. I was one of the few people present during King Fahd's visit to Nazer, and I was impressed by King Fahd's ease and the feeling that his talk came from his heart. He referred to many national and international issues. King Fahd was naturally smart and knowledgeable and able to explain issues clearly and frankly.

12. Al-Dakhil, *Hisham Nazer*, 211.

13. The $18 price target of 1986 was the subject of many rumors, debates, and speculation. Some thought this price had been suggested by the United States when Vice President Bush visited Saudi Arabia in 1986. I spoke with many people, especially inside Saudi Arabia, and discovered that this story was not true. The idea of the $18 price target came from within the Economic Department of the Ministry of Petroleum, and only after careful study and consultation with Saudi decision makers. It was supported by some countries within OPEC as well as by other producers. The decision to adopt the $17 to $19 price range was made during a meeting of five OPEC ministers in a tent in Taif. Prince Saud al-Faisal, who was the second ranking person in the ministry and who became foreign minister nine years later, was one of the officials who attended the meeting.

14. Al-Dakhil, *Hisham Nazer*, 220.

15. Al-Dakhil, *Hisham Nazer*, 220–21.

16. Al-Dakhil, *Hisham Nazer*, 217.

17. In January and February of 1990, Minister Nazer, Prince Abdulaziz, and Ali Al-Naimi (president of Aramco) and a small delegation that included me visited a number of Asian countries hoping to expand Saudi Arabia's oil market

share in the growing Asian market and find good joint ventures. Some Asian countries presented good opportunities for Saudi Arabia, especially through the joint-ownership (with local partners) of refineries and distribution networks. The main targets that year were Japan, Korea, and the Philippines. Deals were made with two of the countries, but reaching a deal with Japan took about fifteen years. During that trip, King Fahd approved increasing the Saudi production capacity.

18. When the invasion of Kuwait took place, I was in London on my annual vacation. Nazer was in Geneva and Prince Abdulaziz was in Marbella, Spain. They were going back to Saudi Arabia, but they asked me to stay in London. I stayed there for about a month, working more than sixteen hours a day. I had many responsibilities. First, briefing the minister and the prince with news, analyses, reactions, and other information via telephone calls and fax. Second, daily briefings with international media, explaining Saudi policies and actions and fighting with those within OPEC, like Algeria and Iran, that were against Saudi Arabia's increased production. I also confronted negative market sentiments about supply shortages, high oil prices, and other matters. When OPEC ministers finally met at the end of the month, I remember the Algerian oil minister Al-Sadeq Abusannah asking me "please stop your media attacks." I also stayed in touch with middle-ranking officials in the United States, especially in the Department of Energy and the Department of State, and we exchanged information and coordinated our messaging to the media and to the international oil market.

19. OPEC and IEA officials didn't talk with each other and behaved as if they were enemies. Any official from the IEA could not talk with people working in OPEC or even the delegations during OPEC meetings. Otherwise, they could be fired. Initiating communications between the two organizations was an interesting process. During OPEC's extraordinary meeting in late August 1990, which sought to allow capable OPEC members to produce as much oil as they could to make up for missing Iraqi and Kuwait oil, the Iranian minister was against the idea. He told the media that IEA's members should release their strategic reserve before OPEC increased production. The Iranians had limited or no production capacity, and their goal was clear—not to allow Saudi to increase production and make oil prices higher. Prince Abdulaziz contacted some IEA officials and asked them to issue a statement indicating that the IEA will not use the strategic reserve first and that OPEC should increase its production beforehand. The Iranian proposal was dismissed, and OPEC decided to allow its capable members to increase production. The communication between the two groups started. It was the beginning of a changing heart and mind. See Ibrahim AlMuhanna, *The Road to Riyadh: From Confrontation to Dialogue* (Riyadh: International Energy Forum, 2007), 26–30.

20. Judith Miller, "Saudi Oil Minister's Family in Mobil Deal," *New York Times*, June 6, 1991. When Minister Nazer expressed his unhappiness to the editor of the *New York Times*, the newspaper published a response to the story quoting Nazer's son, Loay. See "Saudis Explain Venture with Mobil," *New York Times*, June 8, 1991.

21. Sadly, many Saudi ministers have not written their memoirs, and they rarely cooperate with those who want to write their biographies. In the history of Saudi Arabia, only a few ministers have written about their experiences.

3. SADDAM HUSSEIN AND SHEIKH ALI AL-SABAH: INVASION OF A NATION

1. Saif al-Dein al-Dory, *Iraq and Kuwait: Continued and Inherited Crises* (Beirut, Lebanon: Arab Scientific Publishers 2016), 175–77. On May 20, 1990, during the Arab summit in Baghdad, Saddam Hussein spoke about the energy market, oil prices, OPEC quotas, and violations of the quotas. It was the beginning of the crisis.

2. In the 1960s, some Iraqi leaders claimed that Kuwait was part of Iraq and even called for "unification" to be achieved either though diplomacy or war. Other Iraqi leaders used the issue as leverage in bilateral diplomatic negotiations, offering Kuwait formal recognition of its border in exchange for handing over the Islands of Warbah and Bubiyan to Iraq. One proposal was for Kuwait to rent the islands to Baghdad for ninety-nine years in return for recognition.

3. In the early 1960s, Iraqi leader Abd al-Karim Qasim was threatening to take over Kuwait. However, three countries strongly stood against him: Egypt (under the leadership of Gamal Abdel Nasser), Saudi Arabia, and the United Kingdom. The Arab League also sent armed forces from Arab countries to defend Kuwait.

4. Othman al-Omeir told me this story in London more than once in 2018 and 2019. He also mentioned it, indirectly, in his book when describing a personal interview he had with Saddam Hussein and other Arab leaders. Othman al-Omeir, *Interview of the End of the Century* (London: Dar al Saqi, 1996 [in Arabic]).

5. Patrick Cockburn, "Saddam Hussein: Deluded and Defiant, a Dictator Awaits His Nemesis," *The Independent*, March 6, 2003.

6. These facts have been mentioned by many Iraqi officials who used to work with Saddam Hussein, including Issam A. al-Chalabi, the Iraqi oil minister from 1987 to 1990. He noted this during my interviews with him in London in the summer of 2018 and in his book. Issam A. al-Chalabi, *50 Years in the World of Oil* (Beirut, Lebanon: Arabic Establishment for Studies and Publication, 2019 [in Arabic]).

7. Al-Dory, *Iraq and Kuwait*.

8. Many reports and news stories showcase how Saddam Hussein's narcissism and self-centered approach prevented him from taking other leaders' words seriously, especially during the invasion of Kuwait. See, for example, Nick Gier, "Could King Hussein Have Stopped Saddam Hussein?," University of Idaho, July 22, 2009. When international troops became involved in the conflict, King Hussein of Jordan attempted to convince Saddam Hussein to remove his forces from Kuwait. However, the Iraqi leader told him that "the whole world is against me, but God is with me and I will be victorious." Also see "Iraqi Invasion of Kuwait—International Response," *Keesing's Record of World Events* 36 (August 1990), 37631. Before the Iraqi invasion of Kuwait, Tarik Aziz, Saddam Hussein's deputy prime minister and Iraq's foreign minister at the time, met with Egyptian president Hosni Mubarak and King Hussein of Jordan. After their meeting, Mubarak stated that Iraq and Kuwait will likely "arrive at a comfortable and calm, quiet solution." However, Iraq's media began aggressively attacking Kuwait and suggested that Sheikh al-Sabah was operating as an American agent. Mubarak visited Iraq after that (alongside Saudi Arabia and Kuwait) and told the media "that Saddam had assured him that Iraq had no intention of attacking Kuwait or of moving forces toward the Kuwaiti border." Less than two weeks later, Iraq invaded Kuwait.

9. A lot has been written about U.S. Ambassador April Glaspie's meeting with Saddam Hussein just five days before the invasion of Kuwait. If Glaspie had been stronger in her statements to Saddam, some people thought that the war might have been avoided. This is simplistic thinking, especially when we consider Saddam's speeches before and during the conflict; it was clear that he intended to take over Kuwait. See, for example, Kevin M. Woods, David D. Palkki, and Mark E. Stout, eds., *The Saddam Tapes: The Inner Workings of a Tyrant's Regime, 1978–2001* (Cambridge, UK: Cambridge University Press, 2011). According to Abdul-Halim Khaddam, the Syrian vice president from 1984 to 2005, Saddam started sending letters to the Iranian leadership in April 1990 explaining that he would move his troops from the border of the two countries to the Kuwaiti border to preserve peace with Iran. Abdul-Halim Khaddam, "Saddam Sent 'Reassuring Messages' to Iran Before the Kuwait Invasion," *Al Sharq al Awsat* 43 (republished from the archives on May 1, 2021).

10. This speech has been quoted in some Arabic books. See Anees al-Dogadi, *The Secret Life of Saddam Hussein: From Places to Hidden Underground Holes*, 20th ed. (Damascus, Syria: Dar al-Kitab Al-Arabi, 2017).

11. I heard this from some Kuwaiti officials who used to work with Sheikh Ali, but they do not want to be mentioned by name.

12. He used to say this to some of his close friends in the international media. A couple of them told me this, but they do not want their names to be mentioned.

13. See "OPEC Interviews and Press Conferences, Kuwait's Ali al Khalifa al Sabah," *MEES* 33, no. 9 (December 4, 1989).

14. Ahmad al-Rabie, "Qatar Looking for a Rule," *Al Sharq al Awsat*, June 26, 2001.

15. The study was later leaked and published in Arabic on the Kuwaiti website Takh Tekh, but I also confirmed this with Kuwaiti sources who do not want to be named.

16. I personally heard this from King Fahd during his visit to the house of Hisham Nazer. He also talked about the importance of helping the Kuwaitis as close brothers to the Saudis. Saddam didn't answer calls from other Arab leaders either.

17. I heard about this statement by King Fahd from Hisham Nazer on many occasions in 1990.

18. I was with Minister Nazer during his meeting with Sheikh Zayed, and I recorded the details of the visit and the discussions, as well as the discussions with former UAE oil minister Mana Said al Otaiba.

19. Turki al-Dakhil, *Hisham Nazer: Untold Biography* (Dubai: Madarek, 2016 [in Arabic]), 240–41.

20. Al-Chalabi, *50 Years in the World of Oil*, 362–63.

21. Al–Chalabi.

22. Al–Chalabi.

23. Personal interview with Abdulsamad Al Awadi, who was a high-ranking member of the Kuwaiti delegation.

24. Turki al-Dakhil, *Hisham Nazer*.

25. I attended that meeting and heard this discussion personally.

26. Hisham Nazer told me this when I met with him on July 30 to inform him that I was going to London in the evening and to Washington, D.C. later on for my annual vacation.

27. Saad al-Bazzaz, *The Generals Are the Last to Know* (Beirut, Lebanon: Dar al-Hikmah, 1997 [in Arabic]).

28. For more details about the oil accounts and the thinking of some Iraqi officials after the invasion, see Al-Chalabi, *50 Years in the World of Oil.*
29. Immediately after the invasion, Ali Al-Naimi, then president of Saudi Aramco, went to the United States looking for help from American oil and energy service companies to expand Saudi Aramco's production capacity. They all told him that they couldn't do that much. While in Chicago, Aramco's management in Dhahran told Al-Naimi to come back because they could do it on their own (i.e., without any help). Their method is simple: import the needed equipment and materials from all around the world, regardless of price and give the workforce the incentive to work more than twelve hours per day. Many international observers had their doubts about the Saudi narrative of increased production, but some reporters believed the story. See Nicholas Moore and Sidney Weiland, eds., *Frontlines: Snapshots of History* (London: Reuters, 2001), 210.

4. LUIS GIUSTI, THE JAKARTA AGREEMENT, AND ITS AFTERMATH

1. Bernard Mommer, *Global Oil and the Nation State* (Oxford, UK: (Oxford University Press, 2002), 212.
2. Mommer, *Global Oil and the Nation State.*
3. In the 1970s and 1980s, dependency theory was a common school of thought in Latin America and beyond. The basic thesis is that poverty and underdevelopment in these countries (the periphery) was due to the domination of wealthy nations, especially the United States (the core). OPEC was seen as a way to weaken this domination, and the West was fighting back. See Guy F. Erb and Valeriana Kallab, eds., *Beyond Dependency: The Developing World Speaks Out*, 3rd ed. (Washington, D.C.: Overseas Development Council, 1997).
4. Miguel Tinker Salas, *Venezuela: What Everyone Needs to Know* (New York: Oxford University Press, 2015).
5. Ali Al-Naimi, *Out of the Desert: My Journey from Nomadic Bedouin to the Heart of Global Oil* (London: Penguin Random House, 2016), 192.
6. In late 1970 and in the early 1980s, I studied in Wisconsin and later in Illinois and had many American friends in both states. My political science professor noticed my strong interest in U.S. politics and the issue of who "really rules America." He told me, "we, in the Midwest, are farmers. You can stay here for as many years as you like and read all the books about U.S. politics, but you won't fully understand American politics unless you live in the East and interact with people there, especially in New York, Boston, or Washington, D.C." I decided to go to Washington, D.C. for my PhD, which surprised my American friends from the Midwest. They thought Washington, D.C. was a dangerous and difficult place to live. This seems to be how people everywhere tend to feel about their country's capital.
7. Al-Naimi, *Out of the Desert*, 192.
8. Al-Naimi, 77.
9. Leonardo Maugeri, *The Age of Oil: The Mythology, History, and Future of the World's Most Controversial Resource* (Westport, CT: Praeger, 2006).
10. Good studies and analyses about the Jakarta meeting that look at it within the context of the oil market include Robert Mabro, "The Oil Price Crisis of 1998," *Oxford*

Institute for Energy Studies, September 10, 1998; Daniel Yergin, *The Quest: Energy Security, and the Remaking of the Modern World* (New York: Penguin, 2011); Maugeri, *The Age of Oil*; and Robert McNally, *Crude Volatility: The History and Future of Boom-Bust Oil Prices* (New York: Columbia University Press, 2017).

11. Personal interview with Iranian minister Bijan Zanganeh in Vienna during an OPEC meeting in December 2019.

12. Personal interview with Abdalla el Badri in Vienna during an OPEC seminar in 2018.

13. Ian Seymour, "Saudi Oil Minister Calls for Increase in OPEC's Production Ceiling to a More Realistic Level," *MEES*, November 3, 1997.

14. Al-Naimi, *Out of the Desert*, 200. In 2020 I asked Walid Khadduri about it, and he said he agrees with the quote and remembers the events very well.

15. "Saudi Oil Minister Calls for Increase in OPEC's Production Ceiling to a More Realistic Level," *MEES*, November 3, 1997.

16. "Saudi Oil Minister Calls for Increase in OPEC's Production Ceiling"; also see Al-Naimi, *Out of the Desert*.

17. I asked Iranian minister Zanganeh about this issue more than once. He told me that it was his first OPEC meeting as a new minister, but the issue seemed to be bigger than that. The moderate/liberal former President Khatami of Iran (now under house arrest) was trying to have good relations with Saudi Arabia, and Iran was to host the Islamic Summit the following month. Iran's leaders did not want small issues, such as increasing OPEC's ceiling by 2.0 or 2.5 MBD, to create a problem between the two countries.

18. "OPEC Interviews and Press Conferences," *MEES Archive* 40, no.49 (December 8, 1997). The interview with Libya's Abdalla el Badri was done by Walid Khadduri, the executive editor, on November 30.

19. At Jakarta's OPEC meeting, el Badri of Libya said that he trusted the Saudis' judgment and information. I asked him about that meeting in 2019, and el Badri said that the information he had about both the oil markets and the Asian financial crises was not clear. Some OPEC countries did not have good information and research resources, but the information from OPEC's secretariat and others was not as bad as some ministers later suggested. There were many studies about the Asian financial crisis and its impact on economic growth and oil demand. OPEC's secretariat projected the call on OPEC oil for 1998 to be 26.4. The OPEC Economic Commission Board (ECB) had a similar estimate. The Saudi delegation to the board had a higher number (27.2), but that was lower than what Al-Naimi had suggested by 300 MBD. "Saudi Sees Demand on OPEC Oil in 1998 at 27.2 MBD," *Reuters*, November 14, 1997. Moreover, on November 24, 1997, I told the *Reuters News Agency* the following about the call on OPEC oil: "The minimum is 27.5 million, but it could be as high as 28." I was definitely supporting and rationalizing my boss's proposal. I was also trying to create a positive picture of the future of the oil market.

20. Maugeri, *The Age of Oil*, 172. I had many conversations with Maugeri, and I think he was one of the few people who understood the international oil market. He greatly valued the importance of decision makers, information, and the way it was interpreted.

21. "Kuwaiti Oil Minister Calls OPEC Jakarta Meeting a 'Disaster,'" *MEES* 41, no. 42 (October 19, 1998).

22. "New OPEC Deal Excellent for the Market—Saudi's Al-Naimi," *Reuters*, December 1, 1997.

5. PRINCE SAUD AL-FAISAL: AN INTERIM ENERGY LEADER

1. Interview with Nordine Ait-Laoussine, a former Algerian energy minister, in Paris in April 2019.
2. Adrian Lajous, "The Mexican, Saudi and Venezuelan Connection—A Memoir," *Oxford Energy Forum* 100 (May 2015): 4. For more information about the involvement of Robert Mabro in this process, see Ibrahim AlMuhanna, "Robert E. Mabro: Beyond Scholarship to Decision Making, *Oxford Energy Forum* 100 (May 2015): 11–13.
3. Lajous, "The Mexican, Saudi and Venezuelan Connection," 4–11.
4. Peter Fritsch and Thomas T. Vogel Jr., "Venezuela Expands Oil Industry to Dismay of Others in OPEC," *Wall Street Journal,* August 14, 1997.
5. Ali Al-Naimi, *Out of the Desert: My Journey from Nomadic Bedouin to the Heart of Global Oil* (London: Penguin Random House, 2016), 205.
6. Lajous, "The Mexican, Saudi and Venezuelan Connection."
7. Ahmed bin Abdullah al-Malik, "Two Previous Financial Crises and the Third Might Be on the Way, Unless Avoided by High Professionalism," *Al Riyadh,* November 17, 2015.
8. I talked with the late Jammaz al-Suhaimi, deputy governor of SAMA between 1998 and 2004, about this subject many times during 1999 and after that. He told me that he would start every morning in part of 1998 and 1999 by "burning the fingers of traders of Saudi riyal futures and options against the U.S. dollar." By buying Saudi riyal options contracts, al-Suhaimi would prevent the price from going down despite the downward trade volume, and those who were betting that the riyal will fall would lose their bets.
9. Sheikh Hamad al-Sayari told me this during some meetings with him in 2019. He also read an early draft of this book and offered many useful comments.
10. Interviews in Riyadh in February 2020 with Lieutenant General Abdulrahman al-Banyan, former chairman of the General Staff of the Saudi Armed Forces.
11. Reports from this committee went directly to King Fahd or Crown Prince Abdullah, or both. See Ali Al-Naimi, "Saud al Faisal: The General and the Official" (paper presented at the Conference to Commemorate Prince Saud, The Diplomatic Institutes, Riyadh, Saudi Arabia, April 25, 2016 [in Arabic]).
12. Al-Naimi, "Saud al-Faisal." Also see Nizar bin Obed Madani, ed., *Saud al-Faisal: His Life, Personality, Views, Thinking, Work, and Achievements,* 2nd ed. (Riyadh: King Faisal Center for Research and Islamic Studies, 2018). Al-Naimi had a good relationship with Prince Saud and often sought his guidance and help.
13. Steve Liesman, Bhushan Bahree, and Jonathan Friedland, " 'Big 3' Exporters' Accord to Cut Oil Output Signals Seismic Shifts," *Wall Street Journal,* June 23, 1998.
14. There are good studies in English and Arabic about what happened in Jakarta and the process afterwards. See chapter 4, note 10.
15. After Venezuela's oil production and the country's share of OPEC revenues fell under Ali Rodriguez Araque, president of PDVSA, Giusti criticized his successor for allowing the country's oil production to fall while Saudi Arabia continued to maintain its 30 percent market share. Daniel Fisher, "A Friend in Need?," *Forbes,* January 6, 2003. The Venezuelan media published articles by "unofficial spokesmen" that blamed declining oil prices "on the overproduction . . . of Saudi Arabia." Carlos Mendoza Pottellá, "Contemporary Oil Criticism: Dissenting Chronicles on the Opening

and the Oil Power," March 1999, https://petroleovenezolano.blogspot.com/2009/12
/critica-petrolera-contemporanea_24.html#.YWM_oUbMKRZ.

16. John Paul Rothbon, "Interview: Venezuela's Rojas Aims to Cut Volatility," *Reuters*,
June 5, 1998.

17. Email from Luis Giusti June 20, 2020.

18. Bernard Mommer, *Global Oil and the Nation State* (Oxford, UK: (Oxford University
Press, 2002).

19. I have met many Iranian oil ministers and other officials during official visits to Iran,
and it is not easy to deal with them even for commercial transactions. Iranian officials tend not to be straightforward and often don't tell the truth. See, for example,
Farnaz Fassihi, "Iran's Lie, from Jet Crash to Confession," *New York Times* (international ed.), January 27, 2020.

20. Interview with Youcef Yousfi on March 23, 1999, *MEES* 42, no. 13 (March 29, 1999).

21. Phone conversation with Nathaniel Kern on July 22, 2020.

22. Al-Naimi, *Out of the Desert*, 232.

23. I met with Prince Saud many times beginning with the Iraqi invasion of Kuwait in
1990. I am so impressed by him. He was a great political leader who understood
political, economic, and petroleum issues, argued logically, was very friendly and
soft in his approach and voice, and avoided conflict at all levels.

6. HUGO CHAVEZ: THE RISE OF A MAN AND THE DECLINE OF A NATION

1. Bernard Mommer, *Global Oil and Nation State* (Oxford: Oxford University Press,
2002), 222.

2. In Libya under Muammar Gaddafi's rule (1968–2012), the responsibility of international oil policy kept changing: from the head of the national oil company to the
prime minister and to the minister of oil. Although Gaddafi was the final decision
maker, Libyan representatives at international meetings, especially OPEC, seemed
to be given enough space to make decisions that they thought were right.

3. I heard this many times from an Algerian delegation member who attended the
meeting. Moreover, in 1997 Minister Erwin Arrieta banned PDSVA officials from
talking about production numbers, but Giusti did talk about Venezuelan production
and gave the media higher numbers than those provided by the ministry. See *Platts
Oilgram News*, November 19, 1997.

4. Miguel Tinker Salas, *Venezuela: What Everyone Needs to Know* (New York: Oxford
University Press, 2015), 158.

5. See Mommer, *Global Oil and Nation State*.

6. Larry Rohter, "Hasta La Vista, Oil Kings, Venezuela Tightens Grip on State Petroleum Company," *New York Times*, April 17, 1999.

7. Rory Carroll, *Comandante: Hugo Chavez's Venezuela* (New York: Penguin, 2014).
Also see Rory Carroll, *Comandante: The Life and Legacy of Hugo Chavez* (Edin-
burgh, UK: Canongate, 2013).

8. The dependency theory was more common within leftist academic circles in
developing countries, especially in Latin America. Yet Chavez used to talk about
the concept (but not the theory itself). I heard him doing so on two or more
occasions.

9. I heard this from Ali Al-Naimi on many occasions, the last time was during his visit to Riyadh on January 28, 2019.

10. OpeOluwani Akintayo, "Former OPEC Secretary General, Rodriguez Passes Away," *Sweet Crude Reports*, November 25, 2018. Also see "OPEC Mourns the Death of Alí Rodríguez, a 'Legend' of the Organization," November 21, 2018, El Diario, https://www.eldiario.es/economia/opop-lamenta-ali-rodriguez-organizacion_1_1827151.html; and "Dr Ali Rodriguez Araque Former OPEC Secretary General Dies," *OPEC Bulletin* (December 2018), 54.

11. For this and other developments within the Venezuelan oil sector, see Mommer, *Global Oil and Nation State*; Miguel Tinker Salas, *The Enduring Legacy: Oil, Culture, and Society in Venezuela* (Durham, NC: Duke University Press, 2009); and Tinker Salas, *Venezuela: What Everyone Needs to Know*.

12. See Carroll, *Comandante: Hugo Chavez's Venezuela*, 160.

13. Carroll, *Comandante: The Life and Legacy of Hugo Chavez*, 160.

14. Carroll, 163.

15. Yehude Simon, as quoted in Carroll, *Comandante: Life and Legacy of Hugo Chavez*, 267.

16. For comments by Chavez and Ahmadinejad about the U.S. dollar, see Jad Mouawad, "Political Crack Opens at Rare OPEC Meeting," *New York Times*, November 18, 2007; Souhail Karam and Simon Webb, "OPEC Summit Ends in Division over Weak Dollar," *Reuters*, November 18, 2007; and Sebatian Abbot, "OPEC Interested in Non-Dollar Currency," *Associated Press*, November 18, 2007.

7. KING ABDULLAH, GEORGE W. BUSH, AND GORDON BROWN: THE SHADOWS OF 2008

1. Andrew Rawnsley, "Moody, Angry, Naive: Yes, He Was Flawed but Gordon Brown Did Save the World," *The Guardian*, December 7, 2014.

2. "Verbatim," *Time Magazine*, June 30, 3008.

3. Linda Heard, "Brown's Chutzpah Payoff," *Arab News*, June 6, 2008.

4. Kathryn Caggianelli, "Time to Fight Back," *Troy Record*, May 25, 2008.

5. I talked with some Kuwaiti officials, members of parliament, and Abdulsamad Al Awadi, who all confirmed this opinion.

6. Abdullah al Fozan, "Why Have We Been Nice to Oil Consumers Against the Interest of Our Children and Grandchildren," *Al Watan*, June 14, 2008.

7. Daniel Yergin, "What Lower Oil Prices Mean for the World," *Financial Times*, November 10, 2008.

8. Sechin and the top Russian officials seemed to change their minds and seek closer cooperation with OPEC in January 2009. Sechin sent a letter to OPEC's secretary-general asking him to speed up the signing of a memorandum of understanding between OPEC and the Russian Ministry of Energy. He also emphasized the importance of collective action from all oil-producing countries to maintain a balanced oil market. More important was the address about international energy cooperation by Russian president Dmitry Medvedev on February 18, 2009. He said, "We must not allow the question of energy cooperation, energy talks to take place without our participation because Russia has to claim a role in all

the diverse global energy processes." http:www.en.kremlin.ru/events/president/transcripts/3231.

9. James Tapsfield and Jamie Grierson, "Brown Warns over Oil Price Fluctuations," *The Independent*, December 19, 2008; and "Oil Summit Opens in London: Speeches," Getty Images, December 19, 2008, (clip #700688122).

10. When I began working at the Saudi Ministry of Petroleum, I closely followed different sources of information about international oil markets (such as supply, demand, and inventory levels), especially when it came to Saudi production and supply. I also established good working and good personal relationships with analysts from some oil research houses. I noticed that definitions around what oil is and the meaning and sources of supply and demand differed widely among them.

11. The only expert who noticed the difference between the actual Saudi production and what was being reported by the international media (secondary sources) was Joel Couse, who worked with Total and prepared the company's monthly market report (it was not available to the public). His methodology looked at oil imports from Saudi oil by different customers, which helped him make good estimates (certainly better than those of others, such as Tanker Tracker).

12. During major economic crises, such as that of 2008, liberal economies (including those from the United States, which was under a pro–free market conservative Republican administration) interfered in the financial markets by increasing regulations, bailing out companies, and even buying some of their shares. See, for example, Adam Tooze, *Crashed: How a Decade of Financial Crises Changed the World* (New York: Penguin, 2018). Also see chapter 8 of this book.

13. In the oil market, it is almost impossible to have completely accurate information about supply, demand, and commercial stocks. The margin of error may vary from one month to another. I believe that the margin of error in normal situations is between 1 percent and 2 percent. During economic and energy crises, it could increase to 5 percent (I confirmed this expectation with some oil experts, including Ayed al-Qahtani, the head of research at OPEC). What makes the issue more complicated is that there are so many steps in the oil market: oil well production, pipelines, gas separation plants, export storage and facilities, loading schedules, shipping, refineries and their storage at both ends, refined products' distribution, and consumers and their usage (cars, airplanes, and more). For example, before the end of the twentieth century, many people were anticipating major disruptions in the world's energy chain as a result of Y2K. At that time, the gasoline tank of the average American consumer was 40 percent filled. If Americans increased their fill level to 60 percent or 70 percent, it would have created a major crisis in the international oil market, especially for U.S. refiners and product distribution chains.

8. BARACK OBAMA, DONALD TRUMP, AND JOE BIDEN: A REVOLVING U.S. ENERGY POLICY

1. King Abdullah and President Barack Obama initially had a good relationship. When the two leaders met in London during the G20 summit in 2009, Obama bowed to the king, which received a lot of criticism in the United States. However, in later years, King Abdullah began to feel uncomfortable with U.S. policy, especially around four

major issues. First, Obama supported the 2011 uprising in Egypt and the ousting of Hosni Mubarak, who was a close ally of Saudi Arabia and a close friend of King Abdullah. Second, Obama was against Gulf Cooperation Council (GCC) countries sending troops into Bahrain during the uprising in 2013. Third, Obama softened U.S. policy on the Syrian revolution, which was supported by Saudi Arabia. Finally, the United States was the major player behind the Iranian nuclear deal, which Saudi Arabia was not happy about, especially because they had not been consulted. I discussed these issues with Abdulrahman H. Al-Saeed, a former adviser to the royal court.

2. To be objective, some journalists balance their stories by asking for different opinions about the effects of official statements. When Al-Naimi met with selected media personnel in Doha, Qatar, on March 20, 2012, as part of the campaign to lower the market price, I asked participating journalists to report the interview straightforwardly and without injecting the opinions of others (especially those expressing negative attitudes). I also asked to see their stories before publication, not to censor the content or to object to the way it was written but to make sure negative opinions were not included in the name of balanced reporting.

3. One journalist refused to attend Minister Al-Naimi's meeting in Doha on March 20, 2012, claiming that the Saudis should not tell him how to write his story. Yet he wrote a story similar to that of the others, and his boss in New York gave approval for the story knowing that I had read it before it was released.

4. Ali Al-Naimi. "Saudi Arabia Will Act to Lower Soaring Oil Prices," *Financial Times*, March 28, 2012.

5. Personal interview with Abdulrahman H. Al-Saeed, former adviser in the royal court, in Riyadh on January 2, 2020.

6. Saudi Arabia has used its spare production capacity to meet a growth in demand many times, including the surge in demand from China and India. See, for example, Bassam Fattouh and Andreas Economou, "Saudi Arabia: Capacity Management," *Forum* 120 (February 1, 2020): 23–26.

7. "U.S. Must Not Be 'Hostage' to Foreign Oil—Bush," *Irish Times*, February 20, 2006.

8. Conspiracy theories about oil often become common during crises, especially when prices collapse as they did in 1968, 1988, and in 2014–2015. See Ibrahim AlMuhanna, "International Media and Petroleum Crises" (paper presented at the annual meeting of the Saudi Association of Media and Communication, Riyadh, April 10, 2007).

9. Peter Schweizer, *Victory: The Reagan Administration's Secret Strategy That Hastened the Collapse of the Soviet Union* (New York: Atlantic Monthly Press, 1994).

10. I also heard this from other Saudi officials. Ali Al-Naimi was with Vice President Bush during his visit to the Eastern Region of Saudi Arabia, and he never mentioned the issue of oil prices. Al-Naimi also quotes Bill Ramsey, a career U.S diplomat, who said: "We came to the conclusion that we had a common interest in a stable oil market." Ali Al-Naimi, *Out of the Desert: My Journey from Nomadic Bedouin to the Heart of Global Oil* (London: Penguin Random House, 2016), 234.

11. Al-Naimi, *Out of the Desert*. It is difficult to know the exact production figures of large oil-producing countries such as Saudi Arabia or the United States. The problem is usually related to the method of estimating the numbers the country uses, alongside the timing of this estimate.

12. With regard to the oil market and OPEC+'s policy, Trump's tweets started to lose their importance by the end of 2018. He later resorted to direct personal communication

and discussions with important oil-producing leaders. For an interesting report about Trump's tweets, see Mark Lander and Katie Rogers, "Following the Leader on Twitter," *New York Times*, March 9–10, 2019.

13. Personal interviews with Gro Anundskaas, the international adviser to the Norwegian Energy Ministry, in 2018 and 2019.

14. It is interesting to study the evolution of U.S. oil sanctions on Iran. In 1995 CONOCO, an American oil company, signed a deal to develop two Iranian offshore oil fields. Senator Chuck Schumer of New York led the fight against this, and new U.S. laws prohibited American oil companies from investing in Iran. By being prohibited from developing the Iranian oil, American companies complained that non-American oil companies would take advantage of this, so the U.S. government expanded the sanctions to include other international oil companies, investors, and oil technology. No doubt, the behavior of Iran, especially during the presidency of Ahmadinejad (2005–2013), who worked to export the Iranian revolution and intervene in other countries' domestic affairs, contributed to expansion of the sanctions.

15. It should be noted that the cost of oil production in the United States is among the highest in the world. It's likely that the United States would prefer a price above $50/BBL. When West Texas Intermediate (WTI) oil prices went very low in late March 2020, the United States took the lead internationally to bring them back up.

16. After the Iraqi invasion of Kuwait in August 1990, both Minister Hisham Nazer and Prince Abdulaziz asked me to stay and work in London. I had three responsibilities. First, to observe major oil-related events and keep them informed through phone and fax. Second, to brief the international media about major oil developments and Saudi policy. Third, to coordinate with some American officials, especially in the Department of Energy, on oil developments and to share common messages to the media and the market.

17. Statement to me from Majid al-Moneef on May 7, 2020.

18. For example, Othman al-Khowaiter, an engineer and Aramco's previous vice president, is active on twitter and holds the opinion that Saudi Arabia should not increase its oil production and should keep the oil in the ground to increase oil prices.

19. At a speech at a Reform Club dinner in London on February 13, 2014, I suggested that U.S interests and involvement in the Middle East are due to many reasons. They include connections with Israel, religious considerations, and intervention from regional powers such as Iran and Turkey, as well as any power vacuum that is likely to be filled by major international powers such as Russia and China. Oil is just one reason among many. During 2019–2020, events related to the U.S.-Iranian conflict proved this point. After becoming president in 2017, Trump promised to withdraw U.S. troops from the Middle East, but he did the opposite. When some Iraqi government officials asked the Americans to withdraw their troops and close the U.S. military base in 2019, the Trump administration took a strong position, warning Iraq against making this request. The president said that the United States does not need the Middle East's oil, and the United States had been a net oil exporter from the beginning of 2019. It is the third largest oil exporter, only after Saudi Arabia and Russia. Yet as a superpower the United States will continue its involvement in the Middle East and in other important regions around the world for political, economic, militaristic, and even cultural reasons.

20. See "OPEC+ Baku Deliberations Complicated by U.S. Sanctions," *Argus Media*, March 18, 2019. Also see "Sanctions on Iran Have Negative Effects on Energy Markets: Novak," *Tehran Times*, March 18, 2019.

21. The evolution of the oil producer-consumer dialogue is an interesting illustration of a change in U.S. thinking, especially with regard to cooperation in the international oil market and the issue of energy management. When France, in cooperation with Norway and Venezuela, called for a meeting of the energy ministers of oil-producing and oil-consuming countries in the summer of 1991, the U.S. administration did not support the idea. However, after a lot of pressure from friends and allies, the United States decided to participate but kept a low profile. When the head of the U.S. team, Bill Ramsey, talked positively about the meeting to the international media, Washington was not happy about it. In 2000, when Saudi Arabia proposed creation of the secretariat of IEF, Washington was not very supportive, although Saudi Arabia was able to convince the United States to go along with the idea and contribute to its budget. We had to make some changes to the structure of the secretariat to make it acceptable to the United States, and twenty years later, during the most antiglobal administration, Washington nominated an American as IEF secretary-general. Moreover, former U.S. secretary of energy Rick Perry told me during his visit to Riyadh in late 2019 (after he decided to leave the government and go back to Houston) that he would seriously consider having the ministerial meeting of the IEF in Houston.

22. Francois Murphy, "U.S. Not Concerned by Any New OPEC Output Cut, Brouillette Says," *Reuters*, February 11, 2020.

9. ALI AL-NAIMI: THE ROAD TO DOHA

1. This report is interesting. Even though it's very well done, its authors were not named. *The Waning Era of Saudi Oil Dominance: Current Challenges and Future Threats to Saudi Arabia's Influence over the Oil Market* (Ergo, February 8, 2012).

2. Glada Lahn and Paul Stevens, *Burning Oil to Keep Cool: The Hidden Energy Crisis in Saudi Arabia* (London: Chatham House, December 2011).

3. I heard this from Ali Al-Naimi, as well as from other people who were involved in the board meeting. Al-Naimi and Ibrahim al-Assaf, the minister of finance, were very close friends and trusted each other.

4. Thomas L. Friedman, "A Pump War?," *New York Times*, October 14, 2014.

5. Friedman, "A Pump War?" Although Friedman stated that it could have been his "imagination" at the beginning of this article, if it was only his imagination, he wouldn't have written such a piece.

6. Peter Waldman, "Buying Time: The Saudi Plan to Extend the Age of Oil," *Bloomberg Market*, April 2015, 26–35.

7. Ibrahim AlMuhanna, "The International Oil Market: A View of the Current Status and the Future" (paper presented in Arabic during the Saudi Economic Association's Annual Conference, Riyadh, April 8, 2015).

8. Ali Al-Naimi, *Out of the Desert: My Journey from Nomadic Bedouin to the Heart of Global Oil* (London: Penguin Random House, 2016), 282–87.

9. Even though the meeting should have been secret, the information about what happened was leaked to the international media and the market. See Al-Naimi, *Out of the Desert*, 282–86.

10. John Defterios interview with Ali Al-Naimi, CNN, December 23, 2014. In that interview Al-Naimi strongly denied that Saudi policy was targeting U.S shale or Russian production.

11. Bassam Fattouh told me this and also said the same thing to major international media outlets.

12. Summer Said, "Saudi Prince Disagrees with Oil Minister on Petroleum Prices," *Wall Street Journal*, October 14, 2014.

13. Abdulaziz al-Dakheel, "With Oil Shock We Should Worry About the Saudi Economy," December 9, 2014, and republished by al Magal, an Arabic website, in 2019. Also see Abdulaziz al-Dakheel, "Another Reading of the New Saudi Budget," January 2, 2015, Al Magal.

14. Ahmed al-Malik, "Two Previous Financial Crises and the Third Might Be On the Way," *al Riyadh*, November 17, 2015.

15. During my conversation with Gro Anundskaas, she confirmed the special petroleum relationship between Saudi Arabia and Norway on different levels and for many years; she also mentioned the importance of personalities in this relationship.

16. AlMuhanna, "The International Oil Market." Also see "The Oil Market Lacks an Anchor: Saudi Oil Official," *Petroleum Argus*, October 12, 2015.

17. Peter Waldman, "Crown Prince Mohammed bin Salman Is Preparing Saudi Arabia for the End of Oil," *Bloomberg Businessweek*, April 25, 2016.

18. The information about this was leaked to almost all the reporters and oil analysts who were covering the meeting, but some of it was distorted by both the media and their sources.

19. Vladimir Soldatkin, Sam Wilkin, and Tom Finn, "The Global Oil Deal That Never Came to Be," *Reuters*, April 18, 2016.

10. VLADIMIR PUTIN: PLACING RUSSIA ON THE GLOBAL OIL MAP

1. Russia was the first major power to recognize the newly established Saudi Arabia in February 1926. Both countries cut their political ties in the 1960s until 1990, but they continued their trade relations during this period.

2. Interview with Andrei Glebovich on *Russia Today* (n.d.). I confirmed the authenticity of the interview with two Russian government officials.

3. See Angela Stent, *Putin's World: Russia Against the West and With the Rest* (New York: Hachette, 2019). Also see "Russia: Distressed Oligarchs," *Energy Compass*, October 17, 2008, 5.

4. Many studies discuss the Russian oil sector during Yeltsin's time. See, for example, Daniel Yergin, *The Quest: Energy Security, and the Remaking of the Modern World* (New York: Penguin, 2011); and Rachel Maddow, *Blowout: Corrupted Democracy, Rogue States, Russia, and the Richest, Most Destructive Industry on Earth* (New York: Crown, 2019).

5. Many oil analysts and experts who followed Russian oil production believed Russia did not make these cuts in 1998. Gary Ross, the former executive chairman and head of Global Oil for PIRA Energy Group, told me this some time in 1999.

6. See Darya Korsunskaya and Olesya Astakhova, "Exclusive: Russia's Sechin Raises Pressure on Putin to End OPEC Deal," *Reuters*, February 8, 2019. In late October of 2019, one month after the Saudi oil facilities in Abqaiq and Khurais were attacked, Sechin said that the world should "reassess Saudi Arabia's role as the unconditionally reliable oil supplier." Julian Lee, "Slinging Mud Won't Secure the World's Oil Supply," *Bloomberg Quint*, October 27, 2019.

7. Stent, *Putin's World*, 348–49.

8. Edward L. Morse and James Richard, "The Battle for Energy Dominance," *Foreign Affairs*, March/April 2002.

9. Maddow, *Blow Out*, xiv–xv.

10. Maddow, xviii.

11. See "TEXT: Saudi-Russian Joint Statement on Oil Market Cooperation," *Reuters*, September 5, 2016.

12. The Russian News Agency, *Tass*, September 1, 2010.

13. Ibrahim AlMuhanna, "Global Oil Markets: Past Pessimism, Future Optimism" (presentation in Arabic at the Twenty-Fourth Forum on the Fundamentals of the Oil and Gas Industry, Organization of Arab Petroleum Exporting Countries, Kuwait, April 12, 2017).

14. I heard this from the Indian oil minister during the Offshore Northern Seas (ONS) conference in Stavingar, Norway, in 2018. Apparently he wasn't aware that I was from Saudi Arabia because he later tried to change his tone. When oil prices began going up in early 2021, he again began blaming oil producers.

15. "Charter Marks Milestone for OPEC+ Alliance," *Petroleum Argus*, July 5, 2019.

16. "Charter Marks Milestone."

17. Personal phone interview with Abdel Monem Said Aly, in Cairo, Egypt, April 18, 2020.

18. Daniel Byman and Kenneth M. Pollack, "Beyond Great Forces: How Individuals Still Shape History," *Foreign Affairs*, November/December 2019.

19. Michael Carpenter, "Putin Has Just Made Two Huge Mistakes—And His Timing Couldn't Be Worse," *Washington Post*, April 29, 2020. The writer was referring to the following two mistakes: Putin's stance at the OPEC+ meeting on March 6, 2020, when faced with the Saudi proposal to cut production, and Putin's response to the coronavirus pandemic.

11. CROWN PRINCE MOHAMMED BIN SALMAN AND PRINCE ABDULAZIZ BIN SALMAN: THE FORTY-FIVE DAY OIL SHOCK

1. Khalid al-Falih became energy minister on May 7, 2016, and he began working on Aramco's IPO immediately. He asked me and others for help with the media for the IPO, especially international media. Al-Falih assemble a large team that covered almost every area in support of a successful IPO. He and other people within the government had concerns about some aspects of the IPO and asked for further studies, such as potential legal problems if Aramco was listed and traded on the New York Stock Exchange or on the London Exchange.

2. Interview with Abdallah Jum'ah on March 24, 2020.
3. Many people from the ministry, including me, and from Aramco were involved in developing this strategy: Suleiman al-Herbish, Majid al-Moneef, Ibrahim al-Mishari, and Samir al-Tubayyeb. The ministry is currently working on a new, comprehensive energy strategy.
4. Personal phone interview with Ahmed al-Subaey, October 2020.
5. Saudi Arabia provides financial assistance to less advanced Arab and Islamic countries, as well as to other developing nations. During the late eighties and early nineties, when Saudi oil production was increasing, Hisham Nazer told me that we should not publish the real figure because some Arab leaders, such as the Syrians, will ask for more financial help, citing increasing Saudi oil production. In the early years of the twenty-first century, for instance, Syria's oil production was increasing and reached close to one million barrels per day, but the Syrian government claimed that the actual figure was between 0.5 and 0.6 MBD. When I privately asked the Syrian minister of energy about this, he said that President Hafez al-Assad was asking Saudi Arabia and other Gulf countries for additional financial aid, but if Syria published its actual production level, these countries might refuse his request for more financial assistance.
6. Ghassan al-Shibl, the former head of Local Content and Government Procurement Authority (LCGPA), told me that he used to coordinate closely with Prince Abdulaziz regarding local content. The prince gave local content on the Saudi energy sector special attention, not only pushing for it but also enforcing it to the fullest extent that the legal process permits.
7. I heard this from the Iranian minister in December 2019, during the first OPEC meeting after Prince Abdulaziz became energy minister. During the OPEC and OPEC+ meetings of March 4–6, the Iranian delegation came to Vienna with a major difficulty. The coronavirus was spreading in Iran, and many countries, including Austria, did not allow Iranians to visit. However, the OPEC secretariat insisted that the Austrian government allow them to enter the country and attend the meeting. During the meeting, the majority of ministers and delegates avoided direct contact with the Iranians, but Prince Abdulaziz shook hands with Minister Zanganeh.
8. Interview with Turki Althunayyani, consultant to the minister and supervisor of legal affairs at the ministry. He worked closely with the prince durnig the Aramco IPO. Riyadh, December 2020.
9. Personal interview with Fahd al Toryf, adviser at the ministry of energy, in Riyadh, July 10, 2020.
10. From 2016 to 2019, Aramco's IPO was one of the most talked about oil issues among media, experts, and in financial and petroleum circles. International banks had different estimates of the company's worth, ranging between $1.2 billion and $2 billion. Some people had doubts about the success of its listing, especially restricting it to the national market.
11. See Valarie Marcel, *Oil Titans: National Oil Companies in the Middle East* (London: Chatham House, 2006).
12. Some major banks and companies listed on the Saudi stock market (Tadawul) are 30 percent or more owned by the Public Investment Fund (PIF). They include SABIC, Ma'aden, STC, Alinma Bank, and al Ahli National Bank, which was merging with

SAMBA (formerly the Saudi-American Bank). The PIF might name people to the companies' boards, but it does not intervene in their business activities.

13. Many times during the oil crises from 1997 to 1999, oil producers acted late and made cuts little by little, extending the recovery time by a year and a half. In 2008, OPEC acted quickly and made big cuts (three times within three months), and the life span of the crisis was only six months.

14. I talked with al-Aama on many occasions during 2020 and 2021 about this subject. This is from one of those conversations.

15. See, for example, David Brooks, "Vladimir Putin, the Most Influential Man in the World," *New York Times*, April 2, 2018.

16. I heard from some delegates during the meeting that the head of a state of OPEC countries tried to call Putin, but they could not get through to him.

17. Vitaly Yermakov and James Henderson, "The New Deal for the Oil Market: Implications for Russia's Short-Term Tactics and Long-Term Strategy," *Oxford Institute*, April 2020.

18. Yermakov and Henderson, "The New Deal for the Oil Market."

19. It was reported that Kirill's wife and Putin's daughter had a close friendship. See, for example, "Report: Russian Financier in Erik Prince's Seychelles Meeting Traced Back to Putin," *Daily Beast*, April 1, 2018 (originally reported in the *Financial Times*); and "Friend of Putin's Daughter, Banker with $10 Billion: Kirill Dmitriev, a Possible Link Between the Kremlin and Trump," *The Scoop*, March 9, 2018.

20. I talked with several Washington insiders and experts about Secretary Brouillette, his personality, and his relationships in the White House and in the U.S. oil industry. They all confirmed his likability and good personality.

21. Phone interview with Joel Couse, chief economist at the IEA, Paris, April 15, 2020.

22. Julian Lee, "Saudi Arabia Lays Down the Law to the Oil Market," *Bloomberg*, June 7, 2020.

23. Grant Smith, Salma El Wardany, Dina Khrennikova, and Javier Blas, "OPEC+ Extends Oil Cut in Win for Saudi-Russian Alliance," *Bloomberg*, June 7, 2020.

CONCLUSION: THOUGHTS ABOUT THE FUTURE

1. Yan Xuetong, *Leadership and the Rise of Great Powers* (Princeton, NJ: Princeton University Press, 2019), 206.

INDEX